MW01077685

DICTIONARY

OF

AMERICANIZED FRENCH-CANADIAN NAMES

Onomastics and Genealogy

Marc Picard

CLEARFIELD

Copyright © 2013
Marc Picard
All Rights Reserved.

Published for Clearfield Company by
Genealogical Publishing Company
Baltimore, Maryland
2013

ISBN 978-0-8063-5645-7

Made in the United States of America

INTRODUCTION

1. The origin and development of French-Canadian surnames

The vast majority of the most common family names in Québec today are French in origin, and so are a great many in Acadia as well as other parts of Canada and the United States. For the most part, they are the offshoots of the surnames that were brought over by the immigrants who settled in *La Nouvelle-France* in the 17th and 18th centuries. Some 400 years later, it should come as no surprise to find that important differences, both linguistic and distributional, have developed between the surnames found in France and those of its erstwhile colony. Indeed, there are enough such differences to make francophone onomastic research in North America a field of study unto itself, one that, surprisingly, has received very little serious attention when one considers how much time and effort have been invested in the genealogical study of these names.

From a linguistic standpoint, the family names borne by current or former native speakers of Canadian French (CF) can be divided into two broad categories:

(1) those that are French in origin, i.e., that were brought to North America by colonists from France and, in a few cases, from Belgium (*Wallonie*) and Switzerland (*Suisse romande*);
(2) those that are not French in origin, though they may emanate from what is now France territorially (*Bretagne, Pays basque, Alsace-Lorraine*).

Each of these categories of family names can in turn be subdivided into two groups:

(1) a. the French names that have undergone no orthographical or phonological changes in CF;
    b. the French names that have undergone idiosyncratic orthographical and/or phonological changes in CF, or that were created post-colonially.
(2) a. the foreign names that have undergone no orthographical changes or non-adaptive phonological changes in CF;
    b. the foreign names that have undergone idiosyncratic orthographical and/or phonological changes in CF.

Moreover, in terms of the etymological transparency of the surnames that constitute the object of this study, there are three different scenarios that present themselves. Thus, if we exclude (2a) which is outside the realm of CF onomastics proper, the following situations will obtain for each of the aforementioned categories of names to be studied (1a, 1b, 2b):

Type I
• some names have clearcut, self-evident and unequivocal etymologies;
Type II
• some names do not have transparent etymologies or have more than one possible source, but strong evidence of one type or another (linguistic, genealogical, geographical, historical, etc.) can be brought forth in support of some particular origin;
Type III
• some names have obscure or opaque etymologies that either cannot be proven beyond a reasonable doubt or cannot be ascertained at all.

iii

2. French names with no modifications

Many of the French family names that one finds in North America today, such as *Benoît, Bernard, Bertrand, Denis, Dubois, Dufour, Dupuis, Fontaine, Fournier, Gauthier, Girard, Lacroix, Lambert, Leclerc, Lefebvre, Marchand, Martin, Ménard, Mercier, Moreau, Morin, Pelletier, Perron, Picard, Poirier, Renaud, Richard, Robert, Rousseau, Roy, Séguin, Vincent,* to name but a few, have identical counterparts in Europe. They were brought over to New France by the early settlers and have not been altered either orthographically or phonologically. Since the origin of surnames like these can usually be found in the dictionaries of Dauzat, Morlet or Tosti, they are generally of Type I and represent the least problematic group of names on the whole.

Still, there remains a sizeable residue of cases that do require some research. These cases can be grouped into one of the two following categories:

- those where the original names borne by the first settlers do not appear in any of the dictionaries of French family names;
- those where such dictionaries propose alternative etymologies or etymologies that are at variance with other sources.

2.1 Unmodified names not found in dictionaries

The first scenario can be exemplified with the names *Arès* and *Sansfaçon* (Type I), *Patenaude* and *Côté* (Type II), and *Chèvrefils* and *Robitaille* (Type III). *Arès* is a surname that was brought over by Jean Arès dit Sansfaçon, who hailed from Agen in the département of Lot-et-Garonne, and since it is a placename in the adjacent département of Gironde (both of which are in Aquitaine), there can be little doubt about its source. *Sansfaçon*, which was borne not only by Jean Arès but also by five other early settlers, is transparently an agglutination of the expression *sans façon*, a nickname meaning 'open, honest, unaffected'.

At first glance, *Patenaude* seems to be completely obscure but since we know that the original bearer of the name was Nicolas Patenaude or Patenostre, and that three of his sons were known as Patenaude or Patenotre, this tells us that it is a phonologically altered form of *Pateno(s)tre*, a nickname for a maker of rosaries derived from *pater noster* 'our father', the opening words of the Lord's Prayer.

On the other hand, *Côté* seems totally transparent since *côté* means 'side' but the problem is that it is unclear what such a nickname might relate to. As is often the case, however, an alternate spelling can help to point us in the right direction. The first colonist with this name was Jean Côté or Costé, and the possibility that the latter Old French spelling is an alteration of the name *Costy* gains support when one considers (1) that the origin of this name is the Old Norman form *costi* (Old French *costil*) 'hill', and (2) that Jean Côté or Costé was from Mortagne-au-Perche in Normandy.

The surname *Chèvrefils* looks like it means 'goat son' but it is structurally aberrant since *fils* is not attached to any other French names (the equivalents of English *-son* are *de, d', du, à,* e.g., *Depaul, Dalain, Dujean, Ageorges*). There is every indication, however, that it is actually an attempt to francize *Chabrefit/Chabrefy* which literally means 'goat fig' in Occitan (< Latin *caprificus* 'wild fig tree'). Note that the endings *–fils* and *–fit/fy* would have all been pronounced /fi/ prior to the 18th century. The name is particularly prevalent in Dordogne where the hamlet *Chabrefie* is also found, and that is precisely the region where François Chèvrefils dit Lalime came from.

iv

Finally, *Robitaille* can be cited as an example of a name whose origin remains undetermined. It is not a placename and has no known meaning in any historical stage of French. It was brought over by the brothers Pierre, Jean and Philippe Robitaille from the region of Artois in Northern France, and the département of Nord-Pas-de-Calais is still the area where this surname is most heavily concentrated, along with its variants *Robitail*, *Robitaillie*, *Ropitail* and *Ropital*. It is tempting to try to break it up morphologically into *robit+aille* since *-aille* is a common French suffix, e.g., *fer* 'iron' and *ferraille* 'scrap iron', *gris* 'gray' and *grisaille* 'dullness, grayness', *mur* 'wall' and *muraille* 'high wall', but two problems immediately crop up when this is done: *-aille* is not a name-forming suffix and *robit* has no obvious meaning.

2.2 Unmodified names with suspect or variant etymologies

Surnames that fit into this category can be illustrated with *Gagnon* which is the second most common French surname in North America after *Tremblay*. According to Morlet's dictionary of French surnames, *Ga(i)gnon* has two possible sources. In the Massif Central region in the south-central part of France, it could be the Old Occitan word *ganhon* 'piglet'. However, since the Gagnons who emigrated to Canada, namely the brothers Mathurin, Jean and Pierre Gagnon along with their cousin Robert, hailed from Basse-Normandie in the north, such an origin is highly unlikely. The other possible etymology proposed by Morlet is the Old French word *gaignon* which originally meant 'watchdog', then 'rascal, nasty individual', and would thus have applied to someone who had the characteristics of a vicious dog. However, there are good reasons to be suspicious of this etymology as well.

First of all, it oddly and unnaturally isolates *Gagnon* from *Gagne*, which is from Old French *gaaigne* 'arable land', and its numerous derivatives, most of which mean 'plowman'. Morlet lists *Gagnant*, *Gagné*, *Gagnaire*, *Ga(i)gneux*, *Gagneur*, *Gagneor*, *Ga(i)gnoux*, *Gagnadour*, *Gagne-dour*, *Ga(i)gn(i)er*, *Gagneron*, *Gagneret*, *Ga(i)gnerot*, *Gagnereau*, *Gagneraud*, *Gagnot*, *Ga(i)-gnet*, *Gagneau*, *Gaigneaud*, *Gagnault*, *Gagn(i)ère*, *Gagnerie*, and there are surely others. Since *-on* is a very productive suffix in French, e.g., *Berger/Bergeron*, *Vache/Vachon*, *Pierre/Perron*, *Georges/Georgeon*, *Taille/Taillon*, etc., its apparent absence in the *Gagne* family of names is most peculiar. Secondly, as noted above, the original Gagnons were from Basse-Normandie, and this is precisely where the first settlers named *Gagné* hailed from, thus indicating that these were very likely nicknames for plowmen in that region.

3. French names with modifications

As a first approximation, the French surnames that evince some sort of phonological or ortho-graphical alteration between their original or etymological form and their current form can be grouped into two categories:

• those in which modifications were effected before their bearers left France (which includes those cases where two versions of a name, i.e., the original form or something close to it and a derived form, were recorded upon a colonist's arrival, e.g., *Demers*, *Hurtubise*, *Galarneau*, *Coutu* also noted *Dumets*, *Heurtebise*, *Galerneau*, *Cottu* in the earliest records);
• those in which modifications were effected after their bearers left France.

When one finds that a name is not listed in Dauzat, Morlet or Tosti, for instance, the usual procedure is to check in a genealogical database such as Jetté's dictionary, Desjardins' *PRDH*,

Fournier's *Fichier origine* or Beauregard's *Genealogy of the French in North America*. If it is, then one must go in search of the original form.

3.1 Names altered prior to emigration

Take the names *Vaillancourt*, *Coderre* and *Trépanier*, for instance. The first was brought over by Robert Vaillancourt who arrived in the Québec City area around 1665. Since this surname does not appear in any onomastic dictionary, one must turn to genealogy for a possible answer, and a search in this direction reveals that he was also known under the name of *Villencourt*. At first glance, this does not appear to be of much help since this form is also absent from any French family name databases. However, the fact that the migrant in question was a native of Seine-Maritime in Haute-Normandie makes it highly probable that the surname is an alteration of *Willencourt* which comes from a placename the adjacent département of Pas-de-Calais.

The surname *Coderre* was established in Québec thanks to Antoine Émery dit Coderre who arrived in 1665 as a soldier in the Contrecoeur Company of the Carignan-Salières Regiment. Although this is the only spelling found in the various genealogical sources, the existence in France of a number of similar forms, such as *Coderc*, *Couderc*, *Coudert*, *Couder*, *Coudeyre*, can serve to lead us to a very plausible origin, namely the widespread toponym *(Le) Coderc*. This is especially true if one considers that some 20 places so named can be found in Dordogne where Antoine Émery dit Coderre came from. In fact, this can be narrowed down even further since there exists a *Le Coderc* near his hometown of Sarrazac.

As for *Trépanier*, the fact that it was also written *(de) Trépagny* and *d'Estrépagny* clearly points to an alteration of *Étrépagny*, a town in Eure in Haute-Normandie. Given that Romain Trépanier or (de) Trépagny, the original bearer of the surname in Québec, hailed from the bordering département of Seine-Maritime, there is little reason to doubt the origin of the surname. In sum, these three cases serve to illustrate the fact that not all the French-Canadian surnames that differ from their European counterparts were transformed on this side of the Atlantic.

3.2 Names altered after emigration

At the heart of CF onomastics are the family names that have undergone changes since they were first introduced in New France. These can be divided into two groups:

• those which have undergone orthographical changes only;
• those which have undergone phonological changes (with concomitant orthographical changes).

Before addressing these particular issues, however, it should be pointed out that in terms of the three types of scenarios that were outlined in Section 1, most of the names that have undergone modifications can nevertheless be classified as Type I or Type II in that their etymologies are either completely transparent or can be readily ascertained since their original forms can usually be found in one or more sources. Thus, although one might initially be stumped by forms like *Laurendeau*, *Hévey* or *Déziel*, a little digging will reveal that they stem from *Rollandeau* (< *Rolland*, from the Germanic name *Hrodland*), *Devé* (< Old French *desvé* 'crazy, enraged, furious') and *Delguel* (< *Le Guel*, a placename in Aquitaine) respectively.

3.2.1 Orthographical changes

To begin with, a number of names have had their spellings slightly modified in various idiosyncratic and largely unpredictable ways, e.g., *Chapdelaine* > *Chapdeleine*, *Charlebois* > *Charles-*

bois, Villemur > Villemure, Filion > Fillion, Farand > Pharand, Ossant > Aussant, Arel (< Harel) > Ar(r)elle, Marcil > Marcille, Marié > Marier, Essiambre (< Estiambre) > Essiembre, Deshayes > Deshaies, Maheu > Maheux, Desgagnés > Desgagné, Desgroseilliers > Desgroseillers, Pomainville > Pom(m)inville/Pommainville, Hén(e)ault > Hain(e)ault, etc.

A few orthographical changes are more widespread, however. Among the consonants, the most common such modification involves word-initial *h* which is sometimes deleted and sometimes inserted. The confusion as regards this letter stems from the fact that the sound /h/ had largely ceased to be pronounced by the 16th century so that it became impossible to tell from the pronunciation of a vowel-initial name whether it was spelled with *h* or not. Some of the settlers arrived in New France with this sort of alternate spelling of their name, e.g., *Hade/Ade, Harbour/Arbour, Hardouin/Ardouin, Herpin/Arpin, Homier/Aumier,* and the practice was continued for some time after, with some names acquiring *h*, e.g., *Abel > Habel, Élie > Hélie, Émond > Hémond, Imb(e)ault > Himbeault, Yvon > Hivon,* and others losing it, e.g., *Hottote > Autotte, Haguenier > Aga(g)nier, Husereau > Usereau, Harbec > Arbec, Harel > Arel.*

Turning to vowel changes, the one that has probably affected the most names is the introduction of *e* to the common ending *-ault,* as in *Perr(e)ault, Thib(e)ault, Archamb(e)ault,* no doubt due to the presence of this letter in the equally common suffix *-eau,* as in *Martineau, Cousineau, Véronneau.* Although the orthographical ending *-eault* appears to have existed in France, it could not have been very widespread since Jetté's dictionary, for example, does not list any names with that spelling.

What caused the confusion, of course, was the fact that by the 16th century, a number of sound changes had conspired to make *-ault, -eault* and *-eau* homophonous. In other words, all three would have been pronounced /o/, and since this was also the case for *-au, -aut, -aud, -aux, -eaut, -eaud, -eaux* as well as *-ost, -ot,* one can well imagine the indeterminacy that this created, especially since so few people were literate at that time. Thus, the original form *Devau* has yielded the variants *Devaud, Devaut, Devault, Devaux, Deveau, Deveaud, Deveault, Deveaut, Deveaux, Devost.*

The result, then, is that many of the original names in *-ault* now have variants in *-eault* in CF, e.g., *Thiffault/Thiffeault, Hunault/Huneault, Imbault/Imbeault, Hénault/ Héneault, Montambault/ Montambeault,* etc., and this has also been extended to those in *-eau,* e.g., *Baribeau/Baribeault, Amireau/ Amireault, Verreau/Verreault,* etc. In fact, the whole thing has turned into a bit of a free-for-all with the proliferation of alternate spellings like *Aspirault/Aspireault/Aspirot, Boudrault/Boudreau/Boudreault, Journault/Journeau/Journeault/Journeaux, Naud/Nault/Neault, Prénovault/Prénoveau/Prénovost,* etc.

A very frequent change that involves both vowels and consonants is the one that has seen the numerous surnames beginning with *Saint(e),* which are mostly nicknames known as *dit* names, acquire a variant with the abbreviated form *St(e)* so that one can never be sure from the pronunciation alone whether to write, for example, *Saint-Jacques* or *St-Jacques, Saint-Denis* or *St-Denis, Saint-Laurent* or *St-Laurent, Sainte-Marie* or *Ste-Marie, Saint-Pierre* or *St-Pierre,* etc. If one had to guess, however, a good bet would be to use the *St(e)* form since it is by far the most common in the overwhelming majority of cases.

3.2.2 Phonological changes

The phonological modifications, that is, the various sound substitutions, deletions and insertions that French surnames have undergone since their arrival on North American soil, are in the main totally unsystematic and haphazard. The only wide-ranging phonologically based spelling change to speak of is the common replacement of the ending *-et* by *-ette* (and, to a lesser extent, of *-ot* by *-otte* and *-el* by *-elle*). Now since *-et* and *-ette* are the masculine and feminine forms of a common diminutive suffix, e.g., *gras* 'fat', *grasset* 'chubby (masc.)', *grassette* 'chubby (fem.)', anyone unfamiliar with the historical development of surnames in the New World might assume that forms in *-ette* are metronymics. We know, however, that all such names, e.g., *Audette, Vermette, Gaudette, Ouellette, Paquette*, etc., were written with *-et* when their bearers first arrived, and that they are virtually unheard of in France to this day.

What prompted the change was the fact that final-obstruent deletion, which had actually begun to operate in the 14th century, had met with a lot of resistance on the part of grammarians, and so was still in a state of flux in the 17th. Thus, an ending like *-et* would have been pronounced *è* by some speakers and *èt* by others. Presumably, *èt*-type speakers giving their names orally to *è*-type transcribers would have had them mistakenly recorded with an *-ette* ending. The result, at any rate, is that a great many *-et* names now have an *-ette* variant, with the situation being further complicated by the fact that some *-et* names, e.g., *Ouellet, Ouimet, Paquet, Rinfret, Gaudet*, are always pronounced with a final /t/. Conversely, a few names like *Charet* and *Rivet* have acquired the variant spelling *Charest* and *Rivest*, possibly to insure that they be pronounced with a final *è*, as forms with original *-est*, e.g., *Laforest, Genest, Ruest*, normally are.

The vast majority of the names that have undergone phonological changes constitute a totally heterogeneous lot, as mentioned above. Vowels, consonants and even entire syllables are altered at random, and none of the changes, such as metathesis, e.g., *Marchelidon > Marchildon*, or vowel copy, e.g., *Prénovost* (< *Prénouveau*) *> Pronovost*, or consonant dissimilation, e.g., *Gerbert > Jalbert*, are of the sort that normally apply regularly in languages. Although it is sometimes possible to deduce that folk etymology or analogy have been at work, as when the semantically empty *Leureau* was turned into *L'Heureux* 'the happy one', or *Dagory* was transformed to *Gadoury* under the influence of *Gaboury*, there seems to be no rhyme or reason for most of the changes. Following is a cross-section of names illustrating such vocalic and consonantal substitutions, deletions and insertions:

Haguenier > Aga(g)nier	*Jouteau > Juteau*
Alavoine > Avoine	*Malteste > Maltais*
Bourgery > Bourgie	*De Gerlaise > Desjarlais*
Vautrin > Vaudrin	*Hazeur > Lazure*
Légaré > Legaré	*Delguel > Déziel*
Guillot(tte) > Diot(te)	*Reguindeau > Riendeau*
Patoile > Patoine	*De Rainville > Drainville*
Jouvin > Jauvin	*Vassor > Vasseur*
Marchàterre > Marcheterre	*Desranleau > Duranleau*
Noreau > Nareau	*Estiambre > Essiambre*
Forand > Farand/Pharand	*Diel > Yelle*
Juineau > Juneau	*Jamme > Gemme*
Autin > Hottin	*Hotot > Althot*

4. Foreign names with modifications

As one might expect, the modifications that foreign names have undergone have no recognizable patterns at all. Although some of these orthographical and phonological alterations have been quite radical, the situation is basically the same for these names as for the ones in the previous section as regards their relative etymological transparency. In other words, there are surprisingly few Type III surnames, i.e., those having obscure or opaque etymologies. Following are the main sources of these foreign names in CF.

4.1 English names

The most numerous family names borne by genuine North American francophones today, i.e., native French speakers who may or may not be proficient in a second language, are surely those of English and Insular Celtic origin (Irish, Scottish, Welsh), with the latter having been anglicized before their arrival. What is perhaps most surprising about this group of surnames is that so few of them have undergone any type of modification. Thus, it is far from uncommon in Québec and other French-speaking areas to come across individuals with monikers like Marc Johnson, Gaétan Hart, Claude Ryan, Pierre Pettigrew, André McDonald, Anne-Marie Jones, Monique Blackburn, and the like.

Those few anglophones who did have their names altered all seem to have had in common the fact that they found themselves isolated among francophones in the early days of the colony, mostly as a result of having been captured by Indians and then released far from home. If their name had a similar French counterpart, then the alteration was minimal. For example, the name *Edmunds* borne by Thomas Edmunds, an Irishman who had married one Marie Kelly in New England around 1693, and who had arrived in Québec not long after since his first child was born there in 1694, quickly became *Edmond* then *Émond*, and later on, *Aymont* and *Hémond*.

English surnames that did not bear such a resemblance to any French names led to the creation of totally new forms. In some instances, the modifications were minimal, as when *Dicker* was restructured to *Dicaire*, *Stebbens* to *Stébenne*, and *Casey* to *Caissie/Caissy/Quessy*. Other transformations were more radical. Although the variants *Hains/Haince/Hainse/Hince/Hins/Hinse* may not seem too distant from the original *Haynes* orthographically, they do involve the significant phonological changes of /h/-deletion, vowel nasalization and the devoicing of /z/ to /s/. The most complete metamorphosis, however, was probably that undergone by *Farnworth* which gradually evolved to *Farneth*, *Fanef* and *Faneuf* to finally end up as *Phaneuf*.

4.2 German names

The family names of German-language origin, that is, from German-speaking countries as well as Alsace and Lorraine in France, are surely those that have undergone the most extensive alterations in sound and spelling. Now, there would have been relatively few of these in Québec had it not been for one significant event. At the start of the American War of Independence in 1776, some 30,000 German mercenaries were recruited by the British Monarchy to fight the rebels, and out of the estimated 10,000 of these Hessians who fought in Canada, over 1,300 remained in Québec after the hostilities were over. Following is a representative sample of the francization of these and other German names:

Beyer > Payeur	*Hartung > Harton*
Henner > Hénaire	*Hennemann > Heynemand*
Koch > Caux	*Letter > Laître/Lettre*
Mayer > Maheu(x)	*Schumpf > Jomphe*
Dickner > Nickner	*Frœbel/Fröbe > Frève*
Orth > Horth	*Behzer > Piuze*

Moller > Molleur	Gœbel/Göbel > Keable
Grothe > Grothé	Felz > Felx
Göbel > Keable	Schnabel > Schnob

Amringer > Hammarrenger/Marenger/Maringer/Marinier

4.3 Basque and Breton names

Although Basque and Breton are as different as chalk and cheese linguistically, they can be dealt with together by virtue of the fact that both have long been indigenous to France, with the result that they did not undergo very many changes in New France given that they had already been francized to a large extent. Thus, the Breton surnames *Boher, Cadudal, Keréon, Kervoac, Pellan, Prigent* and *Tanguy* had become *Boire* (via *Beauher*), *Catudal, Quirion, Kirouac, Pelland, Prégent* and *Tanguay* before the settlers who bore them ever reached North America. Only a few such names were subsequently altered, e.g., *Hangrion* to *Angrignon, Bellec* to *Bélec, Gour* to *Gourd, Bourhis* to *Boulerice*. Note, however, that some names which had originally undergone no changes later developed one or more variants. For instance, *Kirouac* is now also *Kéroack, Kérouack, Kirouack* while *Arcouet* and *Cadoret* have almost predictably evolved to *Arcouette* and *Cadorette*.

As for Basque names, all those that have left a trace in CF had already undergone some degree of francization before their advent in Canada. Thus, *Basterretxe* had been altered to *Basterretche, Bidegaray* to *Bidegaré, (de) Larrazabal* to *Delarosbil, Etxeverri* to *Etcheverry, Garibay* to *Gariépy, Aosteguia* to *Ostiguy, Iturbide* to *Turbide, Azpiroz* to *Aspirot*. Once in North America, some of these names continued to evolve so that *Basterretche* turned into *Bastarache* while *Bidegaré, Aspirot* and *Etcheverry* acquired the respective variants *Bidégaré, Aspirault/Aspireault* and *Chevarie/Detcheverry/D'Etcheverry*.

4.4 Other foreign names

Only a handful of the foreign names that were not discussed above have undergone any modifications in CF, which is truly remarkable considering that there have been so many hundreds of them over the last four centuries or so, not only from Europe but also more recently from Asia, Africa, the Caribbean and Latin America. What we find is that just as in the case of Breton and Basque surnames, most of the modifications that we can detect were effected before the settlers ever left their homeland.

Particularly interesting in this category are *Vandelac* and *Ipperciel/Ippersiel*, two virtually unrecognizable surnames of Flemish toponymical origin. The first stems from *van Doolaghe* while the second is an alteration of *van Niepenzele* which in Belgium has also become *Hypersiel, Hypersier, Ipersiel, Ipercielle, Ypersiel, Ypersielle, Ypersier, Yperzeele, Yperzielle, Yppersiel*. Finally, *Rodrigues* and *Da Silva* are Portuguese names that arrived in Québec under the guise of *Rodrigue* and *Dasylva*, with the latter subsequently branching out to *Dassilva, Dassylva, Da Sylva/De Sylva*. *Salvaia* and *Rosa* were two Italian names that underwent minor alterations to *Salvail* and *Rose*. Polish *Głąbiński* became *Globensky* while Hungarian *Kovácsy* and *Viola* were changed to *Coache* and *Vignola*.

5. The alteration of French-Canadian surnames in English Canada and the US

Discounting a few seemingly haphazard and unmotivated anglicizations such as *Ward < Benoît, Carey < Busque, Leo < Charpentier, Hoskins < Durepos, Luro < Sirois*, there are two basic ways in which CF surnames were altered when, for largely economic reasons, their bearers ventured in droves out of Québec and Acadia into (1) English Canada, mostly in Ontario and subsequently to Michigan and the surrounding states, and (2) throughout New England. This occurred mainly during the course of the 19th century, though the migratory movement had started in the 18th, especially with the expulsion of the Acadians to Louisiana, and continued into the early part of the 20th.

5.1 Types of anglicization

The most common type of anglicization or americanization one finds is orthographical in nature, involving as it does either the simple elimination of diacritics, e.g., *Levesque < Lévesque, Giguere < Giguère, Cote < Côté, Lague < Lagüe, Lefrancois < Lefrançois, Dentremont < D'Entremont*, or an adaptation to English pronunciation, as in *Pelkey < Pelletier, Shovan < Chauvin, Tibedo < Thibodeau, Lepoint < Lapointe, Itchue < Hétu.*

A second type is composed of French surnames that are replaced by what are perceived to be English equivalents in some sense. On the one hand, there are substitutions which are based solely on the fact that an existing English surname sounds vaguely the same as the French original, e.g., *McQueen < Moquin, Gordon < Godin, Grant < Lagrandeur, Green < Grenier, Blair < Bélair*, though sometimes these conversions are not to actual surnames but simply to ordinary English lexemes, e.g., *Donor < Daunais, Sequin < Séguin, Laundry < Landry, Companion < Compagna, Dragon < Daragon*. On the other hand, some of these lexical substitutions are semantically based in that they constitute attempts at translation. This phenomenon can be divided into four categories, viz., direct translations, partial translations, near translations, and mistranslations.

5.1.1 Direct translations

The simplest type of translation is the one where there exists a straightforward, one-to-one semantic correlation between the French and English words, phrases or given names that make up the surnames: *Butterfly < Papillon, Carpenter < Charpentier, Fish < Poisson, Goodblood < Bonsang, Goodfriend < Bonami*. It is important to note that the meanings attributed to certain translated French names do not correspond to their etymology but simply bear an accidental resemblance to synchronically transparent forms. For example, the origin of *Gaucher* is the Germanic name *Walhari* but this name would nowadays be ineluctably interpreted as *gaucher* 'left-handed' and translated along those lines.

Though there may exist a slight discrepancy between the spelling of a French surname and that of its lexical origin, instances of this type can also be considered to involve a direct translation if the two forms are phonolocially identical and etymologically related. Fitting this type of process are instances like *Buckwheat < Sarrazin* (= *sarrasin*), *Carter < Chartier* (= *charretier*), *Drinkwine < Boivin* (= *bois vin*), *King < Roy* (= *roi*), *Nice < Joly* (= *joli*). A final type of direct translation involves proper names preceded by *Saint* which, as previously noted, is usually abbreviated to *St*, e.g., *Stdennis < St-Denis, Stfrancis < St-François, Stgeorge < St-Georges, Stjames < St-Jacques, Stjohn < St-Jean.*

5.1.2 Partial translations

Most of the surnames that fit into this category involve the determiners *le* 'the (masculine)', *la* 'the (feminine)' and *l'* 'the (prevocalically)'. On the one hand, they may remain as such in the English adaptations while the rest of the name undergoes a direct translation. Examples are

Laforrest < *Laforest, Lamountain* < *Lamontagne, Lapearl* < *Laperle, Lavalley* < *Lavallée, Legray/Lagray* < *Legris*. On the other hand, the determiners may simply be omitted as in *Bird* < *Loiseau, Bishop* < *Lévesque, Brown* < *Lebrun, Cross* < *Lacroix, Happy* < *L'Heureux*.

This type of deletion always occurs when names begin with the preposition + determiner combinations *du* (< *de le*) 'from the (singular)' and *des* (< *de les*) 'from the (plural)', e.g., *Cedar* < *Ducèdre, Oven* < *Dufour, Strong* < *Dufort, Wood* < *Dubois, Fields* < *Deschamps*. Most of the remaining instances of partial translation have in common the fact that only the last word or name is kept in the English adaptation, as in *Leaf* < *Bellefeuille, Wedge* < *Aucoin, Wood* < *Gadbois, Woods* < *Charlebois/Gadbois*.

5.1.3 Near translations

In contradistinction to the names listed in the previous section in which the translated parts are exact renderings of the original elements, there are others where the correlation between French and English is an approximation of some sort, though always in the same semantic area. The simplest cases are those that involve a change in number, i.e., from singular to plural or vice versa, most often with the concomitant omission of initial prepositions and determiners observed in the partial translations above, as in *Gates* < *Barrière* from *barrière* 'gate', *Hickory* < *Desnoyers* from *noyers* 'hickories', *Hill* < *Descôteaux* from *côteaux* 'hills', *Rivers* < *Larivière* from *rivière* 'river', *Threehouse* < *Destroismaisons* from *trois maisons* 'three houses'.

A less prevalent type of near translation is comprised of agglutinated French names only one element of which is rendered faithfully in English: *Fairfield* < *Beauchamp* from *beau champ* 'beautiful field', *Goodnature* < *Belhumeur* from *belle humeur* 'good mood', *Goodroad* < *Beauchemin* from *beau chemin* 'beautiful road', *Walker* < *Marcheterre* from *marche à terre* 'walks on the ground'. Finally, there are translated surnames that simply contain a lexically related element which may or may not be in the same word class, such as *Ashley* < *Lafrenière* from Old French *fresniere* 'ash grove', *Betters* < *Lemieux* from *le mieux* 'the best', *Lander* < *Therrien* from *(propriétaire) terrien* 'landowner', *Fisher* < *Poisson* from *poisson* 'fish', *Gardner* < *Desjardins* from *jardins* 'gardens'.

5.1.4 Mistranslations

These can be divided into two broad categories. One is where a bona fide French word or phrase is rendered in English by a complete or partial form that means something different. For example, we find *Blackbird* < *Létourneau* from *étourneau* 'starling', *Farmer* < *Therrien* from *(propriétaire) terrien* 'landowner', *Flagg* < *Papillon* from *papillon* 'butterfly' misconstrued as *pavillon* 'flag', *Freeheart* < *Généreux* from *généreux* 'generous', *Goodwater* < *Bonneau* from *bon* 'good' and the diminutive suffix *-eau* the combination of which is homophonous with *bonne eau* 'good water'.

The second type of faulty translation involves word associations whereby French names containing synchronically meaningless lexemes, and even mere syllables, are associated with actual like-sounding words and rendered in English as such. Thus, we find *Brooks* < *Rousseau*, from either Old French *rous* 'red-haired' and the diminutive suffix *-eau* or the placename *(Le) Rousseau*, translated as *ruisseaux* 'brooks', *Counter* < *Contois* from *Comtois*, a native of Franche-Comté in France, associated with a derivative of *compter* 'to count' such as *compteur* or *comptoir, Cowan* < *Vachon* derived from *vache* 'cow' which has nothing to do with the anglicized Irish name, *Fish* and *Fisher* < *Poissant* from Old French *poissant* 'powerful' likened to *poisson* 'fish', *Lively* and *Playful* < *Joyal* from Old French *joiel* 'joyous' from which *joy* is extracted and associated with liveliness and playfulness.

While the mistranslations listed above are all based on complete French surnames, others are only effected on parts of them. Such are, for example, *Bean* < *Lefebvre* from Old French *fe(b)vre* 'blacksmith' interpreted as *fève* 'bean', *Foote* < *Frappier* from either a variant of Old French *frepier* 'secondhand clothes dealer' or the placename *(Le) Frappier* with the syllable *-pier* being associated with the homophonous word *pied* 'foot', *Salt* < *Decelle* from the placename *Celle* homophonous with *sel* 'salt', *Sister* < *Levasseur* from Old French *vasseur* 'vassal' with the syllable *-seur* associated with the homophonous word *soeur* 'sister', *Spooner* < *Lécuyer* from *écuyer* 'squire' with *-cuyer* suggestive of *cuiller* 'spoon'.

6. Summary

As outlined above, the establishment and diffusion of French names in North America was essentially a two-part process, not only in historical and geographical terms but also onomastically. In my *Dictionnaire des noms de famille du Canada français: anthroponymie et généalogie*, I covered the first phase of the process by providing the family-name etymologies of the migrants from France and elsewhere who settled in Québec and Acadia in the 17th and 18th centuries. A unique feature of this dictionary was the inclusion of genealogical information on the first bearers of the surnames when it was available, which was usually the case given the remarkably detailed birth, marriage and death records that were kept from the very outset of settlement in New France.

The second stage of the colonization process was the spread of these surnames to various English-speaking parts of North America. The result of this migration was an extensive transformation of the original names due either to the fact that their bearers were illiterate and were at the mercy of monolingual anglophone scribes, or simply because some migrants simply wanted to minimize their foreign status and fit in, as it were. This is what constitutes the object of the present work, which is structured as follows.

The entries that contain data on the original immigrants to French Canada consist of two parts. The first of these is onomastic in nature in that it provides the etymology of the surname and any americanized variants they stem from. The latter are also listed alphabetically in their proper place when the case arises. The second part ideally contains the following information: the name of the first bearer followed by that of his parents, his place of origin, the name of his spouse as well as that of her parents, and the place and date of their marriage. Some of these details may be missing, however, if the genealogical records are incomplete. My own ancestry can serve as an illustration of all this:

Picard, from *Picard*, the nickname of a native of Picardie, a former province in France. — Amer. **Peacor, Pecor, Pecore.**
— *Philippe Destroismaisons dit* **Picard** *(Adrien and Antoinette Leroux) from Montreuil in Pas-de-Calais (Nord-Pas-de-Calais) m. Martine Crosnier (Pierre and Jeanne Rotreau) in Château-Richer, QC in 1669.*

SIGNS AND ABBREVIATIONS

m. : married
Amer. : Americanized
(...) : given name or surname unknown
/ : or
* : unattested family name
< : comes from
> : goes to

REFERENCES

I – Onomastics and Toponymy

Bahlow, Hans (2002). *Dictionary of German Names*. Madison: University of Wisconsin.

Bardsley, Charles Waring (1988) [1901]. *A Dictionary of English and Welsh Surnames*. Ramsbury: Heraldry Today.

Black, George F. 1946. *The Surnames of Scotland*. New York: New York Public Library.

Dauzat, Albert (1977). *Les noms de famille de France*. Paris: Librairie Guénégaud.

Dauzat, Albert (1989), *Dictionnaire étymologique des noms de famille et prénoms de France*. Paris, Larousse.

Dauzat, Albert, and Charles Rostaing (2002). *Dictionnaire étymologique des noms de lieux en France*. Paris: Guénégaud.

Darley, Diana, and Dominique de Fleurian (2001). *Dictionnaire national des communes de France*. Paris: Éditions Albin Michel.

De Bhulbh, Seán (2002). *Sloinnte Uile Éirann – All Ireland Surnames*. Limerick: Comhar-Chumann Íde Naofa Teo.

Deshayes, Albert (1995). *Dictionnaire des noms de famille bretons*. Douarnenez: Le Chasse-Marée/ArMen.

Faure, Roberto, María Asunción Ribes, and Antonio García (2005). *Diccionario de apellidos españoles*. Espasa: Madrid.

Francipane, Michele (2006). *Dizionario ragionato dei cognomi italiani*. Milan: Biblioteca Universale Rizzoli.

Fucilla, Joseph G. (1949) [2003]. *Our Italian Surnames*. Baltimore: Genealogical Publishing Company.

Géoportail (2013). Online at www.geoportail.gouv.fr/.

Germain, Jean, and Jules Herbillon (2007). *Dictionnaire des noms de famille en Wallonie et à Bruxelles*. Bruxelles: Éditions Racine.

Hanks, Patrick, ed. (2003). *Dictionary of American Family Names*. Oxford and New York: Oxford University Press.

Hanks, Patrick, and Flavia Hodges (1988). *A Dictionary of Surnames*. Oxford and New York: Oxford University Press.

Hoffman, William F. (1998). *Polish Surnames: Origins and Meanings*. Chicago: Polish Genealogical Society of America.

Jacob, Roland (2006). *Votre nom et son histoire: les noms de famille au Québec*. Montréal: Les Éditions de l'Homme.

Kálmán, Béla (1978). *The World of Names: A Study in Hungarian Onomatology*. Budapest: Akadémiai Kiadó.

Kohlheim, Rosa and Volker Kohlheim (2005). *Duden Familiennamen: Herkunft und Bedeutung*. Mannheim: Dudenverlag.

MacLysaght, Edward (1997). *The Surnames of Ireland*. Dublin: Irish Academic Press.

Michelena, Luis (1973). *Apellidos vascos*. San Sebastián: Editorial Txertoa.

Montandon, Charles (2013). *Patronymes romands*. Online at suisse-romande.ch/patronymes/.

Morgan, T. J., and Prys Morgan (1985). *Welsh Surnames*. Cardiff: University of Wales Press.

Morlet, Marie-Thérèse (1997). *Dictionnaire étymologique des noms de famille*. Paris: Perrin.

Nègre, Ernest (1990). *Toponymie générale de la France*. Genève: Librairie Droz.

Pégorier, André (1997). *Les noms de lieux en France: glossaire de termes dialectaux*. Paris: Institut Géographique National.

Picard, Marc (2010). *Dictionnaire des noms de famille du Canada français: anthroponymie et généalogie*. Québec: Les Presses de l'Université Laval.

Reaney, P. H., and R. M. Wilson (2005). *A Dictionary of English Surnames*, revised 3rd edition. Oxford and New York: Oxford University Press.

Tosti, Jean (2013). *Le dictionnaire des noms*. Online at jeantosti.com/noms/.

II – Genealogy and Demography

Ancestry World Tree. Online at awt.ancestry.com/cgi-bin/igm.cgi?surname.

Beauregard, Denis (2013). *Genealogy of the French in North America*. Online at www.francogene.com/gfna/gfna/998/index.htm.

Beauregard, Denis (2013). *Index of French Immigrants in North America*. Online at francogene.com/migrants/index.php.

Desjardins, Bertrand (2013). *Le Programme de recherche en démographie historique (PRDH)*. Online at www.genealogie.umontreal.ca/fr/leprdh.htm.

Duchesne, Louis (2006). *Les noms de famille au québec: aspects statistiques et distribution spatiale*. Québec: Institut de la statistique du Québec.

Family Search (2013). Online at familysearch.org.

Fordant, Laurent (2013). *Tous les noms de famille en France entre 1891 et 1990*. Online at www.geopatronyme.com/.

Fournier, Marcel (1992). *Les Bretons en Amérique du Nord des origines à 1770*. Montréal: Société généalogique canadienne-française.

Fournier, Marcel (1992). *De la Nouvelle-Angleterre à la Nouvelle-France*. Montréal: Société généalogique canadienne-française.

Fournier, Marcel (1995). *Les Français au Québec: 1765-1865*. Sillery: Les éditions du Septentrion.

Fournier, Marcel (2001). *Les origines familiales des pionniers du Québec ancien (1621-1865)*. Sainte-Foy: Fédération québécoise des sociétés de généalogie.

Fournier, Marcel (2013) *Fichier Origine*. Online at www.fichierorigine.com/.

GenForum (2013). Online at genforum.genealogy.com/.

Jetté, René (1983). *Dictionnaire généalogique des familles du Québec des origines à 1730*. Montréal: Les Presses de l'Université de Montréal.

Jetté, René, and Micheline Lécuyer (1988). *Répertoire des noms de famille du Québec des origines à 1825*. Montréal: Institut Généalogique J. L. et Associés.

Marchi, François (2013). *Généalogie Québec*. Online at genealogiequebec.info/frames.html.

Merz, Johannes Helmut (2001). *The Hessians of Quebec: German Auxiliary Soldiers of the American Revolution Remaining in Canada*. Hamilton: Merz.

White, Stephen A. (1999). *Dictionnaire généalogique des familles acadiennes*. Moncton: Centre d'études acadiennes.

Wilhelmy, Jean-Pierre (1997). *Les mercenaires allemands au Québec, 1776-1783*. Sillery: Septentrion.

A

Abair, Abaire, Abar, Abare, Abear, Aber, see **Hébert.**

Abner, see **Lemelin.**

Achee, Achey, see **Haché.**

Aikey, Akey, see **Éthier.**

Alain, from Latin *Alanus*, the name of an ancient people from Scythia. — Amer. **Allen.**
— *Simon Alain (André and Catherine Marc) from Rouen in Seine-Maritime (Haute-Normandie) m. Jeanne Maufay (Pierre and Marie Duval) in Québec, QC in 1670.*

Alard, see **Allard.**

Allain, variant of **Alain.** — Amer. **Allen.**
— *Louis Allain from France m. Marguerite Bourg (Antoine and Antoinette Landry) in Port-Royal, NS in 1690.*

Allard, from the Germanic name *Adalhard* composed of *adal* 'noble' and *hard* 'hard, strong'. — Amer. **Alard, Allor, Allord, Allore, Alore.**
— *François Allard (Jacques and Jacqueline Frérot) from Blacqueville in Seine-Maritime (Haute-Normandie) m. Jeanne Languille (Michel and Étiennette *Toucheraine) in Québec, QC in 1671.*

Allary, alteration of *Alarie*, from the Germanic name *Alaric* composed of *ala* 'all' and *ric* 'powerful'. — Amer. **Allery.**
— *René Alarie dit Grandalarie (Antoine and Anne Chebret) from Neuville-de-Poitou in Vienne (Poitou-Charentes) m. Louise Thibault (Michel and Jeanne Soyer) in Neuville, QC in 1681.*

Allen, see **Alain** and **Allain.**

Allery, see **Allary.**

Allor, Allord, Allore, Alore, see **Allard.**

Amans, see **Hamann.**

Ambeau, see **Imbault.**

Amblo, see **Imbleau.**

Amell, see **Hamel.**

Amelot, derived from *Amel*, probably from the Latin name *Amelius*. — Amer. **Amlott.**
— *Jacques Amelot dit Sanspeur (Jacques and Marguerite Pattin) from Dieppe in Seine-Maritime (Haute-Normandie) m. Angélique Godin (Charles and Marie Boucher) in L'Ange-Gardien, QC in 1698.*

Amerault, Amero, see **Amirault.**

Amiotte, alteration of *Amiot*, derived from Old French *ami* 'bosom friend, lover, parent'. — Amer. **Emeott.**
— *Philippe Amiot from Soissons in Aisne (Picardie) m. Anne Convent (Guillaume and Antoinette de Longval) in France c. 1625.*

Amirault, variant of *amiral* 'admiral', an ironic nickname. — Amer. **Amerault, Amero, Amiro, Meraw, Mero, Merrow, Mireau.**

— *François Amireau/**Amirault/Mirault** dit Tourangeau from Touraine in Indre-et-Loire (Centre) m. Marie Pitre (Jean and Marie Pesselet) in Acadia c. 1683.*

Amlaw, Amlin, see **Hamelin.**

Amlott, see **Amelot.**

Ammell, see **Hamel.**

Amo, see **Émond.**

Amore, see **Émard.**

Anas, see **Vanasse.**

Ance, see **Hinse.**

Ano, Anoe, see **Hénault.**

Antaya, origin undetermined. — Amer. **Anteau.**

— *François Pelletier dit **Antaya**, son of Nicolas from Gallardon in Eure-et-Loir (Centre), m. Marguerite-Madeleine Morisseau (Julien and Anne *Brelancour) in Québec, QC in 1661.*

Anthony, see **St-Antoine.**

April, from Latin *(mensis) Aprilis* '(month of) Aphrodite'. — Amer. **Laprel.**

— *Francesco Aprile/François **April** dit Francisque (Giuseppe and Marie Olivier) from Genoa in Italy m. Marie-Geneviève Hayot (Zacharie and Marie-Josèphe Levasseur) in Kamouraska, QC in 1763.*

Arave, see **Arrivé.**

Arbour, probably from the Germanic name *Hardburg* composed of *hard* 'hard, strong' and *burg* 'protection'. — Amer. **Arbeau, Arbo.**

— *Michel Harbour/**Arbour** (Pierre and Jeanne *Predan) from Montmain in Seine-Maritime (Haute-Normandie) m. Marie Constantineau (Julien and Marie Langlois) in Québec, QC in 1671.*

Arcand, from the Germanic name *Arcan*, from *ercan* 'excellent, precious'. — Amer. **Arkin.**

— *Simon **Arcand** dit Bourdelais (Antoine and Jeanne Poulet) from Sainte-Croix-du-Mont in Gironde (Aquitaine) m. Marie-Anne Inard (Paul and Marie Bonheur) in Batiscan, QC in 1687.*

Arcement, see **D'Entremont.**

Arceneau, Arceneaux, see **Arseneau.**

Archambault, from the Germanic name *Arcanbald* composed of *ercan* 'excellent, precious' and *bald* 'bold'. — Amer. **Archambo, Chambo, Shambo.**

— *Jacques **Archambault** (Antoine and Renée Ouvrard) from Dompierre-sur-Mer in Charente-Maritime (Poitou-Charentes) m. Françoise Tourault in Dompierre-sur-Mer c. 1629.*

Arcouette, alteration of *Arcouet*, a variant of *Argoat*, the name of the inland part of Brittany. — Amer. **Arquette, Arquit, Arquitt, Arquitte.**

— *Jean **Arcouet** dit Lajeunesse (Pierre and Élisabeth Martin) from Marennes in Charente-Maritime (Poitou-Charentes) m. Élisabeth Pépin (Guillaume and Jeanne Méchin) in Trois-Rivières, QC in 1671.*

Ariel, see **Harel.**

Arkin, see **Arcand.**

Armey, see **Hermès.**

Arno, see **Renaud.**

Arpin, apparently derived from *harpe* 'harp', the nickname of a harpist. — Amer. **Harper.**

— *Émery Arpin/Herpin dit Poitevin (Pierre and Catherine *Osbéré) from Poitiers in Vienne (Poitou-Charentes) m. Marie-Jacqueline Coulon (Auffray and Françoise Tierce) in Québec in 1689.*

Arquette, Arquit, Arquitt, Arquitte, see **Arcouette.**

Arrivé, from *arrivé* 'arrived', probably the nickname of newcomer to a community. — Amer. **Arave.**

— *Jacques Arrivé dit Delisle (Pierre and Jeanne Rosier) from Ars-en-Ré in Charente-Maritime (Poitou-Charentes) m. Renée (de) Laporte (Jacques and Esther Coindriau) in Ars-en-Ré in 1663.*

Arsement, see **D'Entremont.**

Arseneau, alteration of *Arsonneau*, derived from Old French *arson* 'saddle-tree', the nickname of a maker. — Amer. **Arceneau, Arceneaux, Arseneaux, Snow.**

— *Pierre Arseneau/Arsenault from Poitou-Charentes m. (1) Marguerite Dugas (Abraham and Marguerite Doucet) in Acadia c. 1675; (2) Marie Guérin (François and Anne Blanchard) in Port-Royal, NS c. 1689.*

Ash, Ashe, see **Dufresne.**

Ashla, Ashland, Ashlaw, see **Asselin.**

Ashley, see **Lafrenière.**

Asselin, from the Germanic name *Azzelin*, derived from *adal* 'noble', or an alteration of *Ancelin*, derived from *Ancel*, from the Germanic name *Anshelm* composed of *Ans*, the name of a god, and *helm* 'helmet'. — Amer. **Ashla, Ashland, Ashlaw, Ashley, Ashlin, Ashline, Ashlow, Aslin, Eslin.**

— *Jacques Asselin (Jacques and Cécile Olivier) from Bracquemont in Seine-Maritime (Haute-Normandie) m. Louise Roussin (Jacques and Madeleine Giguère) in Château-Richer, QC in 1662.*

— *René Ancelin/Asselin (François and Jeanne *Ciclon) from L'Hermenault in Vendée (Pays de la Loire) m. Marie Juin (François and Mathurine *Thessereyne) in La Rochelle in Charente-Maritime (Poitou-Charentes) in 1665.*

Atchue, see **Hétu.**

Aubain, see **Aubin.**

Aubé, alteration of the Dutch name *Obee*, origin undetermined. — Amer. **Aubie, Obey, Oby.**

— *Hendrick Obee/Andrew Obey/André Aubé dit Langlais (Hendrick and Aeltje Claes) from Schenectady, NY m. Geneviève Fradet (Jean and Jeanne Élie) in Saint-Vallier, QC in 1715.*

Aubertin, derived from *Aubert*, from the Germanic name *Adalbert* composed of *adal* 'noble' and *berht* 'bright'. — Amer. **Aubertine, Hobart.**

— *Jean Aubertin (Nicolas and Claire Joannette) from Grand-Fayt in Nord (Nord-Pas-de-Calais) m. Claire-Françoise Gauthier (Charles and Catherine Camus) in Boucherville, QC in 1698.*

Aubin, from the Latin name *Albinus*, derived from *albus* 'white'. — Amer. **Aubain, Oben, Obey, Obin.**

— *René Aubin dit Saint-Aubin (André and Marie Nérine) from Ranville in Charente (Poitou-Charentes) m. Françoise Bigras (François and Marie Brunet) in Pointe-Claire,*

QC in 1716.

Aubry, from the Germanic name *Alberic* composed of *alb* 'elf' and *ric* 'powerful'. — Amer. **Aubrey, Obrey.**

— *Jean Aubry from Châlons-sur-Marne in Marne (Champagne-Ardenne) m. Antoinette Guény (Nicolas and Jeanne Pitois) in France c. 1731.*

Aubuchon, from [fils] *au Buchon* '[son] of Buchon', from Old French *buschon* 'lumberjack'. — Amer. **Aubuchont, Aubuschon, Beshaw, Obershaw, Obeshaw, Obuchon, Overshon.**

— *Jacques Aubuchon dit Le Loyal (Jean and Catherine Le Marchand) from Dieppe in Seine-Maritime (Haute-Normandie) m. Mathurine Poisson (Jean and Barbe Broust) in Québec, QC in 1647.*

— *Jean Aubuchon dit/sieur de Lespérance (Jean and Jeanne Gille) from Dieppe in Seine-Maritime (Haute-Normandie) m. Marguerite Sédilot (Louis and Marie Grimoult) in Trois-Rivières, QC in 1654.*

Auclair, from [fils] *au Clair* '[son] of Clair', from the Latin name *Clarus*, from *clarus* 'famous'. — Amer. **Oclair, O'Clair.**

— *Pierre Auclair (Pierre and Suzanne Aubineau) from Saint-Vivien in Charente-Maritime (Poitou-Charentes) m. Marie-Madeleine Sédilot (Étienne and Madeleine Carbonnet) in Québec, QC in 1679.*

Aucoin, from the Germanic name *Alhwin* composed of *alah* 'temple' and *win* 'friend'. — Amer. **Ocoin, O'Coin, O'Quinn, Wedge.**

— *Martin Aucoin (Martin and Suzanne Barboteau) from La Rochelle in Seine-Maritime (Poitou-Charentes) m. Marie Sallé (Denys and Françoise Arnaud) in La Rochelle in 1632.*

Audet(te), derived from the Germanic name *Alda*, from *ald* 'old'. — Amer. **Audett, Odett, Odette, O'Dett, O'Dette.**

— *Nicolas Audet dit Lapointe (Innocent and Vincente Roy) from Maulais in Deux-Sèvres (Poitou-Charentes) m. Madeleine Després (François and Madeleine Le Grand) in Sainte-Famille, Île d'Orléans, QC in 1670.*

Auger, from the Germanic name *Alfgari* composed of *alf* 'elf' and *gari* 'spear'. — Amer. **Augare, Geromette, Oge, Ogea, Ogee, Oshia.**

— *Louis Auger from Saintes in Charente-Maritime (Poitou-Charentes) m. Marie-Antoinette Barabé (Nicolas and Michelle Ouinville) in Québec in 1691.*

— *Charles Lemaître dit Auger (François and Judith Rigaud) from La Rochelle in Charente-Maritime (Poitou-Charentes) m. Madeleine Crevier (Nicolas and Louise Lecoutre) in Montréal, QC in 1689.*

Aupry, probable variant of **Aubry.** — Amer. **Auprey.**

— *Louis-Bertrand Aupry dit Laramée (Jean and Françoise Coeffard) from Bordeaux in Gironde (Aquitaine) m. Anne Dumas (René and Marie Lelong) in Laprairie, QC in 1694.*

Austin, see **Ostiguy.**

Avery, Avey, see **Hévey.**

Ayotte, alteration of *Hayot*, a probable variant of *Haillot*, derived from *haille* 'rag', the nickname of an individual dressed in tatters. — Amer. **Iott.**

— *Thomas Hayot from Soligny-la-Trappe in Orne (Basse-Normandie) m. Jeanne Boucher in Mortagne-au-Perche in Orne in 1629.*

4

B

Babba, see **Babin.**

Babeu, alteration of *Babeuf,* a placename in Gironde (Aquitaine). — Amer. **Babeau, Babeaux, Babeuf, Babbey, Babbie, Babby, Barber.**

   — *André **Babeu** (Jean and Marguerite Boulanger) from Cheray in Charente-Maritime (Poitou-Charentes) m. Anne Roy (Pierre and Catherine Ducharme) in Laprairie, QC in 1689.*

Babin, derived from *bab-,* an onomatopoetic stem denoting pouting or stuttering. — Amer. **Babba, Babine, Burbine.**

   — *Antoine **Babin** from La Chaussée in Vienne (Poitou-Charentes) m. Marie Mercier (... and Françoise Gaudet) in Acadia c. 1662.*

Babineau, derived from **Babin.** — Amer. **Babineaux, Babino.**

   — *Nicolas **Babineau** dit Deslauriers from France m. Marie-Marguerite Granger (Laurent and Marie Landry) in Acadia c. 1687.*

Bachand, alteration of *Bachant,* a placename in Nord (Nord-Pas-de-Calais). — Amer. **Bachamp, Bashaw.**

   — *Nicolas **Bachand** dit Vertefeuille (Nicolas and Marie Pinson) from Saint-Cloud in Hauts-de-Seine (Île-de-France) m. Anne Lamoureux (Louis and Françoise Boivin) in Boucherville, QC in 1692.*

Badeau, from the Germanic name *Badwald* composed of *bad* 'combat' and *wald* 'power, authority'. — Amer. **Badeaux.**

   — *Jacques **Badeau** from La Rochelle in Charente-Maritime (Poitou-Charentes) m. Anne Ardouin (Jean and Anne Mouchard) in La Rochelle c. 1631.*

Badger, see **Baillargeon.**

Bador, Badore, Badour, see **Bédard.**

Bail, from Old French *bail* 'governor, regent, bailiff', an ironic nickname. — Amer. **Bayle.**

   — *Jean-Baptiste **Bail** (Claude and Anne Ballot) from Metz in Moselle (Lorraine) m. Marie-Françoise Sarrazin (Jean-Baptiste and Marie-Rose Charbonneau) in Saint-Eustache, QC in 1787.*

Baillargeon, derived from Old French *baillarge,* a type of barley, the nickname of a producer or seller. — Amer. **Badger.**

   — *Mathurin **Baillargeon** (Thomas and Marie Mignot) from Embourie in Charente (Poitou-Charentes) m. Marie Métayer (Étienne and Jeanne Robine) in Québec in 1650.*

Baker, see **Bélanger** and **Boulanger.**

Balanger, see **Bélanger.**

Baldic, see **Bolduc.**

Baldwin, see **Beaudoin.**

Baliles, see **Bélisle.**

Ballard, from the Germanic name *Balhard* composed of *bal* 'torment, spitefulness' and

5

hard 'hard, strong'. — Amer. **Ballor, Bellor.**

— *Louis Balard/**Ballard** dit Latour (Pierre and Sébastienne Pillin) from Autun in Saô-ne-et-Loire (Bourgogne) m. Marguerite Migneron (Jean and Marie Pavie) in Québec, QC in 1676.*

Ballinger, see **Bélanger.**

Ballor, see **Ballard.**

Balthazar, from the Hebrew name *Beltshatztzar* via Latin *Balthazar*, derived from Babylonian *balat shar usur* 'save the life of the king'. — Amer. **Baltazor, Balthazor.**

— *Martin **Balthazar**/Balthazard dit Saint-Martin (Jean and Marguerite Daille) from Lorraine m. Marie-Marguerite Joubert (Pierre and Marie-Agathe Jarry) in Saint-De-nis-sur-Richelieu, QC in 1761.*

Banyea, see **Bernier.**

Baraw, see **Baril.**

Barbeau, either derived from *barbe*, the nickname of a bearded individual, or from the Latin name *Barbara*, from Greek *barbaros* 'stranger, barbarian'. — Amer. **Barber, Barbo.**

— *François **Barbeau** (Jacques and Jeanne Cornuelle) from Poitiers in Vienne (Poitou-Charentes) m. Marguerite Hédouin (François and Catherine Le Roy) in Québec, QC in 1671.*

— *Jean **Barbeau** dit Boisdoré (Pierre and Madeleine Babin) from Pons in Charente-Maritime (Poitou-Charentes) m. Marie Denoyon (Jean and Marie Chauvin) in Boucherville, QC in 1686.*

Barber, see **Babeu** and **Bombardier.**

Barbo, see **Barbeau.**

Barcelo, alteration of *Barsalou*, a placename in Lot-et-Garonne (Aquitaine). — Amer. **Barceleau.**

— *Gérard **Barsalou** (Jean and Hélène Lamarque) from Agen in Lot-et-Garonne (Aquitaine) m. Marie-Catherine Legras (Jean and Marie-Geneviève Mallet) in Montréal, QC in 1700.*

Barcom, Barcomb, Barcombe, Barcome, Barcum, Barcume, see **Berthiaume.**

Bargeron, see **Bergeron.**

Baril, from *baril* 'barrel', either the nickname of a short and stout individual or a heavy drinker. — Amer. **Baraw, Barrie, Barry, Bary, Berrea, Berry.**

— *Jean **Baril** from Charente-Maritime m. (1) Marie Guillet (Pierre and Jeanne de Saint-Père) in Québec c. 1674; (2) Élisabeth Gagnon (Robert and Marie Parenteau) in Sainte-Famille, Île d'Orléans, QC in 1684; (3) Catherine Dessureaux (François and Marie Bouart) in Batiscan, QC in 1704.*

Barkyoumb, see **Berthiaume.**

Barnabé, from the Greek name *Barnabas*, derived from Aramean *bar* 'son' and *nabha* 'prophecy, exhortation', hence 'son of exhortation'. — Amer. **Barnaby.**

— *René Martin dit **Barnabé**, son of Barnabé from France, m. Marie Mignier (André and Jacquette Michel) in Acadia c. 1693.*

Barney, Barnier, see **Bernier.**

Barno, see **Bruneau.**

Barré, either from *Barré*, a placename in France, or from Old French *barré* 'striped', the nickname of an individual who wore that sort of clothing. — Amer. **Barry, Bora.**

— *Louis-Jean* **Barré** *from Beauvais in Oise (Picardie) m. Marie-Josèphe Bessette (Jean and Madeleine Plamondon) in Chambly, QC in 1722.*

Barrette, alteration of *Baret* via *Barette*, derived from the Germanic name *Baro*, from *ber(n)* 'bear'. — Amer. **Barrett.**

— *Jean* **Barette** *(Guillaume and Thiphaine Carrey) from Beuzeville in Eure (Haute-Normandie) m. Jeanne Bitouset (Antoine and Nicole Duport/Leserf) in Château-Richer, QC in 1661.*

Barrie, see **Baril.**

Barrieau, from the Germanic name *Berwald* composed of *ber(n)* 'bear' and *wald* 'power, authority'. — Amer. **Barrileaux, Barrilleaux, Berrio.**

— *Nicolas* **Barrieau/***Bariault from France m. Martine Hébert (Étienne and Marie Gaudet) in Acadia c. 1682.*

Barrière, either from *(La) Barrière*, a placename in France, or from *barrière* 'gate', the nickname of a toll collector. — Amer. **Barrier, Gates.**

— *René* **Barrière** *dit Langevin (Joseph and Catherine Béranger) from Longué in Maine-et-Loire (Pays de la Loire) m. (1) Marie-Françoise Gareau (Jean and Thérèse Bau) in Chambly, QC in 1728; (2) Agathe Laporte (Paul and Marie-Catherine Savary) in Saint-Mathias, QC in 1746.*

Barrileaux, Barrilleaux, see **Barrieau.**

Barry, see **Baril** and **Barré.**

Barsa, probable alteration of *(Le) Barsac*, a placename in France. — Amer. **Berza, Berzas, Berzat.**

— *André* **Barsa** *dit Lafleur (Étienne and Léonarde *Choseau) from Auriat in Creuse (Limousin) m. Françoise Pilois (Gervais and Hélène Tellier) in Montréal, QC in 1669.*

Barshaw, see **Bergeron.**

Barthelette, Bartlett, see **Berthelette.**

Barton, Bartrand, see **Bertrand.**

Bartro, see **Berthiaume.**

Bary, see **Baril.**

Baryo, see **Bériault.**

Bashaw, see **Bachand** and **Bergeron.**

Bashier, see **Bégin.**

Basile, from the Greek name *Basileios* via Latin *Basilius*, derived from *basileus* 'king'. — Amer. **Bazille, Bezile, Bozile.**

— *Basile Gladu dit* **Basile**, *descendant of Jean from Cognac in Charente (Poitou-Charentes), m. Charlotte Lefebvre (Pierre and Josèphe Saint-Jacques) in Marieville, QC in 1801.*

Bassett, Bassette, see **Bessette.**

Bastarache, alteration of *Bazterretxe, Bazterretchea, Bazterretchia, Bazterretchéa, Bazterréchia* or *Basterech*, placenames in Pyrénées-Atlantiques (Aquitaine). — Amer. **Basterash.**

— *Joannis Basterretche/Jean* **Bastarache** *dit Le Basque from Pyrénées-Atlantiques (Aquitaine) m. Huguette Vincent (Pierre and Anne Gaudet) in Acadia c. 1684.*

Bastien, derived from *Sébastien*, from the Greek name *Sebastianos*, derived from *sebastos* 'venerable'. — Amer. **Bastian, Bastine.**

— *François Roquan/Rocan dit* **Bastien**, *grandson of Pierre from Saint-Martin-de-Ré in*

7

Charente-Maritime (Poitou-Charentes), m. Marie-Marguerite Lacasse (Jean-Baptiste and Barbe Labelle) in Saint-Vincent-de-Paul, QC in 1771.

Baulier, alteration of *Banlier*, derived from *banne* 'wicker basket', the nickname of a maker or seller. — Amer. **Boulia.**

 — *Mathurin **Banlier** dit Laperle from Poitiers in Vienne (Poitou-Charentes) m. Françoise Vernin (Jacques and ...) in Québec c. 1678.*

Bayle, see **Bail.**

Bazille, see **Basile.**

Bazinaw, see **Vézina.**

Beabeau, see **Bibeau.**

Bean, Beane, see **Lefebvre.**

Bearor, see **Bérard.**

Beaubriand, see **Boisbriand.**

Beauchaine, see **Beauchesne.**

Beauchamp, from *Beauchamp*, a placename in France. — Amer. **Boshaw, Bushaw, Fairfield.**

 — *Jean **Beauchamp** dit Le Petit Beauchamp (Michel and Marie Roullet) from La Rochelle in Charente-Maritime (Poitou-Charentes) m. Jeanne Loisel (Louis and Marguerite Charlot) in Montréal, QC in 1666.*

Beauchane, see **Beauchesne.**

Beauchemin, from *beau chemin* 'beautiful road', a nickname apparently from the site of an estate or property. — Amer. **Goodroad, Goodrode.**

 — *Marc-Antoine Hus dit **Beauchemin**, grandson of Paul from Montigny in Seine-Maritime (Basse-Normandie), m. Louise-Ursule Laguerce (Jean-François and Marie-Marguerite Lefebvre) in Sorel, QC in 1735.*

Beauchesne, from Old French *beau chesne* 'beautiful oak', a nickname apparently from the site of an estate or property. — Amer. **Beauchaine, Beauchane, Boshan, Boshane.**

 — *Joseph Bourbeau dit **Beauchesne**, son of Pierre from La Rochelle in Charente-Maritime (Poitou-Charentes), m. Marie-Marguerite-Agathe Bigot (François and Marie-Anne Perrault) in Bécancour, QC in 1732.*

Beaudet(te), derived from *Baud*, from the Germanic name *Baldo*, from *bald* 'bold'. — Amer. **Bodet, Bodette, Boudette.**

 — *Jean **Beaudet**/Baudet (Sébastien and Marie *Baudonier) from Blanzay in Vienne (Poitou-Charentes) m. Marie Grandin (Michel and Marie Le Jeune) in Québec, QC in 1670.*

Beaudin, same origin as **Beaudet(te).** — Amer. **Beaudine, Boda, Bodah, Bodi, Bodie, Bodin.**

 — *René **Beaudin**/Baudin (Charles and Jeanne Moinet) from Niort in Deux-Sèvres (Poitou-Charentes) m. Suzanne Vallée (Pierre and Marie-Thérèse Leblanc) in Beauport, QC in 1687.*

Beaudoin, from the Germanic name *Baldwin* composed of *bald* 'bold' and *win* 'friend'. — Amer. **Baldwin, Beudoin, Boadway, Boardman, Boardway, Bodoh, Bodway, Boudway, Budway.**

 — *Jacques **Beaudoin**/Baudouin (Solon and Anne Gautreau) from La Rochelle in Charente-Maritime (Poitou-Charentes) m. Françoise Durand (Pierre and Noëlle Asselin) in Québec in 1671.*

— *Jean **Beaudoin**/Baudouin (Jean and Jeanne Bretet) from La Jarrie in Charente-Maritime (Poitou-Charentes) m. Charlotte Chauvin (Michel and Anne Archambault) in Montréal, QC in 1663.*

Beaudre, see **Beaudry**.

Beaudreau, alteration of *Baudreau*, from the Germanic name *Baldhari* composed of *bald* 'bold' and *hari* 'army'. — Amer. **Budreau, Budrow**.

— *Urbain **Baudreau** dit Graveline (Jean and Marie Chauveau) from Clermont-Créans in Sarthe (Pays de la Loire) m. Mathurine Juillet (Blaise and Antoinette de Liercourt) in Montréal, QC in 1664.*

Beaudry, from the Germanic name *Baldric* composed of *bald* 'bold' and *ric* 'powerful'. — Amer. **Beaudre, Beaudrie, Bodrie, Boudrie**.

— *Toussaint **Beaudry**/Baudry (Louis and Maixende Godet) from Velluire in Vendée (Pays de la Loire) m. Barbe Barbier (Gilbert and Catherine de Lavaux) in Montréal, QC in 1670.*

Beaulac, from *beau lac* 'beautiful lake', a nickname apparently from the site of an estate or property. — Amer. **Bolack**.

— *Antoine Chapdelaine dit **Beaulac**, son of André from Plomb in Manche (Basse-Normandie), m. Catherine Baudreau (Jean and Françoise Bazinet) in Saint-Ours, QC in 1737.*

Beaulieu, from *(Le) Beaulieu* or *(Le) Beau Lieu*, placenames in France. — Amer. **Beauleau, Beaulier, Bolia, Bolio, Boulieu**.

— *Pierre Hudon dit **Beaulieu** (Jean and Françoise Durand) from Chemillé in Maine-et-Loire (Pays de la Loire) m. Marie Gobeil (Jean and Jeanne Guyet) in Québec, QC in 1676.*

Beaumier, alteration of *Boismé*, a placename in Deux-Sèvres (Poitou-Charentes). — Amer. **Boismier, Bomia, Bomier, Bomya**.

— *Jean Boesmé/**Boismé** (Pierre and Andrée Bounet) from Poitiers in Vienne (Poitou-Charentes) m. Marie Hué (Marc and Marie Crespin) in Québec, QC in 1668.*

Beauparlant, from *beau parlant* 'smooth talker'. — Amer. **Beauparland, Tucker**.

— *Jean **Beauparlant** (Simon and Jeanne Besançon) from Nevers in Nièvre (Bourgogne), m. Marie-Josèphe Moreau (Aimé and Françoise Forestier) in Montréal, QC in 1734.*

Beaupré, either from *(Le) Beaupré*, a placename in France, or from *beau pré* 'beautiful meadow', a nickname apparently from the site of an estate or property. — Amer. **Bopray, Boprey**.

— *Pierre **Beaupré** (Philippe and Esther Sauniée) from Metz in Moselle (Lorraine) m. Thérèse Mercier (Louis and Louise Simon) in Québec, QC in 1725.*

— *Ignace Bonhomme dit **Beaupré**, son of Nicolas from Fécamp in Seine-Maritime (Haute-Normandie), m. (1) Agnès Morin (Noël and Hélène Desportes) in Québec, QC in 1671; (2) Anne Poirier (Vincent and Françoise Pinguet) in Québec in 1691.*

Beauregard, from *Beauregard*, a placename in France. — Amer. **Begor, Begore, Bourgard, Burgard, Burgor**.

— *François Davignon dit **Beauregard** from France m. Madeleine Maillot (Jean and Marie Courault) in Chambly, QC in 1719.*

— *André Jarret, sieur de **Beauregard** (Jean and Perrette Sermette) from Vignieu in Isère (Rhône-Alpes) m. Marguerite Anthiaume (Michel and Marie Dubois) in Montréal,*

Beausoleil, from *Beausoleil*, a placename in France. — Amer. **Beausoliel, Boseley, Bosley, Bousley, Bushley.**

— *Simon Sylvestre dit **Beausoleil** (Simon and Marie *Forninque) from Chirac in Lozère (Languedoc-Roussillon) m. Marguerite Baillargeon (Nicolas and Angélique Niquet) in Sorel, QC in 1763.*

Beauvais, from *(Le) Beauvais*, a placename in France. — Amer. **Bouva, Bouvia, Bova, Bovat, Bovay.**

— *Jacques **Beauvais** dit Saint-Gemme (Gabriel and Marie Cronière) from Igé in Orne (Basse-Normandie) m. Jeanne Soldé (Martin and Julienne Le Potier) in Montréal, QC in 1654.*

— *Joseph-Xavier **Beauvais** (Jacques and Anne-Marie Arbel) from Champagnole in Jura (Franche-Comté) m. Marie-Josèphe Desnoyers (Pierre and Marie-Josèphe Létourneau) in Chambly, QC in 1757.*

Bebeau, Bebo, see **Bibeau.**

Bédard, derived either from Old French *bedier* 'ignorant, stupid' or from *bedon/bedaine* 'paunch, potbelly', the nickname of a pudgy individual. — Amer. **Bador, Badore, Badour, Bedeau, Bedor, Bedore, Bedour.**

— *Isaac **Bédard** from La Rochelle in Charente-Maritime (Poitou-Charentes) m. Marie Girard (Simon and Françoise Giraudet) in La Rochelle in 1644.*

Before, see **Bouffard.**

Bégin, derived from Old French *bégart* 'stupid', the nickname of a silly, foolish, or hypocritical individual. — Amer. **Bashier, Begins, Beshong, Bushong.**

— *Jacques **Bégin** from Honfleur in Calvados (Basse-Normandie) m. Anne *Meloque in Honfleur c. 1623.*

Begor, Begore, see **Beauregard.**

Bélair, from *Belair* or *Bélair*, placenames in France. — Amer. **Bellaire, Blair.**

— *François Janvry dit **Bélair** (Charles and Marie Lefebvre) from Dives in Oise (Picardie) m. Marie-Élisabeth Martel (Louis and Marie-Josèphe Légaré) in Pierrefonds, QC in 1761.*

— *François Cibert/Sibert dit **Bélair** (Pierre and Françoise de la Rapidie) from Cherves-Chatelars in Charente (Poitou-Charentes) m. Marie-Marguerite Gareau (Bernard and Marie-Suzanne Mornay) in L'Assomption, QC in 1762.*

— *Jacques-Philippe Vêtu dit **Bélair** (Philippe and Marie-Madeleine Feret) from Neuville-Bourjouval in Pas-de-Calais (Nord-Pas-de-Calais) m. Marie-Anne Laroche (Jean and Marie-Madeleine Lereau) in Montréal, QC in 1724.*

Béland, from the Germanic name *Berland* composed of *ber(n)* 'bear' and *land* 'land'. — Amer. **Bellow, Bellows.**

— *Jean **Béland** (Jean and Élisabeth Cadran) from Rouen in Seine-Maritime (Haute-Normandie) m. Geneviève Gandin (Barthélemi and Marthe Cognac) in Québec in 1677.*

Bélanger, from the Germanic name *Berngari* composed of *ber(n)* 'bear' and *gari* 'spear'. — Amer. **Baker, Balanger, Ballinger, Belenger, Bellenger, Bellinger, Belonga, Belonge, Belonger, Belongia, Belongie, Belongy, Blongy.**

— *François Bellenger/**Bélanger** apparently from Touques in Calvados (Basse-Normandie) m. Marie Guyon (Jean and Mathurine Robin) in Québec, QC in 1637.*

Beleele, see **Bélisle.**

Belenger, see **Bélanger.**

Belfy, see **Bellefeuille.**

Belgard, Belgarde, see **Bellegarde.**

Belhumeur, alteration of *belle humeur* 'nice disposition', a soldier's nickname. — Amer. **Bellemer, Bellemere, Bellemeur, Bellemore, Bellmer, Goodnature.**

— *Martin Monet dit **Belhumeur** (Jean-Baptiste and Rose Liotard) from Pernes-les-Fontaines in Vaucluse (Provence-Alpes-Côte-d'Azur) m. Marie-Josèphe Boissel (Charles and Marie-Thérèse Daudelin) in Verchères, QC in 1757.*

Bélisle, either an alteration of *Belle Isle* or *Belle-Isle*, placenames in France, or of Old French *belle isle* 'beautiful island', a nickname apparently from the site of an estate or property. — Amer. **Baliles, Beleele, Beliel, Belile, Beliles, Belliel, Bellile, Bilile, Billings, Burlile.**

— *Henri Germain dit **Bélisle**, son of Robert from Lonlay-l'Abbaye in Orne (Basse-Normandie), m. Geneviève Marcot (Jacques and Élisabeth Salé) in Cap-Santé, QC in 1698.*

— *Jacques Goyer dit **Bélisle**, son of Mathurin from Tourouvre in Orne (Basse-Normandie), m. Hélène Courault (Cybard and Françoise Goupil) in Montréal, QC in 1699.*

— *Emmanuel Leborgne dit **Bélisle** (Emmanuel and Catherine Planeau) from Calais in Pas-de-Calais (Nord-Pas-de-Calais) m. Jeanne François (Jacques and Jeanne Gouillon) in La Rochelle in Charente-Maritime (Poitou-Charentes) in 1635.*

Bell, see **Lebel.**

Bellaire, see **Bélair.**

Bellefeuille, apparently from *(La) Bellefeuille, (La) Belle Feuille* or *Belle-Feuille*, placenames in France. — Amer. **Belfy, Leaf.**

— *Louis-Joseph Rivard dit **Bellefeuille**, son of Robert from Tourouvre in Orne (Basse-Normandie), m. Marie-Françoise Lesieur (Charles and Françoise Lafond) in Louiseville, QC in 1717.*

Bellegarde, from *Bellegarde*, a placename in France. — Amer. **Belgard, Belgarde, Bellgard.**

— *Christophe Gerbault dit **Bellegarde** (Élie and Perrine Philippe) from Saumur in Maine-et-Loire (Pays de la Loire) m. Marguerite Lemaître (François and Judith Rigaud) in Québec in 1676.*

Bellemare, apparently from *Bellemare* or *(La) Belle Mare*, placenames in France. — Amer. **Bellemore, Bellmare, Bellmore, Belmore.**

— *Jean Gélinas dit **Bellemare**, grandson of Étienne from Saintes in Charente-Maritime (Poitou-Charentes), m. Jeanne Boissonneau (Vincent and Anne Colin) in Saint-Jean, Île d'Orléans, QC in 1700.*

Bellemer, Bellemere, Bellemeur, see **Belhumeur.**

Bellemore, see **Belhumeur** and **Bellemare.**

Bellenoix, apparently from *La Belle Noix*, a placename in Sarthe (Pays de la Loire). — Amer. **Bellenoit.**

— *Jean-Baptiste Lemaître dit Auger and **Bellenoix**, grandson of François from France, m. Marie-Françoise Lesieur (Julien and Marie-Simone Blanchet) in Yamachiche, QC in 1727.*

Bellerose, from *belle rose* 'beautiful rose', a soldier's nickname. — Amer. **Bellrose, Belrose.**

— *Jean Ménard dit **Bellerose**, son of Jacques from Mervent in Vendée (Pays de la Loi-*

re), m. Élisabeth Valiquet (Jean and Renée Loppé) in Boucherville, QC in 1690.
— Jean Rivat dit **Bellerose** *(Quirin and Anne Desaulx) from Fraimbois in Meurthe-et-Moselle (Lorraine) m. Marie-Angélique Joly (Marc-Antoine and Marie-Anne Boucher) in Berthier-en-Haut, QC in 1760.*

Bellenger, see **Bélanger.**
Belleveau, see **Belliveau.**
Bellgard, see **Bellegarde.**
Belliel, Bellile, see **Bélisle.**
Bellinger, see **Bélanger.**
Belliveau, apparently derived from Old French *beliver* 'to stagger along', the nickname of a drunkard. — Amer. **Belleveau.**
— Antoine **Belliveau**/*Béliveau from La Chaussée in Vienne (Poitou-Charentes) m. Andrée Guyon in France or Acadia c. 1651.*

Bellmare, see **Bellemare.**
Bellmer, see **Belhumeur.**
Bellmore, see **Bellemare.**
Bellor, see **Ballard.**
Bellow, Bellows, see **Béland.**
Bellrose, see **Bellerose.**
Belmore, see **Bellemare.**
Belodeau, see **Bilodeau.**
Belonga, Belonge, Belonger, Belongia, Belongie, Belongy, see **Bélanger.**
Belrose, see **Bellerose.**
Bennett, Bennette, see **Binet(te).**
Benoît, from the Latin name *Benedictus,* from *benedictus* 'blessed'. — Amer. **Bennett, Benware, Benway, Ward.**
— Martin **Benoît** *dit Labrière from France m. Marie Chaussegros in Port-Royal, NS in 1672.*
— Paul **Benoît** *dit Nivernois/Livernois (François and Dimanche Chapelain) from Châtillon-en-Bazois in Nièvre (Bourgogne) m. Élisabeth Gobinet (Nicolas and Marguerite *Lorgeleux) in Montréal, QC in 1658.*

Benore, see **Bernard.**
Benware, Benway, see **Benoit.**
Bérard, from the Germanic name *Berhard* composed of *ber(n)* 'bear' and *hard* 'hard, strong'. — Amer. **Bearor.**
— Gabriel **Bérard** *dit Lépine (Pierre and Isabelle Guillermain) from Château-du-Loir in Sarthe (Pays de la Loire) m. Geneviève Hayot (Jean and Louise Pelletier) in Québec in 1673.*

Bercier, from *bercier,* a regional variant of *berger* 'shepherd'. — Amer. **Rocker.**
— Louis **Bercier** *from Le Bernard in Vendée (Pays de la Loire) m. Anne Cochet in Québec c. 1668.*

Bercume, see **Berthiaume.**
Berger, alteration of *Nürnberger,* derived from *Nürnberg,* a placename in Germany. — Amer. **Shepard.**
— Friedrich Wilhelm Nürnberger/Frédéric-Guillaume **Berger** *(Friedrich Wilhelm and ...) from Hesse-Cassel in Germany m. Marie-Euphrosine Gaudreau (Joseph-Marie and*

Marie-Anne Fortin) in L'Islet, QC in 1787.

Bergeron, derived from *berger* 'shepherd'. — Amer. **Bargeron, Barshaw, Bashaw, Bershaw.**

— *Pierre **Bergeron** from Saint-Saturnin-du-Bois in Charente-Maritime (Poitou-Charentes) m. Catherine Marchand in Saint-Saturnin-du-Bois c. 1642.*

Bériault, alteration of *Bériau,* derived from *Bérier,* from the Germanic name *Berihari* composed of *ber(n)* 'bear' and *hari* 'army'. — Amer. **Baryo.**

— *Vincent **Bériau** dit Poitevin (Jean and Marie Arnaud) from Luçon in Vendée (Pays de la Loire) m. Marie Cordeau (Jean and Catherine Latour) in Québec, QC in 1681.*

Bernard, from the Germanic name *Bernhard* composed of *ber(n)* 'bear' and *hard* 'hard, strong'. — Amer. **Benore, Burnor.**

— *Pierre **Bernard** dit Lajoie (Daniel and Marie Bertrand) from Pons in Charente-Maritime (Poitou-Charentes) m. Marguerite Durand (Pierre and Marie-Thérèse Mondin) in Montréal, QC in 1726.*

— *Pierre **Bernard** (Mathurin and Marie Amiot) from Saint-Étienne-du-Bois in Vendée (Pays de la Loire) m. Marie-Geneviève Giroux (Raphaël and Marie-Madeleine Vachon) in Beauport, QC in 1730.*

Bernier, from the Germanic name *Bernhari* composed of *ber(n)* 'bear' and *hari* 'army'. — Amer. **Banyea, Barney, Barnier, Bonyea.**

— *Jacques **Bernier** dit Jean de Paris (Yves and Michelle *Trevilet) from Paris (Île-de-France) m. Antoinette Grenier (Claude and Catherine ...) in Québec, QC in 1656.*

Berno, see **Bruneau.**

Bero, see **Liboiron.**

Berrea, see **Baril.**

Berrio, see **Barrieau.**

Berry, see **Baril** and **Laframboise.**

Bershaw, see **Bergeron.**

Berthelette, alteration of *Berthelet,* derived from the Germanic name *Berto,* from *berht* 'bright'. —Amer. **Barthelette, Bartlett.**

— *Antoine **Berthelet** dit Savoyard (François and Françoise Ravier) from Héry-sur-Alby in Haute-Savoie (Rhône-Alpes) m. Jeanne Chartier (René and Marguerite Delorme) in Montréal, QC in 1701.*

Berthiaume, from the Germanic name *Berhthelm* composed of *berht* 'bright' and *helm* 'helmet'. — Amer. **Barcom, Barcomb, Barcombe, Barcome, Barcum, Barcume, Barkyoumb, Bartro, Bercume, Burcume, Burkum.**

— *Jacques **Berthiaume** (Pierre and Jacqueline Brion) from Thury-Harcourt in Calvados (Basse-Normandie) m. Catherine Bonhomme (Nicolas and Catherine Gouget) in Québec in 1667.*

Bertrand, from the Germanic name *Berhthramn* composed of *berht* 'bright' and *hramn* 'raven'. — Amer. **Barton, Bartrand, Burton, Burtraw.**

— *Jean **Bertrand** (Jean and Marie Jofret) from Marcillat-en-Combraille in Allier (Auvergne) m. Isabelle Legrain (Adrien and Louise-Thérèse Stebbins) in Saint-Mathias, QC in 1741.*

— *Pierre **Bertrand** dit Desrochers (Jean and Marie Magné) from La Rochelle in Charente-Maritime (Poitou-Charentes) m. Catherine Lemoine (Nicolas and Marguerite Jasselin) in Montréal, QC in 1714.*

Bérubé, variant of *Barabé*, from the Greek name *Barabbas*, derived from Aramean *bar abba* 'son of the father'. — Amer. **Burbee, Burbey, Burby.**

— *Damien **Bérubé** (Robert and Catherine Ferrecoq) from Yvetot in Seine-Maritime (Haute-Normandie) m. Jeanne Savonnet (Jacques and Antoinette Babillet) in L'Islet, QC in 1679.*

Berza, Berzas, Berzat, see **Barsa.**

Besaw, see **Bisson.**

Beshaw, see **Aubuchon.**

Beshong, see **Bégin.**

Besio, see **Bisaillon.**

Bessette, from *(La) Bessette*, a placename in France. — Amer. **Bassett, Bassette, Bessett.**

— *Jean **Bessette** dit Brisetout from Cahors in Lot (Midi-Pyrénées) m. Anne Seigneur (Guillaume and Madeleine Sauvé) in Québec in 1668.*

Bétourné, from Old French *bestorné* 'misshapen', the nickname of a deformed or crippled individual. — Amer. **Bitney.**

— *Adrien **Bétourné** dit Laviolette (Charles and Marguerite ...) from Saint-Crépin-Ibouvilliers in Oise (Picardie) m. Marie Deshayes in Québec c. 1668.*

Betters, see **Lemieux.**

Beudoin, see **Beaudoin.**

Beyett, Beyette, see **Billet.**

Beyor, see **Biard.**

Bezeau, from *Bezeau*, a placename in Vendée (Pays de la Loire). — Amer. **Bisso.**

— *Pierre **Bezeau** (Pierre and Françoise Tulon) from Angers in Maine-et-Loire (Pays de la Loire) m. Renée Millet (René and Madeleine Drouet) in France c. 1665.*

Bezile, see **Basile.**

Bezio, see **Bisaillon.**

Biard, alteration of *Biort*, origin uncertain. — Amer. **Beyor.**

— *Pierre **Biort** (Pierre and Martine Godeau) from Blois in Loir-et-Cher (Centre) m. Marie-Anne Lamarre (Pierre and Marie Paulet) in Montmagny, QC in 1705.*

Bibeau, probably derived from Old French *biberon* 'neck, spout', the nickname of a drinker or a drunkard. — Amer. **Beabeau, Bebeau, Bebo.**

— *François **Bibeau** (Jacques and Jeanne Savineau) from Huré in Charente-Maritime (Poitou-Charentes) m. Louise Énard (Simon and Marie Loubier) in Trois-Rivières, QC in 1682.*

Bienvenu, derived from Old French *bienvenir* 'to greet favorably', a former given name meant to be a good omen. — Amer. **Welcome.**

— *Pierre Fontaine dit **Bienvenu** (Jacques and Claude Giron) from Orléans in Loiret (Centre) m. (1) Marguerite Anthiaume (Michel and Marie Dubois) in Québec in 1692; (2) Marguerite Gentès (Étienne and Catherine Messier) in Varennes, QC in 1700.*

Bigonesse, origin undetermined. — Amer. **Bigness.**

— *Jean **Bigonesse** dit Beaucaire (Antoine and Marie Mousseau) from Nîmes in Gard (Languedoc-Roussillon) m. Marie Raymond (Louis and Madeleine Laroche) in Saint-Philippe-de-Laprairie, QC in 1762.*

Biladeau, see **Bilodeau.**

Bilile, see **Bélisle.**

Billadeau, Billadeaux, Billado, Billeadeau, Billeaudeau, Billedeau, Billedeaux, see **Bilodeau.**

Billet, alteration of *Biguet,* origin uncertain. — Amer. **Beyett, Beyette.**

— *Étienne **Biguet** dit Nobert (Jean and Nicole Levier) from Ponts in Manche (Basse-Normandie) m. Dorothée Dubois (René and Anne-Julienne Dumont) in Champlain, QC in 1691.*

Billideau, see **Bilodeau.**

Billings, see **Bélisle.**

Bilodeau, variant of *Billaudeau,* derived from *Billaud,* from the Germanic name *Biliwald* composed of *bili* 'gentle' and *wald* 'power, authority'. — Amer. **Belodeau, Biladeau, Billadeau, Billadeaux, Billado, Billeadeau, Billeaudeau, Billedeau, Billedeaux, Billideau.**

— *Jacques **Billaudeau/Bilodeau** (Pierre and Jeanne Fleurie) from Poitiers in Vienne (Poitou-Charentes) m. Geneviève Longchamp (Pierre and Marie Desante) in Québec, QC in 1654.*

Bilo, Bilow, see **Boileau.**

Binet(te), derived from **Robert** via *Robinet.* — Amer. **Bennett, Bennette.**

— *René **Binet** (Mathurin and Marie Proute) from Saint-Jean-de-Sauves in Vienne (Poitou-Charentes) m. Catherine Bourgeois (Thomas and Renée Petit) in Québec, QC in 1667.*

Bird, see **Loiseau.**

Bisaillon, probably derived from Old French *bisaille,* a mixture of peas and vetch used for fodder, the nickname of a producer or seller. — Amer. **Besio, Bezio, Bizaillon.**

— *Étienne **Bisaillon** (Benoît and Françoise Dublay) from Saint-Jean-d'Aubrigoux in Haute-Loire (Auvergne) m. Jeanne Roinay (François and Perrine Meunier) in Laprairie, QC in 1685.*

Bishop, see **Lévesque.**

Bisnett, Bisonett, Bisonnett, see **Bissonnet(te).**

Bissette, see **Bizet.**

Bisso, see **Bezeau.**

Bisson, from *(Le) Bisson* or an alteration of *(Le) Buisson,* placenames in France. — Amer. **Besaw.**

— *Gervais **Bisson/Buisson** dit Saint-Côme from Saint-Cosme-en-Vairais in Sarthe (Pays de la Loire) m. Marie Lereau (René and Marguerite Guillin) in Saint-Cosme-en-Vairais c. 1640.*

Bissonnet(te), probable variant of *Bessonnet,* derived from Old French *besson* 'twin'. — Amer. **Bisnett, Bisonett, Bisonnett, Bissonett, Bissonnett.**

— *Pierre **Bissonnet** (Jacques and Guillemette Debien) from Bourg-sous-la-Roche in Vendée (Pays de la Loire) m. Marie Dallon (Michel and Marguerite *Véronne) in Québec, QC in 1668.*

Bitney, see **Bétourné.**

Bizaillon, see **Bisaillon.**

Bizet, derived from *bis* 'greyish-brown', the nickname of an individual with a dark complexion. — Amer. **Bissette.**

— *Jean **Bizet** (Jacques and Françoise Collier) from London in England m. Catherine Quenneville (Jean and Denise Marié) in Montréal, QC in 1697.*

Blackbird, see **Létourneau.**

Blair, see **Bélair.**

Blais, from the Latin name *Blasius.* — Amer. **Blair, Blay.**

— *Pierre Blais (Mathurin and Françoise Pénigaut) from Hanc in Deux-Sèvres (Poitou-Charentes) m. (1) Anne Perrault (Jean and Jeanne Valta) in Sainte-Famille, Île d'Orléans, QC in 1669; (2) Élisabeth Royer (Jean and Marie Targer) in Saint-Jean, Île d'Orléans, QC in 1689.*

Blanchet, derived from *blanc* 'white', the nickname of an individual with light blond hair. — Amer. **Blanchett.**

— *Pierre Blanchet (Noël and Madeleine Valet) from Rosières-en-Santerre in Somme (Picardie) m. Marie Fournier (Guillaume and Françoise Hébert) in Québec, QC in 1670.*

Blay, see **Blais.**

Bleau, variant of *Belleau,* derived from *bel* 'beautiful'. — Amer. **Bleaux, Blow.**

— *Alexis Bleau dit Alexandre (Barthélemi and Barbe Aubry) from Évreux in Eure (Haute-Normandie) m. Marie-Madeleine Charron (Jean and Anne d'Anneville) in L'Ancienne Lorette, QC in 1712.*

Blongy, see **Bélanger.**

Blow, see **Bleau.**

Bluteau, derived from *bluteur* 'bolter', the nickname of an individual who sifted flour. — Amer. **Bluto.**

— *Jacques Bluteau (Clément and Anne Moques) from Le Gué-de-Velluire in Vendée (Pays de la Loire) m. Claire-Françoise Paré (François and Marie Fortier) in Sainte-Famille, Île d'Orléans, QC in 1679.*

Boadway, Boardman, see **Beaudoin.**

Boardo, see **Bourdeau.**

Boardway, see **Beaudoin.**

Bobo, see **Bourbeau.**

Boclair, see **Boisclair.**

Boda, Bodah, see **Beaudin.**

Bodet, Bodette, see **Beaudet.**

Bodi, Bodie, Bodin, see **Beaudin.**

Bodo, see **Thibodeau.**

Bodoh, see **Beaudoin.**

Bodrie, see **Beaudry.**

Bodway, see **Beaudoin.**

Boie, see **Bois.**

Boileau, alteration of *boit l'eau* 'drinks the water', probably an ironic nickname for a heavy drinker. — Amer. **Bilo, Bilow, Bylow.**

— *Pierre Boileau (Edmé and Geneviève Girard) from Poitiers in Vienne (Poitou-Charentes) m. Marguerite Ménard (Maurice and Madeleine Couc) in Boucherville, QC in 1706.*

Bois, from *(Le) Bois,* a placename in France. — Amer. **Boie.**

— *Jacques Bois (René and Reine/Renée Boyer) from Poitiers in Vienne (Poitou-Charentes) m. Anne Soucy (Jean and Jeanne Savonnet) in Rivière-Ouelle, QC in 1704.*

Boisbriand, from *(Le) Bois Briand,* a placename in France. — Amer. **Beaubriand,**

Bombria.

— *Charles Morel dit* **Boisbriand/Boisbrillant**, *descendant of Olivier from Le Gâvre in Loire-Atlantique (Pays de la Loire), m. Marie-Françoise Pinel (Charles-François and Marie-Anne Ouellet) in La Pocatière, QC in 1751.*

Boisclair, from *(Le) Bois Clair*, a placename in France. — Amer. **Boclair.**

— *Jacques Bériau/Blereau dit* **Boisclair** *(Jean and Élisabeth Brault) from Hermeray in Yvelines (Île-de-France) m. Marie-Anne Maranda (Charles and Denise Fiset) in Québec, QC in 1731.*

Boismenu, from *Boismenu* or *(Le) Bois Menu*, placenames in France. — Amer. **Boismenue.**

— *Jean Monet/Moinet dit* **Boismenu** *(Michel and Marie Bretelle) from Dampierre-sur-Boutonne in Charente-Maritime (Poitou-Charentes) m. Thérèse Glory (Laurent and Jacqueline Lagrange) in Pointe-aux-Trembles, QC in 1678.*

Boismier, see **Beaumier.**

Boissy, from *(Le) Boissy*, a placename in France. — Amer. **Bushey.**

— *Julien* **Boissy** *dit La Grillade (Jean and Marie Gourmaux) from Le Givre in Vendée (Pays de la Loire) m. Françoise Grossejambe (Martin and Jeanne Grandchamp) in Québec, QC in 1671.*

Boisvert, either from *Boisvert, Bois-Vert* or *(Le) Bois Vert*, placenames in France, or from *bois vert* 'green wood', a nickname apparently from the site of an estate or property. — Amer. **Bovair, Greenwood.**

— *Étienne Denevers dit* **Boisvert**, *son of Étienne from L'Épine in Marne (Champagne-Ardenne), m. Marie-Jeanne Lemay (Michel and Marie Duteau) in Québec c. 1688.*

— *Jean Joubin dit* **Boisvert** *(Bénigne and Jeanne Rivos) from Saint-Benoît-de-Carmaux in Tarn (Midi-Pyrénées) m. Françoise Renaud (Pierre and Françoise Desportes) in Grondines, QC in 1694.*

Boivin, alteration of *boit vin* 'drinks wine', the nickname of a heavy drinker. — Amer. **Drinkwine.**

— *Pierre* **Boivin** *(Pierre and Anne Lecocq) from Rouen in Seine-Maritime (Haute-Normandie) m. Étiennette Fafard (Bertrand and Marie Sédilot) in Trois-Rivières, QC in 1664.*

Bolack, see **Beaulac.**

Bolduc, alteration of *Bois le Duc*, a placename in France. — Amer. **Baldic, Bolduke, Burgess.**

— *Louis* **Bolduc** *(Pierre and Gillette Pijard) from Paris (Île-de-France) m. Élisabeth Hubert (Claude and Isabelle Fontaine) in Québec, QC in 1668.*

Bolia, Bolio, see **Beaulieu.**

Bombard, see **Labombarde.**

Bombardier, from *bombardier* 'artilleryman'. — Amer. **Barber.**

— *André* **Bombardier** *dit Labombarde and Passepartout (Jean and Marie-Françoise Guillin) from Lille in Nord (Nord-Pas-de-Calais) m. Marguerite Demers (Jean-Baptiste and Cunégonde Masta) in Montréal, QC in 1706.*

Bombria, see **Boisbriand.**

Bomia, Bomier, Bomya, see **Beaumier.**

Bonami, from *bon ami* 'good friend'. — Amer. **Goodfriend.**

— *Raymond* **Bonami** *dit Lespérance (Jean and Gabrielle Miaulet) from Loriol-du-*

Comtat in *Vaucluse (Provence-Alpes-Côte d'Azur)* m. *Marie-Madeleine Thibodeau in Chambly, QC in 1762.*

Bonenfant, from *bon enfant* 'good child'. — Amer. **Bonefont, Goodchild, Gutchell.**
— *Jean-Baptiste* **Bonenfant** *(Louis and Hilairette Macaud) from Saint-Martin-de-Fraigneau in Vendée (Pays de la Loire)* m. *Élisabeth Balsé (Jean and Anne Brisseau) in La Flotte in Charente-Maritime (Poitou-Charentes) in 1745.*

Bonneau, either from *(Le) Bonneau,* a placename in France, or derived from *bon* 'good'. — Amer. **Bonno, Bono, Bunno, Goodwater.**
— *Jean* **Bonneau** *(Jean and Marie Jouanneau) from Saint-Quentin-lès-Troo in Loir-et-Cher (Centre)* m. *Marie-Madeleine Moreau (Pierre and Marie-Madeleine Lemire) in Québec, QC in 1712.*
— *Joseph* **Bonneau** *dit La Bécasse (Pierre and Marie Lambert) from Vernoux-en-Gâtine or Vernoux-sur-Boutonne in Deux-Sèvres (Poitou-Charentes)* m. *Marie-Madeleine Duchesne (Pierre and Catherine Rivet) in Saint-François, Île d'Orléans, QC in 1684.*

Bonnet(te), either from *(Le) Bonnet,* a placename in France, or derived from *bon* 'good'. — Amer. **Bonnett.**
— *Louis* **Bonnet** *dit Latour (Jean and Marie-Anne Trilha) from Latour-de-France in Pyrénées-Orientales (Languedoc-Roussillon)* m. *Marie-Geneviève Petit (Joseph and Marie-Geneviève Lemaire) in Verchères, QC in 1760.*

Bonnevie, from *bonne vie* 'good life', a well-wishing name. — Amer. **Bonvie.**
— *Jacques* **Bonnevie** *dit Beaumont from Paris (Île-de-France)* m. *Françoise Mius (Philippe and ...) in Acadia c. 1701.*

Bonneville, from *(La) Bonneville,* a placename in France. — Amer. **Bonville.**
— *François Bouteille dit* **Bonneville** *(Simon and Michelle Masson) from Thauron in Creuse (Limousin)* m. *Marie-Jeanne Charron (Pierre and Catherine Pillard) in Québec c. 1706.*

Bonno, Bono, see **Bonneau.**

Bonsang, alteration of *Bonsaint,* from *bon saint* 'good saint', probably an ironic nickname. — Amer. **Goodblood.**
— *Paul Prévost dit* **Bonsaint,** *descendant of François from Avranches in Manche (Basse-Normandie),* m. *Marguerite Gamache (Abraham and Anastasie Pelletier) in Saint-Roch-des-Aulnaies, QC in 1834.*

Bonvie, see **Bonnevie.**

Bonville, see **Bonneville.**

Bonvouloir, from *bon vouloir* 'goodwill', the nickname of a friendly or amiable individual. — Amer. **Goodwill.**
— *Julien Delière/Deslierres/Deslières dit* **Bonvouloir** *(René and Émérence Godard) from Laval in Mayenne (Pays de la Loire)* m. *Marie-Marthe Daragon (François and Marie Guillemet) in Montréal, QC in 1717.*

Bonyea, see **Bernier.**

Booska, see **Bousquet.**

Bopray, Boprey, see **Beaupré.**

Bora, see **Barré.**

Bordeau, Bordeaux, Bordo, see **Bourdeau.**

Bornais, from *(Le/Les) Bornais,* a placename in France. — Amer. **Burness.**
— *Aimé* **Bornais** *(Aimé and Marguerite *Dartenai) from Paris (Île-de-France)* m. *Ma-*

rie-Geneviève Papillon (Étienne and Geneviève Garnier) in Neuville, QC in 1727.

Boseley, see **Beausoleil.**

Boshan, Boshane, see **Beauchesne.**

Boshaw, see **Beauchamp.**

Bosley, see **Beausoleil.**

Boss, see **Bourgeois.**

Bossé, from Old French *bossé* 'hunchbacked'. — Amer. **Bossee, Bossie, Bussey.**

— *Louis **Bossé** (Jean and Anne Guillon) from Chabournay in Vienne (Poitou-Charentes) m. Angélique Bouchard (Nicolas and Anne Roy) in Cap-Saint-Ignace, QC in 1692.*

Botineau, derived from *Botin,* same origin as **Boutin.** — Amer. **Bottineau.**

— *Pierre **Botineau** (Mathurin and Marie Aubron) from Nantes in Loire-Atlantique (Pays de la Loire) m. Marie-Angélique Fournaise (François and Angélique Serre) in Lavaltrie, QC in 1760.*

Boucha, see **Boucher.**

Bouchard, from the Germanic name *Burchard* composed of *burg* 'protection' and *hard* 'hard, strong'. — Amer. **Bushaw, Bushor, Bushore.**

— *Claude **Bouchard** dit Le Petit Claude (Jacques and Noëlle Touschard) from Saint-Cosme-en-Vairais in Sarthe (Pays de la Loire) m. Louise Gagné (Louis and Marie Michel) in Québec, QC in 1654.*

Boucher, from *boucher* 'butcher'. — Amer. **Boucha, Bouche, Bouchey, Bouchie, Boushee, Boushey, Bush, Busha, Bushay, Bushee, Bushey, Bushie, Bushy.**

— *Jean **Boucher** (Quatrin and Jeanne Denis) from Chaix in Vendée (Pays de la Loire) m. Marie-Madeleine Paré (Robert and Françoise Lehoux) in Beaupré, QC in 1678.*

— *Marin **Boucher** from Mortagne-au-Perche in Orne (Basse-Normandie) m. (1) Julienne Baril (Jean and Raoulline Crête) in Mortagne-au-Perche in 1611; (2) Perrine Mallet (Pierre and Jacqueline Liger) in Saint-Langis-lès-Mortagne in Orne c. 1628.*

Boudette, see **Beaudet.**

Boudreau, alteration of *Boudrot,* derived from *Boudier,* from the Germanic name *Bodhari* composed of *bod* 'messenger' and *hari* 'army'. — Amer. **Boudreaux, Boudro, Budro, Budroe, Budrow.**

— *Michel Boudrot/**Boudreau** from La Rochelle in Charente-Maritime (Poitou-Charentes) m. Michelle Aucoin in France or Acadia c. 1641.*

Boudrie, see **Beaudry.**

Boudway, see **Beaudoin.**

Bouffard, from Old French *bouf(f)ard* 'glutton'. — Amer. **Before, Boufford.**

— *Jacques **Bouffard** (Jean and Marguerite Le Portier) from Rouen in Seine-Maritime (Haute-Normandie) m. Anne Leclerc (Jean and Marie Blanquet) in Saint-Pierre, Île d'Orléans, QC in 1680.*

Boulanger, from *boulanger* 'baker'. — Amer. **Baker.**

— *Claude Lefebvre dit **Boulanger** (Louis and Marie Verneuil) from Vigny in Val d'Oise (Île-de-France) m. Marie Arcular (Jean and Catherine Coin) in Sainte-Famille, Île d'Orléans, QC in 1669.*

Boulay, from *(Le) Boulay,* a placename in France. — Amer. **Buley.**

— *Robert **Boulay** from Loisé in Orne (Basse-Normandie) m. Françoise Grenier in Loisé in 1658.*

Boulerice, alteration of the Breton name *Bourhis,* from *bourc'his* 'burgher'. — Amer.

Boulerisse, Bulrice, Bulris, Bulriss.
— *Jean* **Bourhis** *dit Le Breton (Jean and Hélène Le Rousseau) from Brest in Finistère (Bretagne) m. Marie Demers (André and Marie Chefdeville) in Montréal, QC in 1686.*
Boulia, see **Baulier.**
Boulieu, see **Beaulieu.**
Bourassa, derived from Old French *bourras* 'coarse canvas', the nickname of a maker or seller. — Amer. **Bourasaw, Bourasso, Bourisaw, Boursaw, Brassaw, Brasseau, Bursaw.**
— *François* **Bourassa** *(François and Marguerite Dugas) from Saint-Hilaire-de-Loulay in Vendée (Pays de la Loire) m. Marie Leber (François and Jeanne Testard) in Contrecoeur, QC in 1684.*
— *Jean* **Bourassa**/*Bourasseau (Jacques and Françoise Fouchard) from Saint-Fulgent in Vendée (Pays de la Loire) m. (1) Perrette Vallée (Nicolas and Madeleine Major) in Québec, QC in 1665; (2) Catherine Poitevin (Guillaume and Françoise Macré) in Québec, QC in 1676.*
Bourbeau, variant of *Bourbaud,* apparently from the Germanic name *Burgbald* composed of *burg* 'protection' and *bald* 'bold'. — Amer. **Bobo, Burbo.**
— *Pierre* **Bourbeau** *dit Lacourse (Élie and Marie Noiron) from La Rochelle in Charente-Maritime (Poitou-Charentes) m. Anne Bénard (René and Marie Sédilot) in Québec in 1676.*
Bourdeau, derived from Old French *bo(u)rde* 'smallholding', the nickname of a tenant farmer. — Amer. **Boardo, Bordeau, Bordeaux, Bordo, Bourdeaux, Bourdo, Bourdow, Burdeau, Burdo.**
— *Pierre* **Bourdeau** *(Pierre and Catherine Junier) from Saint-Jean-d'Aubrigoux in Haute-Loire (Auvergne) m. (1) Marie Faye (Mathieu and Marguerite-Françoise Moreau) in Laprairie, QC in 1689; (2) Marguerite Lefebvre (Pierre and Marguerite Gagné) in Laprairie, QC in 1700.*
Bourdon, from *(Le) Bourdon,* a placename in France. — Amer. **Bourdo.**
— *Jacques* **Bourdon** *(Jean and Marguerite Legris) from Rouen in Seine-Maritime (Haute-Normandie) m. Marie Ménard (Jacques and Catherine Forestier) in Boucherville, QC in 1672.*
Bourdow, see **Bourdeau.**
Bourett, Bourette, see **Bourret.**
Bourgard, see **Beauregard.**
Bourgault, variant of *Bourgaud,* from the Germanic name *Burgwald* composed of *burg* 'protection' and *wald* 'power, authority'. — Amer. **Bourgo, Burgo.**
— *Gilles* **Bourgaud**/*Bourgault dit Lacroix (Jacques and Marguerite Dumay) from Saint-Alban in Côtes-d'Armor (Bretagne) m. Marie-Marthe Gazaille (Jean and Jeanne Touzé) in Québec in 1694.*
Bourgeois, from *bourgeois* 'burgher', the nickname of an individual who lived in a market town. — Amer. **Boss, Bourgois, Bullock, Burgess, Bushway.**
— *Jacques* **Bourgeois** *from France m. Jeanne Trahan (Guillaume and Françoise Corbineau) in Acadia c. 1643.*
Bourget, alteration of *Bourgeais,* same origin as **Bourgeois.** — Amer. **Bourgette.**
— *Pierre Bourgeais/***Bourget** *dit Lavallée (Pierre and Marie Roux) from Bardécille in Charente-Maritime (Poitou-Charentes) m. Marie Jean (Vivien and Élisabeth Drouet) in*

Lauzon, QC in 1691.

Bourgo, see **Bourgault.**

Bourgois, see **Bourgeois.**

Bourisaw, see **Bourassa.**

Bourque, alteration of *(Le) Bourg,* a placename in France. — Amer. **Bourke, Burk, Burke.**

— *Antoine Bourg/**Bourque** (Simon and Hélène Lecompte) from Martaizé in Vienne (Poitou-Charentes) m. Antoinette Landry in Acadia c. 1642.*

Bourret, probable alteration of *Bourré,* from the Germanic name *Bodrad* composed of *bod* 'messenger' and *rad* 'counsel' — Amer. **Bourett, Bourette, Bourrette, Boury.**

— *Gilles **Bourret**/Bourré dit Lépine (Jean and Marie Danguy) from Saint-Georges-de-Rouelley in Manche (Basse-Normandie) m. Marie Bellehache (Pierre and Marie Burelle) in Québec in 1673.*

Boursaw, see **Bourassa.**

Boury, see **Bourret.**

Boushee, Boushey, see **Boucher.**

Bousley, see **Beausoleil.**

Bousquet, from *(Le) Bousquet,* a placename in France. — Amer. **Booska, Bousquette, Buska, Buskey.**

— *Jean **Bousquet** (Jean and Isabelle Hilaret) from Tonneins in Lot-et-Garonne (Aquitaine) m. Catherine Fourrier (Claude and Marie Pennetier) in Montréal, QC in 1672.*

Bouta, Boutah, Boutain, see **Boutin.**

Boutaugh, see **Boutot.**

Bouthillette, alteration of *Bouteiller* via *Boutillet,* same origin as **Bouthillier.** — Amer. **Boutiette.**

— *Jacques **Boutillet**/Bouteiller (Jean and Anne *Ficton) from Bordeaux in Gironde (Aquitaine) m. Marguerite Verreau (Barthélemi and Marthe Quitel) in Château-Richer, QC in 1699.*

Bouthillier, alteration of *Bouteiller,* derived from *bouteille* 'bottle', either the nickname of a maker or of a cupbearer. — Amer. **Butler.**

— *André **Bouteiller** (André and Jeanne Chobelet) from Saint-André-Treize-Voies in Vendée (Pays de la Loire) m. Angélique Chapacou (Simon and Marie Pacaud) in Boucherville, QC in 1686.*

Boutiette, see **Bouthillette.**

Boutin, derived from the Germanic name *Boto,* from *bod* 'messenger'. — Amer. **Bouta, Boutah, Boutain.**

— *Antoine **Boutin** dit Laplante (Jean and Georgette Bonneau) from Vernon in Vienne (Poitou-Charente) m. Geneviève Gandin (Barthélemi and Marthe Cognac) in Québec, QC in 1665.*

Boutot, alteration of *Thiboutot,* same origin as **Thibodeau.** — Amer. **Boutaugh.**

— *Jacques **Thiboutot** (Jacques and Marie Carel) from Cliponville in Seine-Maritime (Haute-Normandie) m. Marie Boucher (Jean-Galleran and Marie Leclerc) in Rivière-Ouelle, QC in 1675.*

Bouva, Bouvia, see **Beauvais.**

Bouvier, from *bouvier* 'herdsman, cattleman'. — Amer. **Bovia.**

— *Michel **Bouvier** (Louis and Anne Darondeau) from La Flèche in Sarthe (Pays de la*

Loire) m. Mathurine Desbordes in Montréal, QC in 1663.

Bouyea, see **Boyer.**

Bova, see **Beauvais.**

Bovair, see **Boisvert.**

Bovat, Bovay, see **Beauvais.**

Bovia, see **Bouvier.**

Boyer, either from *(Le) Boyer,* a placename in France, or a regional variant of **Bouvier.** — Amer. **Bouyea, Boyea.**

— *Charles Boyer (Pierre and Denise *Retonel) from Vasles in Deux-Sèvres (Poitou-Charentes) m. Marguerite Ténard (Barthélemi and Jeanne Govin) in Montréal, QC in 1666.*

Bozile, see **Basile.**

Brabant, from *(Le) Brabant,* a placename in France. — Amer. **Brabo.**

— *Pierre Brébant/Brabant dit Lamothe (Pierre and Suzanne Daugert) from Aubigny-sur-Nère in Cher (Centre) m. Anne Goupil (Nicolas and Marie Pelletier) in Québec in 1671.*

Braconnier, from Old French *braconnier,* derived from *braque* 'pointer', the nickname of an individual who led this kind of gun dog. — Amer. **Bracconier, Brockney, Brockway.**

— *Jean Braconnier dit Parisien (Jean and Marguerite Legros) from Paris (Île-de-France) m. Françoise Chapelain (Bernard and Éléonore Mouillard) in Saint-Laurent, Île d'Orléans, QC in 1700.*

Branchaud, probable variant of *Branchereau,* derived from *Brancher,* from the Latin name *Pancratius* via *Brancatius,* from Greek *pankration* 'pancratia', an athletic contest combining wrestling and boxing. — Amer. **Brancheau, Branshaw.**

— *Charles Branchaud/Branchereau dit Lacombe (Jacques and Antoinette Vincend) from Macqueville in Charente-Maritime (Poitou-Charentes) m. Marthe Garand (Pierre and Renée Chanfrain) in Saint-Laurent, Île d'Orléans, QC in 1694.*

Brandimore, see **Brindamour.**

Branshaw, see **Branchaud.**

Brassard, origin uncertain. — Amer. **Brassor.**

— *Antoine Brassard from Normandie m. Françoise Méry in Québec, QC in 1637.*

Brassaw, Brasseau, see **Bourassa.**

Brassor, see **Brassard.**

Brault, from the Germanic name *Berwald* composed of *ber(n)* 'bear' and *wald* 'power, authority'. — Amer. **Braud, Breaud, Breaux, Bro, Broe, Brow.**

— *Vincent Breau/Brault from France m. Marie Bourg (Antoine and Antoinette Landry) in Acadia c. 1661.*

Breen, see **Briand.**

Brelia, see **Brière.**

Bresett, Bresette, Bressett, Bressette, see **Brisset(te).**

Breton, from *Breton,* the nickname of a native of Bretagne, a former province in France. — Amer. **Burton, Butler.**

— *Jean Élie/Hélie dit Breton (Jean and Jeanne Mounier) from Ménéac in Morbihan (Bretagne) m. Jeanne Labbé (Charles and Marie François) in Sainte-Famille, Île d'Orléans, QC in 1669.*

22

Breyette, see **Brouillet(te).**

Briand, variant of *Brien*, from Breton *brient* 'preeminence, privilege', probably the nickname of a pretentious individual. — Amer. **Breen.**

— *Pierre-François **Briand**/Brillant (Laurent and Jacquette Martin) from Saint-Malo in Ille-et-Vilaine (Bretagne) m. Renée Marchand (Louis and Marie Godin) in Port-Toulouse (St. Peters), NS c. 1730.*

Briard, either from *Briard*, the nickname of an individual from *Brie*, a region east of the Parisian basin, or a variant of *Bréard*, from the Germanic name *Berhard* composed of *ber(n)* 'bear' and *hard* 'hard, strong'. — Amer. **Brillard, Preo.**

— *Pierre Lejeune dit **Briard** from France m. ... Doucet (Germain and ...) in Port-Royal, NS c. 1650.*

Bricault, derived from Old French *bric* 'crazy, stupid, foolish'. — Amer. **Bricco, Bricko.**

— *Jean **Bricault** dit Lamarche (Julien and Perrine Roussel) from Vay in Loire-Atlantique (Pays de la Loire) m. Marie Chénier (Jean and Jacqueline Sédilot) in Montréal, QC in 1674.*

Brickey, see **Briqué.**

Bricko, see **Bricault.**

Brière, from *La Brière*, a placename in France. — Amer. **Brelia.**

— *Jean **Brière** (Charles and Marie Lepec) from Clarbec in Calvados (Basse-Normandie) m. Jeanne Grandin (Antoine and Jeanne Voinel) in Québec, QC in 1671.*

Brillard, see **Briard.**

Brindamour, from *brin d'amour* 'bit of love', a soldier's nickname. — Amer. **Brandimore.**

— *Étienne Giraud dit **Brindamour** (Jacques and Louise Caillou) from Vouneuil-sous-Biard in Vienne (Poitou-Charentes) m. Marie Berthiaume (Noël and Marie-Françoise Girard) in Montréal, QC in 1760.*

Brine, see **Lebrun.**

Briqué, origin undetermined. — Amer. **Brickey.**

— *Louis-Étienne Vivier dit **Briqué**, descendant of Pierre from Thiré in Vendée (Pays de la Loire), m. Marie-Suzanne Perrault (Albert and Marie-Louise Létourneau) in Saint-Philippe in 1782.*

Brisard, derived from *briser* 'to break', the nickname of a violent individual. — Amer. **Brissard.**

— *Jean **Brisard** dit Saint-Germain (François and Marie Benoist) from Saint-Germain-du-Seudre in Charente-Maritime (Poitou-Charentes) m. Marie-Anne (de) Gerlaise (Jean and Jeanne Trudel) in Trois-Rivières, QC in 1714.*

Brisset(te), derived from *Bris*, from the Latin name *Brictius*. — Amer. **Bresett, Bresette, Bressett, Bressette, Brissett.**

— *Jacques **Brisset** from France m. Jeanne Fétis in France c. 1647.*

— *Jean **Brisset** (Jean and Marguerite Gabory) from Saint-Laurent-de-la-Salle in Vendée (Pays de la Loire) m. Geneviève Trut (Mathurin and Marguerite Gareman) in Batiscan, QC in 1693.*

Bro, see **Brault.**

Brochu, origin uncertain. — Amer. **Brushey.**

— *Jean **Brochu** (Louis and Renée/Louise Guichet) from Montaigu in Vendée (Pays de* *la Loire)* m. Nicole Saulnier *(Pierre and Jeanne Chevillard) in Sainte-Famille, Île d'Orléans, QC in 1669.*

Brockney, Brockway, see **Braconnier.**

Brodeur, from *brodeur* 'embroiderer'. — Amer. **Brother, Brothers.**

— *Jean **Brodeur** dit Lavigne (Jean and Françoise Frogeret) from Nieul-le-Dolent in Vendée (Pays de la Loire) m. Marie-Anne Messier (Michel and Anne Lemoine) in Boucherville, QC in 1679.*

Broe, see **Brault.**

Brooks, see **Rousseau.**

Brousseau, either from *(Le) Brousseau* or *Le Brosseau,* placenames in France. — Amer. **Bruso, Brusseau, Brusso.**

— *Denis **Brosseau** (Jean and Perrine Gobin) from Saint-Sébastien-sur-Loire in Loire-Atlantique (Pays de la Loire) m. Marie-Madeleine Hébert (Guillaume and Marguerite Meunier) in Québec in 1670.*

— *Jean **Brousseau** (Jean and Marie Belion) from Langon in Vendée (Pays de la Loire) m. Anne Greslon (Jacques and Jeanne Vignault) in Québec, QC in 1683.*

Brother, Brothers, see **Brodeur.**

Brouillet(te), from *(Le) Brouillet,* a placename in France. — Amer. **Breyette, Brouillett, Broulette, Bruette, Bruya, Bruyea, Bruyette.**

— *Michel **Brouillet** dit Laviolette (Jacques and Renée Vassière) from Grouex in Vienne (Poitou-Charentes) m. Marie Dubois (Guillaume and Isabelle Lasoeur) in Québec in 1670.*

Brow, see **Brault.**

Brown, see **Lebrun.**

Bruette, see **Brouillet(te).**

Brûlé, from *(Le) Brûlé,* a placename in France. — Amer. **Bruleigh, Bruley.**

— *Antoine **Brûlé** dit Francoeur (Antoine and Madeleine Aubry) from Amiens in Somme (Picardie) m. Françoise-Angélique Méline (Louis and Marie-Anne Massard) in Montréal, QC in 1711.*

Brunais, see **Brunet(te).**

Bruneau, either derived from *brun* 'brown-haired', or an alteration of *Druineau,* derived from **Drouin.** — Amer. **Barno, Berno, Bruno, Burneau, Burno.**

— *François **Bruneau**/Druineau (Robert and Françoise Charbonnier) from Neuvicq-le-Château in Charente-Maritime (Poitou-Charentes) m. Marie Prévost (Antoine and Marie Prévost) in Québec, QC in 1669.*

— *Joseph Petit dit **Bruneau** (Henri and Élisabeth Fontaine) from Paris (Île-de-France) m. Marie Chenay (Bertrand and Marie-Madeleine Bélanger) in Québec, QC in 1675.*

Brunet(te), derived from *brun* 'brown-haired'. — Amer. **Brunais, Brunett, Bruney.**

— *Alexis **Brunet** dit Dauphiné (Jean and Jeanne Robart) from Ancenis in Loire-Atlantique (Pays de la Loire) m. Marie-Josèphe Harnois (Joseph and Angélique Petit) in Québec, QC in 1732.*

— *Mathieu **Brunet** dit Létang (Jacques and Jacqueline *Recheine/*Prohuie) from Rai in Orne (Basse-Normandie) m. Marie Blanchard (Jean and Martine Lebas) in Québec, QC in 1667.*

Bruno, see **Bruneau.**

Brushey, see **Brochu.**

Bruso, Brusseau, Brusso, see Brousseau.
Bruya, Bruyea, Bruyette, see Brouille(te).
Buckwheat, see Sarrazin.
Budreau, see Beaudreau.
Budro, Budroe, see Boudreau.
Budrow, see Beaudreau and Boudreau.
Budway, see Beaudoin.
Buley, see Boulay.
Bullock, see Bourgeois.
Bulrice, Bulris, Bulriss, see Boulerice.
Bunno, see Bonneau.
Burbee, Burbey, see Bérubé.
Burbine, see Babin.
Burbo, see Bourbeau.
Burby, see Bérubé.
Burcume, see Berthiaume.
Burdeau, Burdo, see Bourdeau.
Burgard, see Beauregard.
Burgess, see Bolduc and Bourgeois.
Burgo, see Bourgault.
Burgor, see Beauregard.
Burk, Burke, see Bourque.
Burkum, see Berthiaume.
Burlile, see Bélisle.
Burneau, see Bruneau.
Burness, see Bornais.
Burno, see Bruneau.
Burnor, see Bernard.
Bursaw, see Bourassa.
Burton, see Bertrand and Breton.
Burtraw, see Bertrand.
Bush, Busha, see Boucher.
Bushaw, see Beauchamp and Bouchard.
Bushay, Bushee, see Boucher.
Bushey, see Boissy and Boucher.
Bushie, see Boucher.
Bushley, see Beausoleil.
Bushong, see Bégin.
Bushor, Bushore, see Bouchard.
Bushway, see Bourgeois.
Bushy, see Boucher.
Buska, Buskey, see Bousquet.
Busque, probable alteration of *Le Busc, Le Bosc* or *Le Boscq*, placenames in France. — Amer. **Carey.**
— *Jean* **Busque** *(André and Marie Rivet) from Dunkerque in Nord (Nord-Pas-de-Calais) m. Catherine Prieur (Joseph and Hélène Méchin) in Québec, QC in 1719.*

Bussey, see **Bossé**.
Butler, see **Bouthillier** and **Breton**.
Butterfly, see **Papillon**.
Bylow, see **Boileau**.

C

Cada, see **Cadet.**

Cadaret, Cadarette, see **Cadoret(te).**

Cadet, either from *(Le) Cadet,* a placename in France, or from *cadet* 'youngest child'. — Amer. **Cada.**

— *Michel **Cadet** (Michel and Élisabeth Lefebvre) from Niort in Deux-Sèvres (Poitou-Charentes) m. Geneviève Gauthier (Jean and Angélique Lefebvre) in Québec, QC in 1703.*

Cadieux, derived from Breton *cad* 'battle', probably the nickname of a combatant. — Amer. **Kiah.**

— *Jean **Cadieux** (Pierre and Renée Foureau) from Luché-Pringé in Sarthe (Pays de la Loire) m. Marie Valade (André and Sarah Cousseau) in Montréal, QC in 1663.*

Cadoret(te), from the Breton name *Catuuoret* composed of *cad* 'combat' and *uuoret* 'help, rescue', hence 'help in combat'. — Amer. **Cadaret, Cadarette, Cadreact, Cataract.**

— *Georges **Cadoret** (Pierre and Barbe Deslauriers) from Vannes in Morbihan (Bretagne) m. Barbe Boucher (Pierre and Marie-Anne Saint-Denis) in Château-Richer, QC in 1686.*

Cadran, alteration of *Catrin* via *Cadrin,* from the Greek name *Aikaterine* via Latin *Katharina.* — Amer. **Cadreau.**

— *Nicolas **Catrin/Cadrin** (Thomas and Marguerite Larsonneur) from Méru in Oise (Picardie) m. Françoise Delaunay (Nicolas and Anne-Antoinette Durand) in Sainte-Famille, Île d'Orléans, QC in 1679.*

Cadreact, see **Cadoret(te).**

Cadreau, see **Cadran.**

Callihoo, see **Gladu.**

Camaraire, alteration of the German name *Kämmerer,* from Middle High German *kæmmerer* 'chamberlain, treasurer'. — Amer. **Cameron.**

— *Jacob Christoph **Kaemmerer/**Jacques-Christophe Camerer (Jacob Christoph and Suzan Schneider) from Gotha in Germany m. Marguerite Guignard (Jean-Baptiste and Élisabeth Nadeau) in Saint-Jean-Port-Joli, QC in 1785.*

Campbell, see **Duhamel.**

Campeau, probably from *Campeau,* a placename in Gironde (Aquitaine). — Amer. **Campau, Campeaux, Campo, Compau, Compeau, Compeaux, Compo.**

— *Étienne **Campeau** (Léonard and Françoise Maugé) from Brive-la-Gaillarde in Corrèze (Limousin) m. Catherine Paulo (Pierre and Renée *Cordetelle) in Montréal, QC in 1663.*

Canell, Cannell, see **Quesnel.**

Cantin, alteration of *Quentin,* from the Latin name *Quintinus,* derived from *quintus* 'fifth (-born)'. — Amer. **Contin.**

— Nicolas **Quentin** dit Lafontaine (Louis and Marie des Mousseaux) from Gonneville-sur-Honfleur in Calvados (Basse-Normandie) m. Madeleine Roulois (Micheline and Jeanne Maline) in Québec, QC in 1660.

Canuel, derived from *canu,* a regional variant of *chenu* 'hoary, white-haired'. — Amer. **Canuelle.**

— Jean-Louis Canuet/**Canuel** (Guillaume and Françoise Lecoq) from Ver in Manche (Basse-Normandie) m. Marie Proulx (Pierre and Agathe Destroismaisons) in Rimouski, QC in 1751.

Caouette, alteration of *Caouet,* from *cah(o)uet* 'screech owl', probably the nickname of an individual with a shrill voice. — Amer. **Cowett, Cowette.**

— Pierre **Caouet**/Cahouet (Jean and Marie Vallée) from Landerneau in Finistère (Bretagne) m. Anne Gaudreau (Gilles and Anne Pineau) in Cap-Saint-Ignace, QC in 1693.

Capistran, apparently from *Capistran,* the French name for the Italian city of Capestrano. — Amer. **Capistrand, Capistrant.**

— Marc-Antoine Hus dit **Capistran,** grandson of Paul from Montigny in Seine-Maritime (Haute-Normandie), m. Marie-Anne Binet (François and Marie-Françoise Vachon) in Québec, QC in 1726.

Carbonneau, regional variant of *Charbonneau,* derived from *charbon* 'coal', the nickname of a producer or seller. — Amer. **Carbino.**

— Esprit **Carbonneau** dit Provençal (Antoine and Marguerite Petit) from Aix-en-Provence in Bouches-du-Rhône (Provence-Alpes-Côte-d'Azur) m. Marguerite Landry (Guillaume and Gabrielle Barré) in Sainte-Famille, Île d'Orléans, QC in 1672.

Carey, see **Busque.**

Carie, see **Quéret.**

Carignan, apparently from *(Le) Carignan,* a placename in France. — Amer. **Carrigan.**

— Joseph Bénard/Besnard dit **Carignan,** son of René from Villiers-au-Bouin in Indre-et-Loire (Centre), m. Marguerite Faye (Mathieu and Marguerite-Françoise Moreau) in Laprairie, QC in 1689.

Cariveau, see **Corriveau.**

Carkey, see **Cartier.**

Caron, either from *(Le) Caron,* a placename in France, or from a regional variant of **Charron.** — Amer. **Carro, Carrow, Coro, Corro, Corron, Corrow.**

— Claude **Caron** from Saint-Jean-d'Aubrigoux in Haute-Loire (Auvergne) m. Madeleine Varennes in Saint-Jean-d'Aubrigoux c. 1670.

— Robert **Caron** from France m. Marie Crevet (Pierre and Marie Le Mercier) in Québec, QC in 1637.

Carpenter, see **Charpentier.**

Carpentier, regional variant of **Charpentier.** — Amer. **Carpenter.**

— Claude **Carpentier** (Florent and Marie Guerlet) from Neuville-Ferrières in Seine-Maritime (Haute-Normandie) m. Marguerite de Sainte-Foy/Bonnefoy (Pierre and Marie Andrieu) in Québec, QC in 1671.

Carrie, see **Quéret.**

Carrier, from *carrier* 'quarryman, quarrier', also 'carrier, carter'. — Amer. **Coyer.**

— Jean **Carrier** (Jean and Jeanne Dodin) from Saint-Georges-d'Oléron in Charente-Maritime (Poitou-Charentes) m. Barbe Halay (Jean-Baptiste and Mathurine Valet) in Québec, QC in 1670.

Carrière, from *(La) Carrière,* a placename in France. — Amer. **Courier, Currier.**
— *Pierre Jamme dit* **Carrière** *(Jean and Charlotte Husse) from Lantheuil in Calvados (Basse-Normandie) m. Marie-Madeleine Barbary (Pierre and Marie Lebrun) in Lachine, QC in 1689.*

Carrigan, see **Carignan.**

Carriveau, see **Corriveau.**

Carro, Carrow, see **Caron.**

Cart, Carte, see **Charette.**

Carter, see **Charette** and **Chartier.**

Cartier, either from *(Le) Cartier,* a placename in France, or an alteration of *carretier,* a regional variant of *charretier* 'carter'. — Amer. **Carkey, Carter, Kirkey, Quarter.**
— *Guillaume* **Cartier** *(Julien and Françoise Bourdain) from Drain in Maine-et-Loire (Pays de la Loire) m. Marie-Étiennette Garnier (François and Jacqueline Freslon) in Neuville, QC in 1685.*

Casa, see **Caza.**

Casaubon, from *Casaubon,* a placename in Pyrénées-Atlantiques (Aquitaine). — Amer. **Cassaubon, Cassibo, Cazaubon, Cazobon.**
— *Martin* **Casaubon** *(Jean and Françoise Maisonneuve) from Saint-Jean-de-Luz in Pyrénées-Atlantiques (Aquitaine) m. Françoise Le Pellé (Jean and Jeanne Isabel) in Champlain in 1689.*

Casavant, probable alteration of *Casaban* or *Cazaban,* placenames in France. — Amer. **Casavoy, Cassavant, Cassavaugh, Cassavaw, Cassavoy, Cassevah, Cassevoy.**
— *Jean* **Casavant** *dit Ladébauche (Jean and Marie Guignière) from Auch in Gers (Midi-Pyrénées) m. Jeanne Charpentier (Jean and Barbe Renaud) in Contrecoeur, QC in 1681.*

Cascagnet, alteration of *(Le) Castanier,* a placename in France. — Amer. **Cascagnette, Cascanette, Caskenette, Caskinett, Caskinette.**
— *Mathieu Castanier/Castagnet/***Cascagnet** *(Bernard and Marie Bacon) from Langoiran in Gironde (Aquitaine) m. Angélique Boesmé (Jean and Marie-Madeleine Bon) in Québec, QC in 1740.*

Cassaubon, see **Casaubon.**

Cassavant, Cassavaugh, Cassavaw, Cassavoy, see **Casavant.**

Cassaw, see **Caza.**

Cassevah, Cassevoy, see **Casavant.**

Cassibo, see **Casaubon.**

Cataract, see **Cadoret(te).**

Catura, Caturia, see **Couturier.**

Cauchois, derived from *Caux,* the nickname of an individual from that region in Normandie. — Amer. **Cushway.**
— *Jacques* **Cauchois** *dit Duclos (Pierre and Marie *Terelle) from Rouen in Seine-Maritime (Haute-Normandie) m. Élisabeth Prudhomme (Louis and Roberte Gadois) in Montréal, QC in 1683.*

Cauchon, regional variant of *chausson* 'slipper', the nickname of a maker or seller. — Amer. **Cushing.**
— *Jean* **Cauchon** *from Dieppe in Seine-Maritime (Haute-Normandie) m. (1) Marguerite Cointerel in Dieppe c. 1619; (2) Jeanne Abraham in Dieppe in 1633.*

Causley, see **Cazelet.**

Caya, alteration of *Cailla*, a placename in Vendée (Pays de la Loire). — Amer. **Cayo.**

— *Pierre **Cailla** (Thomas and Florence Gernie) from Bourg-sous-la-Roche in Vendée (Pays de la Loire) m. Olive Landry (Antoine and Andrée *Commaillelle) in Trois-Riviè-res, QC in 1664.*

Cayer, alteration of *Caillé*, a placename in France. — Amer. **Cayea, Currier.**

— *Jacques **Caillé** from Fontenay-le-Comte in Vendée (Pays de la Loire) m. Marie-An-drée Gervais in Fontenay-le-Comte c. 1664.*

Cayo, see **Caya.**

Caza, apparently from *Caza*, a placename in Lot-et-Garonne (Aquitaine). — Amer. **Ca-sa, Cassaw.**

— *Jean-Baptiste-Amable Lebeau dit Beaufils and **Caza**, grandson of Pierre from Paris (Île-de-France), m. Marie-Marthe Gerbault (Charles and Angélique Dumay) in Louise-ville, QC in 1777.*

Cazaubon, see **Casaubon.**

Cazelet, alteration of *(Le) Cazalet*, a placename in France. — Amer. **Causley.**

— *Jean-Baptiste **Cazelet** dit Languedoc (Jean and Claire Boudon) from Montpellier in Hérault (Languedoc-Roussillon) m. Marie-Françoise Faucher (François-de-Sales and Marie-Charlotte Belleau) in Neuville, QC in 1761.*

Cazobon, see **Casaubon.**

Cedar, see **Ducèdre.**

Centerbar, see **St-Aubin.**

Chabot, from *(Le) Chabot*, a placename in France. — Amer. **Jabotte, Shepard, Sher-bert.**

— *Mathurin **Chabot** (Jean and Jeanne Rode) from Nalliers in Vendée (Pays de la Loi-re) m. Marie Mesange (Robert and Madeleine Lehoux) in Québec, QC in 1661.*

Chagnon, from *(Le) Chagnon*, a placename in France. — Amer. **Shonio, Shonyo.**

— *François **Chagnon** dit Larose (Pierre and Louise Aubry) from Descartes in Indre-et-Loire (Centre) m. Catherine Charron (Pierre and Catherine Pillard) in Québec in 1679.*

Chaisson, see **Chiasson.**

Chalifoux, either an alteration of *Chalfour*, an older form of *Chaufour*, a placename in France, or a regional variant of *chaufour* 'lime kiln', the nickname of an operator. — Amer. **Chilafoux.**

— *Paul Chalifou/Chalifour/**Chalifoux** (Paul and Marie Gaborit) from La Rochelle in Charente-Maritime (Poitou-Charentes) m. Jacquette Archambault (Jacques and Fran-çoise Tourault) in Québec, QC in 1648.*

Chaloux, alteration of *Chalou*, a placename in France. — Amer. **Sharlow.**

— *Pierre-François **Chalou** dit Saint-Pierre (Pierre-François and Catherine Challet) from Javarzay in Deux-Sèvres (Poitou-Charentes) m. Marie Barbeau (Jean and Marie Denoyon) in Québec, QC in 1723.*

Chaltry, see **Chartré.**

Chalut, probable alteration of *Chalua*, a placename in Deux-Sèvres (Poitou-Charentes). — Amer. **Shallow.**

— *François **Chalut** dit Lagrange (Pierre and Jeanne Thibodeau) from Limalonges in Deux-Sèvres (Poitou-Charentes) m. Marie Amaury (Jean and Marie Vigny) in Québec* *in 1695.*

Chamard, from *(Le) Chamard*, a placename in France. — Amer. **Shumar, Shumard.**

— *Pierre* **Chamard** *(Jean and Jeanne Pipet) from Saint-Hilaire-du-Bois in Charente-Maritime (Poitou-Charentes) m. Florimonde Rableau (Mathurin and Marie Dubois) in Québec, QC in 1665.*

Chamberland, from Old French *chamberlan* 'chamberlain'. — Amer. **Chamberlain.**

— *Simon* **Chamberland** *(René and Catherine David) from Chantonnay in Vendée (Pays de la Loire) m. Marie Boileau (René and Joachine Seran) in Sainte-Famille, Île d'Orléans, QC in 1669.*

Chambo, see **Archambault.**

Champagne, either from *Champagne*, a former province in France, or from *(La) Champagne*, a placename in France. — Amer. **Champagn, Champaign, Champain, Champany, Champine, Shampine.**

— *Étienne Huyet/Huguet dit Poncelet and* **Champagne** *(Pierre and Marguerite Saumé) from Sormonne in Ardennes (Champagne-Ardenne) m. Barbe Forestier (Étienne and Marguerite Lauzon) in Montréal, QC in 1718.*

Champeau, alteration of *Champoux*, a placename in France. — Amer. **Shampo.**

— *Pierre* **Champoux** *dit Jolicoeur (André and Marie Lavaux) from Eymet in Dordogne (Aquitaine) m. Geneviève Guillet (Pierre and Jeanne Saint-Père) in Québec c. 1680.*

Champigny, derived from *Champigny-sur-Marne*, a placename in Val-de-Marne (Île-de-France). — Amer. **Champie, Champney, Shampay.**

— *Jean Deslandes dit* **Champigny** *(Philippe and Anne Delost) from Champigny-sur-Marne in Val-de-Marne (Île-de-France) m. Élisabeth Ronceray (Jean and Jeanne Servignan) in Boucherville, QC in 1688.*

Champine, see **Champagne.**

Champney, see **Champigny.**

Chantal, from *(Le) Chantal*, a placename in France. — Amer. **Shontell, Shontelle.**

— *Pierre* **Chantal** *dit Lafleur (Jean and Louise Chort) from Bergerac in Dordogne (Aquitaine) m. Marie-Angélique Martin (Joachim and Anne-Charlotte Petit) in Saint-Pierre, Île d'Orléans, QC in 1696.*

Chantell, see **Quintal.**

Chaput, probable alteration of Old French *chapuis* 'carpenter'. — Amer. **Shappee, Shappy, Shepard, Sheperd.**

— *Nicolas* **Chaput** *(Antoine and Claudine Reber) from Noidans-le-Ferroux in Haute-Saône (Franche-Comté) m. Angélique Gauthier (Mathurin and Nicole Philippeau) in Pointe-aux-Trembles, QC in 1689.*

Charbonneau, derived from *charbon* 'coal', the nickname of a producer or seller. — Amer. **Charbeneau, Cole, Sharbino, Sharbono.**

— *Olivier* **Charbonneau** *from Marans in Charente-Maritime (Poitou-Charentes) m. Marie Garnier in Marans c. 1656.*

Charette, probable alteration of *Chauray* via *Choret*, a placename in Deux-Sèvres (Pays de la Loire). — Amer. **Cart, Carte, Carter, Cherette, Cherrette, Scherette, Sharette, Sharrett, Sharrette, Shaurette, Shorett, Shorette, Shurette.**

— *Mathieu* **Choret** *(Mathieu and Jeanne Serre) from La Rochelle in Charente-Maritime (Poitou-Charentes) m. Sébastienne Veillon (Maixent and Bernarde Venet) in La Rochelle in 1647.*

Charland, probably derived from Old French *charrel* 'cart', the nickname of a cartwright or wheelwright. — Amer. **Charlon, Sharland.**

— *Claude Charland dit Francoeur (Jean and Catherine Mavile) from Châteauroux in Indre (Centre) m. (1) Jacqueline Desbordes (Dimanche and Radegonde Valentin) in Québec, QC in 1652; (2) Jeanne Pelletier (Simon and Marie Large) in Québec, QC in 1661.*

Charlebois, alteration of *Charles bois* 'Charles wood', apparently a placename. — Amer. **Charleboix, Woods.**

— *Jean Charlebois dit Jolibois and Joly (Antoine and Marie Dosquet) from Saint-André-du-Bois in Gironde (Aquitaine) m. Marthe Perrier (Jean and Marie Gaillard) in Montréal, QC in 1686.*

Charleville, apparently from *Charleville*, a placename in France. — Amer. **Sharleville.**

— *Joseph Chauvin dit Charleville, grandson of Jean from Fresquienne in Seine-Maritime (Haute-Normandie), m. Marie-Geneviève-Monique Rivard (Antoine and Marie Briard) in Kaskaskia, IL in 1740.*

Charlon, see **Charland.**

Charpentier, from *charpentier* 'carpenter'. — Amer. **Carpenter, Leo.**

— *Denis Charpentier dit Sansfaçon (François and Marie Méteyer) from Coulommiers in Seine-et-Marne (Île-de-France) m. Marie-Anne Despernay (Laurent and Jeanne Cambron) in Boucherville, QC in 1688.*

— *Jean Charpentier dit Lapaille (Cyprien and Catherine Thérel) from Veulettes-sur-Mer in Seine-Maritime (Haute-Normandie) m. Barbe Renaud (Vincent and Marie Martin) in Québec, QC in 1661.*

— *Joseph Lalague dit Charpentier (Raymond and Jeanne Caemont) from Moncrabeau in Lot-et-Garonne (Aquitaine) m. Catherine Therrien (Louis and Catherine Bidet) in Sainte-Foy, QC in 1726.*

Charron, from *charron* 'cartwright, wheelwright'. — Amer. **Sharon, Sharron, Sharrow, Shurn.**

— *Charles Charron dit Larose and Cabanac (Pierre and Marie-Françoise Selle) from Chartres in Eure-et-Loir (Centre) m. Élisabeth Poupard (René and Marie Gendron) in Montréal, QC in 1713.*

— *Pierre Charron dit Ducharme (Pierre and Judith Martin) from Meaux in Seine-et-Marne (Île-de-France) m. Catherine Pillard (Pierre and Marguerite Moulinet) in Montréal, QC in 1665.*

Chartier, either an alteration of *charretier* 'carter', or of the English name *Carter*, from *carter*. — Amer. **Carter, Sharkey, Shorkey.**

— *Guillaume Chartier dit Robert (Jacques and Marguerite Loysel) from La Flèche in Sarthe (Pays de la Loire) m. Marie Faucon (Pierre and Marie Berger) in Montréal, QC in 1663.*

— *John Carter/Jean-Joseph Chartier (Samuel and Mercy Brooks) from Deerfield, MA m. Marie Courtemanche (Antoine and Marguerite Vaudry) in Rivière-des-Prairies, QC in 1718.*

Chartrand, probably derived from Old French *chartrer* 'prison guard'. — Amer. **Chartraw, Chartreau, Shartrand, Shatraw.**

— *Thomas Chartrand (Louis and Hermine Queval) from Ectot-lès-Baons in Seine-Maritime (Haute-Normandie) m. (1) Thècle Hunault (Toussaint and Marie Lorgueil) in*

Montréal, QC in 1669; (2) Jeanne Matou (Philippe and Marguerite Doucinet) in Montréal, QC in 1679.

Chartré, alteration of Old French *chartrer* 'prison guard'. — Amer. **Chaltry, Sheltra.**

— *François Chartré (Pierre and Michelle Deschamps) from Saint-Pierre-du-Chemin in Vendée (Pays de la Loire) m. Apolline Morin (André and Marguerite Moreau) in Charlesbourg, QC in 1692.*

Chartreau, see **Chartrand.**

Chassé, alteration of *Chassey*, a placename in France. — Amer. **Chase, Hunter.**

— *Jean-François Chassé/Chassey (Sébastien and Élisabeth Grandmaître) from Combeaufontaine in Haute-Saône (Franche-Comté) m. (1) Marie-Josèphe Mignault (Pierre and Jeanne Autin) in Kamouraska, QC in 1735; (2) Marie-Angélique Asselin (Louis and Marie-Angélique Dubé) in Kamouraska, QC in 1757.*

Châteauneuf, from *Châteauneuf*, a placename in France. — Amer. **Shatney.**

— *Jean Desranleau dit Châteauneuf (Jacques and Jeanne *Durinost) from Chaunay in Vienne (Poitou-Charentes) m. Marie-Madeleine Trottier (Jean-Baptiste and Geneviève Lafond) in Batiscan, QC in 1698.*

Châtelain, from *châtelain* 'lord', an ironic nickname. — Amer. **Chatlin.**

— *François Châtelain/Chastelain (François and Catherine Royer) from Paris (Île-de-France) m. Marguerite Cardin (Maurice and Marie-Madeleine Duguay) in Trois-Rivières, QC in 1729.*

Châtigny, probable alteration of *Châtilly*, a placename in Dordogne (Aquitaine). — Amer. **Shorty.**

— *Vincent Châtigny dit Lépine from Bézenac in Dordogne (Aquitaine) m. Françoise Aubry (Louis and Julienne Juhel) in Québec c. 1676.*

Chatlin, see **Châtelain.**

Chaussé, probable alteration of Old French *chaussier*, derived from *chausse* 'sock, hose', the nickname of a maker or seller. — Amer. **Chosa, Chosay, Chosse, Shosey.**

— *François Han/Jahan dit Chaussé (Gaspard and Martine Voglet/Roguelet) from Poitiers in Vienne (Poitou-Charentes) m. Marie-Madeleine Prunier (Nicolas and Antoinette Legrand) in Repentigny, QC in 1685.*

Chauvin, either from *Chauvin*, a placename in France, or derived from *chauve* 'bald'. — Amer. **Chovin, Shovah, Shovan, Shovar, Shoven, Shover.**

— *Jean Chauvin (François and Marie-Catherine Duval) from Fresquienne in Seine-Maritime (Haute-Normandie) m. Marie-Madeleine Courtois (Jean and Catherine Daniel) in Boucherville, QC in 1702.*

— *Pierre Chauvin dit Le Grand Pierre (René and Catherine Avard) from Solesmes in Sarthe (Pays de la Loire) m. Marthe Hautreux (René and Françoise *La Chamallière) in Montréal, QC in 1658.*

Cheff, alteration of the German name *Schäffer*, either a variant of *Schaffer*, from Middle High German *schaffœre* 'steward, bursar', or of *Schäfer*, from Middle High German *schœfœre* 'shepherd'. — Amer. **Sheff.**

— *Andreas Gerhart Schäffer from Germany m. (1) Johanna Dorothea Maher in Germany in 1778; (2) Marie-Louise Beauvais (Étienne and Élisabeth Gibouleau) in Rigaud, QC in 1804.*

Chenard, probable alteration of *Chanal* or *Chenal*, placenames in France. — Amer. **Snow.**

— Guillaume **Chenard**/Chenal/Chanal (Michel and Marguerite Bret) from Darnets in Corrèze (Limousin) m. Marie-Anne Parent (François and Catherine Binet) in Beauport, QC in 1752.

Chenette, alteration of Le Chesnay or Le Chênet, placenames in France. — Amer. **Chennette, Shennett, Shennette.**

— Bertrand Chesnay/Chenay/**Chênet** dit/sieur de La Garenne (Nicolas and Catherine-Marguerite de La Vigne) from Yffiniac in Côtes-d'Armor (Bretagne) m. Élisabeth Aubert (Charles and Jacqueline Lucas) in Château-Richer, QC in 1671.

Chênevert, from Chênevert, a placename in Deux-Sèvres (Poitou-Charentes). — Amer. **Chenevare, Chenvert, Chinavare, Shanaway, Shinavar, Shinevar, Shinevare, Shinevarre.**

— Moïse Morin dit **Chenevert** (Aaron and Jeanne Boutin) from Niort in Deux-Sèvres (Poitou-Charentes) m. Madeleine Monin (Gilles and Marthe Richaume) in Québec, QC in 1707.

Chennette, see **Chenette.**

Chenvert, see **Chênevert.**

Cherette, Cherrette, see **Charette.**

Chiasson, derived from chiasse 'diarrhea', the nickname of an individual with chronic dysentery. — Amer. **Chaisson, Chesson.**

— Guyon **Chiasson** dit Lavallée (Pierre and Marie Péroché) from La Rochelle in Charente-Maritime (Poitou-Charentes) m. Jeanne Bernard (... and Andrée Guyon) in Acadia c. 1665.

Chicoine, probable alteration of cigogne 'stork', the nickname of a long-legged individual. — Amer. **Shequin.**

— Pierre **Chicoine** (Gilles and Perrine Boisaubert) from Channay-sur-Lathan in Indre-et-Loire (Centre) m. Madeleine Chrétien (Toussaint and Françoise Bertault) in Montréal, QC in 1670.

Chilafoux, see **Chalifoux.**

Chinavare, see **Chênevert.**

Choinière, apparently an alteration of La Chaunière, a placename in France. — Amer. **Sweeney.**

— Jean Sabourin dit **Chaunière,** son of Jean from Montalembert in Deux-Sèvres (Poitou-Charentes), m. Françoise Venne (Jacques and Marguerite Provost) in Pointe-aux-Trembles, QC in 1701.

Cholette, alteration of (Le) Cholet, a placename in France. — Amer. **Sholette, Shoulette.**

— Sébastien **Cholet** dit Laviolette (Sébastien and Perrine Hilaire) from Aubigné-sur-Layon in Maine-et-Loire (Pays de la Loire) m. Ann Heard (Benjamin and Elizabeth Roberts) in Montréal, QC in 1705.

Choquet, origin uncertain. — Amer. **Shackett, Shackette.**

— Nicolas **Choquet** dit Champagne (Nicolas and Claude Gruet) from Amiens in Somme (Picardie) m. Anne Julien (Pierre and Marie Pepin) in Montréal, QC in 1668.

Chosa, Chosay, Chosse, see **Chaussé.**

Chouinard, derived from Old French choue 'screech owl', a nickname related to some characteristic of this bird. — Amer. **Sweeney, Sweenor, Swenor, Swinyer.**

— Jacques **Chouinard** (Charles and Élisabeth Valin) from Beaumont-la-Ronce in Indre-et-Loire (Centre) m. Louise Jean (Pierre and Françoise Favreau) in Québec, QC in

1692.

Chovin, see **Chauvin.**

Chrétien, from the Latin name *Christianus,* derived from Greek *khristos* 'anointed'. — Amer. **Christian.**

— *Michel **Chrétien** (Jacques and Catherine Nivert) from Loches in Indre-et-Loire (Centre) m. Marie Meunier (Claude and Catherine Charpentier) in Québec, QC in 1665.*

— *Vincent **Chrétien** from France m. Anne Leclerc (Jean and Perrette Brunel) in Québec c. 1668.*

Churco, Churcott, see **Turcot(te).**

Cicotte, see **Sicotte.**

Cinq-Mars, alteration of *Saint-Mars,* a placename in France. — Amer. **Seymour, Stmars.**

— *Marc-Antoine Gobelin dit **Saint-Mars/Cinq-Mars** (Pierre and Madeleine Lebel) from Savignies in Oise (Picardie) m. Françoise Chapelain (Bernard and Éléonore Mouillard) in Saint-Laurent, Île d'Orléans, QC in 1692.*

Cire, see **Cyr.**

Cirier, derived from *cire* 'wax', the nickname of a maker or seller. — Amer. **Cyrier.**

— *Martin **Cirier** dit Argenteuil (Nicolas and Catherine Prévost) from Argenteuil in Val-d'Oise (Île-de-France) m. Marie-Anne Beaune (Jean and Marie-Madeleine Bour-gery) in Detroit, MI in 1710.*

Claymore, see **Clément.**

Cleaves, see **Cliche.**

Clément, either from *Clément,* a placename in France, or from the Latin name *Clemens,* from *clemens* 'lenient, indulgent'. — Amer. **Claymore.**

— *Pierre **Clément** dit Larivière (Pierre and Catherine ...) from Tarascon in Bouches-du-Rhône (Provence-Alpes-Côte-d'Azur) m. Marie Prézeau (Michel and Marie Chancy) in Montréal, QC in 1702.*

Clermont, from *Clermont,* a placename in France. — Amer. **Clements.**

— *Jean-Baptiste Lemarquis dit **Clermont** (Thomas and Anne Dalvan) from Saint-Malo in Ille-et-Vilaine (Bretagne) m. Anne Lapierre (François and Jeanne Rimbault) in Acadia c. 1730.*

Cliche, regional variant of Old French *clice* 'braided wicker', the nickname of a maker. — Amer. **Cleaves, Clisch, Clish.**

— *Nicolas **Cliche** (Nicolas and Catherine Poète) from Noyon in Oise (Picardie) m. Marie-Madeleine Pelletier (Georges and Catherine Vanier) in Beaupré, QC in 1675.*

Clodgo, see **Gladu.**

Cloutier, from *cloutier* 'nail maker, nail seller'. — Amer. **Clookey, Cloukey, Cluchey, Cluckey, Clukey, Clutchey, Nailor, Naylor.**

— *Zacharie **Cloutier** (Denis and Renée Brière) from Mortagne-au-Perche in Orne (Basse-Normandie) m. Sainte Dupont in Mortagne-au-Perche in 1616.*

Coache, alteration of the Hungarian name *Kovácsy,* derived from *kovács* 'blacksmith'. — Amer. **Coash.**

— *János Kovácsy/Jean **Coache** (Ferenc and Katalin Bognar) from Buzica in Slovakia m. Marie Duclos (François and Charlotte Mathieu) in Laprairie, QC in 1785.*

Coallier, variant of *Couaillier,* probably derived from regional French *couaille* 'coarse wool, cloth, rag', the nickname of a maker or seller. — Amer. **Quillia, Qulia.**

*— Philibert **Coallier** (Pierre and Anne *Steverin) from Novion-Porcien in Ardennes (Champagne-Ardennes) m. Marie-Thérèse Favreau (Pierre and Marie-Anne Perrault) in Boucherville, QC in 1757.*

Coasch, see **Coache.**

Cody, see **Côté.**

Cognac, from *Cognac,* a placename in France. — Amer. **Conyac.**

*— Pierre **Cognac** dit Léveillé (Jean-Claude and Marie Perrault) from L'Abergement-de-Varey in Ain (Rhône-Alpes) m. Marie-Josèphe Lefort (Jean-Baptiste and Marie-Charlotte Ménard) in Chambly, QC in 1757.*

Cole, see **Charbonneau.**

Collette, alteration of *Collet,* derived from *Nicolas,* from the Greek name *Nikolaos* via Latin *Nicolaus,* from *nike* 'victory' and *laos* 'people', hence 'prevailing among the people'. — Amer. **Collett, Collins.**

*— Pierre-Joseph **Collet** (Jean and Marie-Thérèse Dupont) from Amiens in Somme (Picardie) m. Marguerite Courtois (Bertrand and Marie Halay) in Charlesbourg, QC in 1689.*

Colomb, Colombe, see **Coulombe.**

Colt, Coltey, Colty, see **Poulin.**

Columb, Columbe, see **Coulombe.**

Come, see **Vien(s).**

Comeau, probably derived from *Come/Côme,* from the Greek name *Kosmas,* from *kosmos* 'world, universe'. — Amer. **Comeaux, Commo, Como.**

*— Pierre **Comeau** from France m. Rose Bayon in Acadia c. 1649.*

Comète, alteration of *Comet,* same origin as **Comeau.** — Amer. **Comette, Commette.**

*— Noël **Comet** (Étienne and Marie-Thérèse Bélanger) from Béziers in Hérault (Languedoc-Roussillon) m. Marie-Marguerite Magnan (Pierre and Marie-Jeanne Robidou) in Saint-Constant, QC in 1770.*

Comings, see **Vien(s).**

Comiré, origin undetermined. — Amer. **Commire.**

*— Nicolas Camiré/**Comiré**/Comirey (Jean and Françoise Conin) from Margilley in Haute-Saône (Franche-Comté) m. (1) Juliette Pernet in Percey-le-Grand in Haute-Saône en 1725; (2) Marie-Geneviève Marchand (Louis and Jeanne Bourassa) in Lauzon, QC in 1741.*

Commette, see **Comète.**

Commire, see **Comiré.**

Commo, Como, see **Comeau.**

Compagna, alteration of *Campagnac* via *Campagna,* a placename in France. — Amer. **Companion.**

*— Mathias **Campagna** (Mathurin and Jacquette Suire) from Angoulins in Charente-Maritime (Poitou-Charentes) m. Suzanne Aubineau in Québec in 1667.*

Compau, Compeau, Compeaux, Compo, see **Campeau.**

Contois, alteration of *Comtois,* the nickname of a native of Franche-Comté, a former province in France. — Amer. **Counter.**

*— Louis Gilbert dit **Comtois** (Louis and Marie Lagoutte) from Besançon in Doubs (Franche-Comté) m. Anne Jacques (Louis and Antoinette Leroux) in Charlesbourg, QC*

in 1722.

Condon, probably from *Caunton*, a placename in England. — Amer. **Conto.**

— *Georges **Condon**, son of John from Ireland, m. Marie Sauvé (Antoine and Marie-Anne Robillard) in Vaudreuil, QC in 1782.*

Contant, regional variant of *Constant*, from the Latin name *Constantius*, derived from *constans* 'consistent, solid'. — Amer. **Glad, Gladd.**

— *Étienne **Contant**/Content (Pierre and Marguerite Grosnier) from Burie in Charente-Maritime (Poitou-Charentes) m. Anne Laîné (Emmanuel and Jeanne Legrand) in Sainte-Famille, Île d'Orléans, QC in 1669.*

Contin, see **Cantin.**

Conto, see **Condon.**

Conyac, see **Cognac.**

Coolong, see **Coulombe.**

Coopee, see **Goupil.**

Corbeil, alteration of *Gourbil* via *Gourbeil*, origin uncertain. — Amer. **Corbelle, Curby, Kirby.**

— *André **Corbeil**/Gourbeil/Gourbil dit Tranchemontagne (Jean and Marie Bernard) from Saint-Porchaire in Charente-Maritime (Poitou-Charentes) m. Charlotte Poutré (André and Jeanne Burel) in Pointe-aux-Trembles, QC in 1695.*

Corbin, derived from Old French *corb* 'raven', a nickname related to some characteristic of this bird. — Amer. **Corbine.**

— *Louis **Corbin** dit Lacroix (François and Catherine Vesval) from Le Tanu in Manche (Basse-Normandie) m. Marie-Catherine Martin (François and Marie-Angélique Pelletier) in Cap-Saint-Ignace, QC in 1754.*

Coro, see **Caron.**

Corriveau, origin uncertain. — Amer. **Cariveau, Carriveau.**

— *Étienne **Corriveau** (François and Marguerite Bernard) from Fontclaireau in Charente (Poitou-Charentes) m. Catherine Bureau (Jacques and Marguerite Vernier) in Sainte-Famille, Île d'Orléans, QC in 1669.*

Corro, Corron, Corrow, see **Caron.**

Côté, variant of *Costé*, a probable alteration of *Le Costil*, a placename in Normandie. — Amer. **Cody, Cota, Cotey, Coty.**

— *Jean **Côté**/Costé from Mortagne-au-Perche in Orne (Basse-Normandie) m. Anne Martin in Québec, QC in 1635.*

Cotuan, probable alteration of *Coduan*, a placename in Côtes-d'Armor (Bretagne). — Amer. **Cutwa, Cutway.**

— *Pierre **Cotuan** (Pierre and Julie Fournier) from Saint-Louis in Bretagne m. Marie-Louise Champoux (Antoine and Marie-Geneviève Houde) in Île-Perrot, QC in 1794.*

Coty, see **Côté.**

Couchene, see **Courchesne.**

Couillard, probable alteration of Old French *coillart* 'uncastrated animal', the nickname of a libertine. — Amer. **Coullard, Queor.**

— *Pierre **Couillard** (Pierre and Marguerite Durandel) from Ballon in Charente-Maritime (Poitou-Charentes) m. Jeanne Bilodeau (Jean and Françoise Poupard) in Trois-Rivières, QC in 1666.*

Coulombe, from the Latin name *Columba*, from *columba* 'dove'. — Amer. **Colomb, Co-**

lombe, Columb, Columbe, Coolong.

— *Louis Coulombe/Colombe (Jacques and Rolline Drieu) from Le Neubourg in Eure (Haute-Normandie) m. Jeanne Boucault (Nicolas and Marguerite Thibault) in Sainte-Famille, Île d'Orléans, QC in 1670.*

Counter, see Contois.

Courchesne, from Old French *cour chesne* 'oak court', a nickname apparently from the site of an estate or property. — Amer. **Couchene, Courchain, Cushing.**

— *Jean-Baptiste Foucault dit Courchesne, son of Jean-François from Dordogne, m. Marguerite Bergeron (François and Étiennette Leclerc) in Trois-Rivières, QC in 1708.*

Courier, see Carrière.

Cournoyer, from *cour noyer* 'walnut court', a nickname apparently from the site of an estate or property. — Amer. **Courneya, Courneyea, Cournia, Cournyea.**

— *Pierre Hus dit Cournoyer, son of Paul from Montigny in Seine-Maritime (Haute-Normandie), m. Jeanne Vanet (Charles and Catherine Magnan) in Saint-François-du-Lac, QC in 1700.*

Courtemanche, from *Courtemanche*, a placename in France. — Amer. **Courtmanche, Shortsleeve, Shortsleeves.**

— *Antoine Courtemanche dit Jolicoeur (Pierre and Marie Houdé) from Bannes in Sarthe (Pays de la Loire) m. Élisabeth Haquin/Aquin (Abraham and Marie *de Calogues) in Montréal, QC in 1663.*

Cousineau, derived from Old French *cousin* 'friend, crony'. — Amer. **Cousino.**

— *Jean Cousineau (Guy and Marie *Pepuchon) from Jumilhac-le-Grand in Dordogne (Aquitaine) m. Jeanne Bénard (Mathurin and Marguerite Viard) in Montréal, QC in 1690.*

Coutcher, see Couture.

Coutlée, alteration of *Coutelet*, derived from Old French *coutel* 'knife', the nickname of a maker or seller. — Amer. **Coutley.**

— *Louis Coutelet dit Marchàterre (François and Marie Boursier) from Vitry-sur-Seine in Val-de-Marne (Île-de-France) m. Marie-Geneviève Labossée (Jacques and Marie Vacher) in Montréal, QC in 1742.*

Couture, from *(La) Couture*, a placename in France. — Amer. **Coutcher, Cutcher.**

— *Guillaume Couture (Guillaume and Madeleine Mallet) from Rouen in Seine-Maritime (Haute-Normandie) m. Anne Émard (Jean and Marie Bineau) in Québec, QC in 1649.*

Couturier, derived from Old French *couture* 'cultivated land', the nickname of a farmer. — Amer. **Catura, Caturia, Taylor.**

— *Jacques Couturier (Jean and Marie Aumont) from Gonneville-en-Auge in Calvados (Basse-Normandie) m. Catherine Anenontha (Nicolas Arendanki and Jeanne Otrihouandit) in Québec in 1672.*

Couvillion, Covyeau, Covyeow, see Quévillon.

Cowan, see Vachon.

Cowett, Cowette, see Caouette.

Coyer, see Carrier.

Crépeau, derived from Old French *cresp(e)* 'frizzy, curly'. — Amer. **Crapo, Crepeaux.**

— *Maurice Crépeau (Jean and Suzanne Fumoleau) from Les Roches-Baritaud in Vendée (Pays de la Loire) m. Marguerite Laverdure (Martin and Jacqueline Leliot) in*

Québec in 1665.

Cross, see **Lacroix**.

Croteau, from *(Le) Croteau*, a placename in France. — Amer. **Croto, Crotteau, Crotto**.
— *Vincent Croteau (André and Marguerite Métayer) from Veules-les-Roses in Seine-Maritime (Haute-Normandie) m. Jeanne Godequin (Jacques and Jeanne Dupuis) in Québec in 1669.*

Cuillerier, derived from *cuiller* 'spoon', the nickname of a maker or seller. — Amer. **Spooner**.
— *René Cuillerier dit Léveillé (Julien and Julienne Piau) from Mareil-sur-Loir in Sarthe (Pays de la Loire) m. Marie Lucos (Léonard and Barbe Poisson) in Montréal, QC in 1665.*

Cumm, Cummings, see **Vien(s)**.

Curby, see **Corbeil**.

Currier, see **Carrière** and **Cayer**.

Curwick, see **Kérouac**.

Cushing, see **Cauchon** and **Courchesne**.

Cushway, see **Cauchois**.

Cutcher, see **Couture**.

Cutwa, Cutway, see **Cotuan**.

Cyr, either from the Greek name *Kurikos* via Latin *Cyricus*, derived from *kuros* 'supreme power, authority', or an alteration of *sire* 'sire, lord', an ironic nickname. — Amer. **Cire, Cyre, Sear, Sears, Syr, Syre**.
— *Pierre Cyr/Sire from France m. Marie Bourgeois (Jacques and Jeanne Trahan) in Acadia c. 1670.*

Cyrier, see **Cirier**.

Cyrway, see **Sirois**.

D

Dabiew, see **Debien.**

Dagenais, from *d'Agenais* 'from Agenais', the nickname of an individual from that region in Aquitaine. — Amer. **Dashnau, Dashnaw, Dashner, Dashnow.**

— *Pierre **Dagenais** dit Lépine (Arnaud and Andrée Poulet) from La Rochelle in Charente-Maritime (Poitou-Charentes) m. Anne Brandon (Daniel and Jeanne Proli) in Montréal, QC in 1665.*

Dagesse, alteration of *d'Agès* 'from Agès', a placename in France. — Amer. **Lagesse, Lagest, Lajesse.**

— *Jean **Dagès**/Dagert (Antoine and Jeanne *Cortedouat) from Castaignos-Souslens in Landes (Aquitaine) m. Marie-Anne Douillard (René and Marie-Anne Demers) in Montréal, QC in 1758.*

Daha, see **Deshaies.**

Daigle, alteration of *d'Aigre* 'from Aigre', a placename in Charente (Poitou-Charentes). — Amer. **Deagle, Digue.**

— *Olivier Daigre/**Daigle** from Aigre in Charente (Poitou-Charentes) m. Marie Gaudet (Denis and Martine Gauthier) in Port-Royal, NS in 1666.*

Daigneault, alteration of *Daniau*, a variant of **Daniel.** — Amer. **Danyew, Danyow, Denue.**

— *Michel **Dagneau**/Dagnaux, sieur d'Ourville/de Douville (Robert and Jacqueline Mayne) from Deux-Jumeaux in Calvados (Basse-Normandie) m. Marie Lamy (Isaac and Marie *de Chevrainville) in Sorel, QC in 1688.*

Dalpé, alteration of *Delpé*, derived from *Le Pey*, a placename in France. — Amer. **Delphia.**

— *Jean **Delpé** dit Pariseau (Jean and Marguerite Delmas) from Rodez in Aveyron (Midi-Pyrénées) m. Renée Lorion (Mathurin and Jeanne Bizet) in Montréal, QC in 1674.*

Dandurand, either from *d'Andurand*, an alteration of Old French *endurant* 'patient', or from the old title of respect *dam* and *Durand*, either from *(Le) Durand*, a placename in France, or from the Latin name *Durandus*, apparently derived from *durare* 'to last, endure'. — Amer. **Dandaraw, Dandro, Dandrow.**

— *Antoine **Dandurand** dit Marchàterre (Jean and Marguerite La Beauce) from Paris (Île-de-France) m. Marie Vérieu (Nicolas and Marguerite Hiardin/Hyardin) in Sainte-Famille, Île d'Orléans, QC in 1696.*

Danette, see **Donat.**

Daniel, from the Hebrew name *Dani'el* composed of *dan* 'judge' and *El* 'God', hence 'God is my judge'. — Amer. **Daniels.**

— *Jean-Baptiste **Daniel** dit Jolibois (Antoine and Catherine Seppe/Sappet) from Rhône-Alpes m. Geneviève Semeur (Marc and Catherine Drapeau) in Saint-Vincent-de-Paul, QC in 1759.*

Danis, variant of *Dany*, derived from **Daniel.** — Amer. **Danna, Donna, Downey.**

— Honoré **Danis**/Dany dit Tourangeau (Martin and Étiennette Badouille) from Mont-louis-sur-Loire in Indre-et-Loire (Centre) m. Perrine Lapierre (Pierre and Claude Le-clerc) in Montréal, QC in 1666.

Dano, see **Deneau**.

Danyew, Danyow, see **Daigneault**.

Daoust, either from d'aoust, derived from Old French aoust 'harvest', probably the nick-name of a seasonal worker, or from D'Aoust, derived from a regional variant of Au-guste, from the Latin name Augustus, from augustus 'saint, majestic, venerable'. — Amer. **Deau, Doe, Dow**.

— Guillaume **Daoust** (Nicolas and Jeanne Aubert) from Sissonne in Aisne (Picardie) m. Marie-Madeleine Lalonde (Jean and Marie Barbant) in Lachine, QC in 1686.

Dapo, see **Dépault**.

Daragon, either from Daragon or d'Aragon 'from Aragon', placenames in France. — Amer. **Dragon**.

— François **Daragon** dit Lafrance from France m. Marie Guillemet (Nicolas and Ma-rie Selle) in Québec c. 1697.

Dashnau, Dashnaw, Dashner, Dashnow, see **Dagenais**.

Daudelin, from d'Audelin '[son] of Audelin', from the Germanic name Aldalin, derived from ald 'old'. — Amer. **Dodelin, Dolan, Dolen, Douglas, Dudley**.

— Nicolas **Daudelin** (Jacques and Jeanne Lépine) from Rouen in Seine-Maritime (Haute-Normandie) m. Anne Girard (Michel and Françoise Graffard) in Château-Ri-cher, QC in 1665.

Daunais, alteration of d'Aunay 'from Aunay', a placename in France. — Amer. **Doaner, Donah, Doner, Doney, Donner, Donor**.

— Antoine **Daunay** (Louis and Jeanne Gavatte) from Luçon in Vendée (Pays de la Loire) m. Marie Richard (Pierre and Anne Masson) in Québec in 1669.

Dauphinais, alteration of Dauphiné, a former province in France. — Amer. **Duffany, Duffiney, Duffiny, Duffney, Duphiney**.

— Jean-Baptiste **Dauphiné** dit Saint-Jean (Pierre and Marie-Catherine *Magumes) from La Nouaille in Creuse (Limousin) m. Marie-Antoinette Desrochers (Pierre and Marie-Anne Rouleau) in Baie-du-Febvre, QC in 1759.

Daviau, derived from David, from the Hebrew name Dawidh 'beloved, friend'. — Amer. **Davieau, Davieaux, Davio, Devoid**.

— Julien **Daviau** dit Prêtàboire (Gilles and Françoise Guimier) from Saint-Germain-des-Prés in Maine-et-Loire (Pays de la Loire) m. Marie-Geneviève Ledoux (Nicolas and Marie-Geneviève Auger) in Varennes, QC in 1757.

Davignon, from d'Avignon 'from Avignon', a placename in France. — Amer. **Deveneau, Devenow, Devino**.

— François **Davignon** dit Beauregard from France m. Madeleine Maillot (Jean and Marie Courault) in Chambly, QC in 1719.

Davio, see **Daviau**.

Deaett, Deaette, see **Guillet(te)**.

Deagle, see **Daigle**.

Deary, see **Déry**.

Deau, see **Daoust**.

Debarge, see **Théberge**.

Debien, from *de Bien* '[son] of Bien', a regional variant of *Vivien*, from the Latin name *Vivianus*, derived from *vivus* 'alive'. — Amer. **Dabiew, Debiew, Debyah.**
— *Étienne **Debien**/Desbiens (Denis and Suzanne ...) from Moulismes in Vienne (Poitou-Charentes) m. Marie Campeau (Étienne and Catherine Paulo) in Montréal, QC in 1691.*

Debo, see **Dubeau.**

Debyah, see **Debien.**

Decaire, see **Dicaire.**

Decant, see **De Quindre.**

Decare, see **Dicaire.**

Decarreau, see **Descarreaux.**

Decato, see **Descôteaux.**

Decelle, from *de Celle* 'from Celle', a placename in France. — Amer. **Decell, Deselle, Deselles, Desselle, Desselles, Salt, Sault.**
— *Gabriel Celle/**Decelle** dit Duclos (Jean and Colette Roquet) from Nonant in Calvados (Basse-Normandie) m. Barbe Poisson (Jean and Barbe Broust) in Montréal, QC in 1651.*

Dechaine, see **Deschênes.**

Dechambeau, see **Deschambault.**

Dechand, see **Deschamps.**

Dechene, see **Deschênes.**

Declue, see **Duclos.**

Decota, Decoteaux, Decoto, see **Descôteaux.**

Default, Defoe, see **Dufault.**

Deford, see **Dufort.**

Defore, see **Dufour.**

Defrain, Defraine, Defresne, see **Dufresne.**

Degagné, probable alteration of *des Gasniers* via *Desgagnés*, derived from *Les Gasniers*, a placename in Ille-et-Vilaine (Bretagne). — Amer. **Degonia.**
— *Jacques **Desgagnés** (Robert and Marguerite Voisin) from Ducy-Sainte-Marguerite in Calvados (Basse-Normandie) m. Geneviève Pelletier (François and Marguerite-Madeleine Morisseau) in Montréal, QC in 1690.*

Deganne, alteration of *Gane*, from the Germanic name *Wano*, derived from *wan* 'hope, expectation'. — Amer. **Degan.**
— *François **Gane** (Germain and Marie Valet) from Geffosses in Manche (Basse-Normandie) m. Marie-Josèphe Bourhis (Jean and Marie Demers) in Longueuil, QC in 1725.*

Degon, see **Dugas.**

Degonia, see **Degagné.**

Degree, see **Dugré.**

Degreenia, Degrenier, see **Dugrenier.**

Dehais, see **Deshaies.**

Deitte, see **Guillet, Guillette.**

Dejarlais, see **Desjarlais.**

Dekett, see **Duquet, Duquette.**

Delage, from *de Lage* 'from Lage' or *de L'Age* 'from L'Age', placenames in France. —

Amer. **Delodge, Deloge, Delosh.**

— *Jean* **Delage** *dit Lavigueur (Jean and Michelle de la Mazerole) from Exideuil in Charente (Poitou-Charentes) m. Anne Chalifou (Paul and Jacquette Archambault) in Beauport, QC in 1692.*

— *Laurent* **Delage** *dit Larivière from France m. Marie-Renée Bezeau (Pierre and Renée Millet) in Québec c. 1693.*

Delancett, Delancette, see **Lalancette.**

Delane, see **Lalonde.**

Delard, alteration of *de Le Lard* 'from Le Lard', a placename in France. — Amer. **Delore.**

— *François Dellard/***Delard** *(Guillaume and Jeanne Verdon) from Lascabanes in Lot (Midi-Pyrénées) m. Marie-Thérèse Therrien (Guillaume and Marie-Anne Jahan) in Saint-Laurent, Île d'Orléans, QC in 1748.*

Delarm, see **Delorme.**

Delaunay, from *de L'Aunay* 'from L'Aunay', a placename in France. — Amer. **Deloney.**

— *Pierre* **Delaunay** *(Gilles and Denise Dubois) from Sarthe (Pays de la Loire) m. Françoise Pinguet (Henri and Louise Lousche) in Québec, QC in 1645.*

Delaurier, see **Deslauriers.**

Delaware, see **Drouin.**

Delisle, from *de Lisle* 'from Lisle' or *de L'Isle* 'from L'Isle', placenames in France. — Amer. **Delille.**

— *François Bienvenu dit* **Delisle** *(Michel and Hélène Guyart) from Saint-Pierre-le-Vieux in Vendée (Pays de la Loire) m. Geneviève Charron (Jean and Anne d'Anneville) in Detroit, MI c. 1701.*

Delodge, Deloge, see **Delage.**

Deloney, see **Delaunay.**

Delore, see **Delard.**

Delorey, see **Deslauriers.**

Delorge, see **Desloges.**

Deloria, Delorier, Deloriers, see **Deslauriers.**

Delorme, apparently from *de Lorme* 'from Lorme' or *de L'Orme* 'from L'Orme', placenames in France. — Amer. **Delarm.**

— *Joseph Lemay dit* **Delorme,** *son of Michel from Chênehutte-Trèves-Cunault in Maine-et-Loire (Pays de la Loire), m. Agnès-Madeleine Gaudry (Nicolas and Agnès Morin) in Québec in 1686.*

Delory, see **Deslauriers.**

Delosh, see **Delage.**

Delphia, see **Dalpé.**

Delude, see **Dulude.**

Demar, Demara, see **Desmarais.**

Demarce, see **Demers.**

Demarie, Demarr, Demarre, see **Desmarais.**

Demars, Demarse, Demarsh, see **Demers.**

Demas, see **Demers** and **Dumas.**

Demerais, see **Desmarais.**

Demers, alteration of *Dumets,* derived from *Le Metz,* a placename in France. — Amer.

Demarce, Demars, Demarse, Demarsh, Demas.
— *André Dumets/**Demers** (Jean and Barbe Mauger) from Dieppe in Seine-Maritime (Haute-Normandie) m. Marie Chefdeville (Jean and Marguerite Gesseaume) in Mont-réal, QC in 1654.*
— *Jean Dumets/**Demers** (Jean and Barbe Mauger) from Dieppe in Seine-Maritime (Haute-Normandie) m. Jeanne Voidy (Michel and Catherine *Dorbelle) in Montréal, QC in 1654.*
Demo, see **Guimond.**
Demoe, Demont, see **Dumont.**
De Montbrun, apparently from *Montbrun*, a placename in France. — Amer. **Demonbreun.**
— *Jean Boucher, sieur de **Montbrun**, grandson of Gaspard from Mortagne-au-Perche in Orne (Basse-Normandie), m. Françoise-Claire Charet (Étienne and Catherine Bissot) in Lauzon, QC in 1692.*
Demore, see **Desmarais.**
Deneau, alteration of *Deniau*, derived from **Daniel.** — Amer. **Dano, Denaut, Denio, Denno, Deno.**
— *Marin **Deniau** dit Destaillis from Luché-Pringé in Sarthe (Pays de la Loire) m. Louise-Thérèse-Marie Lebreuil (Jean and Marie Lecomte) in Montréal, QC in 1659.*
Deniger, origin undetermined. — Amer. **Denesha.**
— *Bernard **Deniger** dit Sansoucy from Bordeaux in Gironde (Aquitaine) m. Marguerite Raisin in Québec c. 1670.*
Denio, see **Deneau** and **Denoyon.**
Denis, from the Greek name *Dionysios*. — Amer. **Dennis, Denny.**
— *Pierre **Denis** dit Lapicardie (Pierre and Marie-Anne Flamand) from Fresnoy-le-Grand in Aisne (Picardie) m. Marie-Charlotte Charbonneau (Jean and Agathe Chaussé) in Lachine, QC in 1719.*
— *Simon Goyette dit **Denis**, descendant of Pierre Goguet from Marans in Charente-Maritime (Poitou-Charentes), m. Marguerite Patenaude (Alexandre and Marguerite Suzor) in Henryville, QC in 1873.*
Dennis, see **St-Denis.**
Denno, see **Deneau.**
Denny, see **Denis.**
Deno, see **Deneau.**
Denoya, Denoyer, see **Desnoyers.**
Denoyon, from *de Noyon* 'from Noyon', a placename in France. — Amer. **Denio.**
— *Jean **Denoyon** (Jean and Jeanne Franchart) from Rouen in Seine-Maritime (Haute-Normandie) m. Marie Chauvin (Marin and Gilette Banne) in Trois-Rivières, QC in 1665.*
D'Entremont, from *d'Entremont* 'from Entremont', a placename in France. — Amer. **Arcement, Arsement.**
— *Philippe Mius, sieur d'**Entremont** from Normandie m. Madeleine Hélie in Acadia c. 1649.*
Denue, see **Daigneault.**
Deo, see **Dion.**
Deon, see **Dion** and **Dionne.**

Dépault, alteration of *Delepeau*, from either *de Le Pau* 'from Le Pau', *de L'Epau* 'from L'Epau' or *de L'Epeau* 'from L'Epeau', placenames in France. — Amer. **Dapo, Depeau, Despaw.**

— *Louis **Delepeau** (François and Jeanne Hulin) from Champeaux in Manche (Basse-Normandie) m. Marie-Josèphe Leroux (Germain and Marie-Anne Pépin) in Sorel, QC in 1751.*

Deplanty, Deplaunty, see **Duplanty.**

De Quindre, origin undetermined. — Amer. **Decant.**

— *Louis-Césaire Dagneau, sieur de **Quindre**, son of Michel from Deux-Jumeaux in Calvados (Basse-Normandie), m. Marie-Françoise Picoté (François-Marie and Marie-Catherine Trottier) in Montréal, QC in 1736.*

Deraleau, Deranleau, see **Desranleau.**

Deresh, Deroch, see **Desroches.**

Derocha, Deroche, Derochea, see **Desrochers.**

Derochie, see **Durocher.**

Derochier, see **Desrochers.**

Deroin, see **Drouin.**

Derose, Derosia, Derosie, see **Desrosiers.**

Derouche, see **Desrochers.**

Derouchie, see **Durocher.**

Derouen, see **Drouin.**

Derousseau, see **Desruisseaux.**

Deruchie, see **Durocher.**

Derush, see **Desroches.**

Derusha, see **Desrochers** and **Durocher.**

Derushe, see **Durocher.**

Derushia, see **Desrochers.**

Deruso, see **Desruisseaux.**

Derway, Derwin, see **Drouin.**

Déry, alteration of *d'Héry* 'from Héry', a placename in France. — Amer. **Deary.**

— *Nicolas **Déry** from France m. Élisabeth Bertrand in France c. 1656.*

Desair, Desaire, see **Deserre.**

Desalliers, from *des Alliers*, apparently derived from *Les Alliers*, a placename in France. — Amer. **Dezalia.**

— *Joseph Aubuchon dit **Desalliers**, son of Jacques from Dieppe in Seine-Maritime (Haute-Normandie), m. Marie-Louise Dandonneau (Pierre and Françoise Jobin) in Champlain, QC in 1688.*

Desarmeau, Desarmeaux, see **Desormeaux.**

Desaulniers, from *des Aulniers*, apparently derived from *Les Aulniers*, a placename in Seine-Maritime (Haute-Normandie). — Amer. **Desonia, Desonie.**

— *Jean-Baptiste Lesieur dit **Desaulniers**, son of Charles from Ozeville in Manche (Basse-Normandie), m. Marie-Élisabeth Rivard (Julien and Élisabeth Thunay) in Batiscan, QC in 1707.*

Desautels, from *des Autels*, derived from *Les Autels*, a placename in France. — Amer. **Deshautelle, Deshotel, Deshotels, Desotell, Desotelle, Dezotell, Dezotelle, Disotell, Disotelle.**

— Pierre **Desautels** dit Lapointe (Thomas and Marie Buisson) from Malicorne-sur-Sarthe in Sarthe (Pays de la Loire) m. (1) Marie Rémy (Nicolas and Marie *Vener) in Montréal, QC in 1666; (2) Catherine Lorion (Mathurin and Françoise Morinet) in Montréal, QC in 1676.

Desaw, see **Dussault**.

Descarreaux, from des Carreaux, derived from Les Carreaux, a placename in France. — Amer. **Decarreau**.

— Denis Derome dit **Descarreaux** (Jean and Marie Goullier) from Myennes in Nièvre (Bourgogne) m. Jacqueline Roulois (Michel and Jeanne Maline) in Québec, QC in 1657.

Deschaine, see **Deschênes**.

Deschambault, alteration of des Chambaults, derived from Les Chambaults, a placename in Maine-et-Loire (Pays de la Loire). — Amer. **Dechambeau**.

— Jacques-Alexis (de) Fleury, sieur **Deschambault** (Jacques and Perrine Gabard) from Montaigu in Vendée (Pays de la Loire) m. Marguerite (de) Chavigny (François and Éléonore de Grandmaison) in Québec, QC in 1671.

Deschamps, from des Champs, derived from Les Champs, a placename in France. — Amer. **Dechand, Deschand, Deschaw, Deshaw, Deshon, Deshong, Dishaw, Dishon, Dishong, Dishongh, Duchen, Fields**.

— Toussaint Hunault dit **Deschamps** (Nicolas and Marie Benoist) from Saint-Pierre-ès-Champs in Oise (Picardie) m. Marie Lorgueil (Pierre and Marie Bruyère) in Montréal, QC in 1654.

— Nicolas-Joseph **Deschamps** dit Cloche from Saint-Martin-de-Ré in Charente-Maritime (Poitou-Charentes) m. Judith Doiron (Charles and Françoise Gaudet) in Pigiquid, NS in 1733.

Deschane, see **Deschênes**.

Deschâtelets, from des Châtelets, apparently derived from Les Châtelets, a placename in France. — Amer. **Deshetler**.

— Joseph Pineau/Pinot dit **Deschâtelets**, son of Pierre from Le Mans in Sarthe (Pays de la Loire), m. Catherine Richer (Pierre and Dorothée Brassard) in Batiscan, QC in 1693.

Deschaw, see **Deschamps**.

Deschenaux, from des Chenaux, apparently derived from Les Chenaux, a placename in France. — Amer. **Dishneau, Dishno**.

— René Pineau dit Laperle and **Deschenaux**, son of Pierre from Le Mans in Sarthe (Pays de la Loire), m. Catherine Janvier (Jean and Dorothée Dubois) in La Pérade, QC in 1705.

Deschênes, from des Chênes, apparently derived from Les Chênes, a placename in France. — Amer. **Dechaine, Dechene, Deschaine, Deschane, Deshane**.

— Jacques Miville dit **Deschênes**, son of Pierre from Fribourg in Switzerland, m. Catherine de Baillon (Alphonse and Louise de Marle) in Québec, QC in 1669.

Descôteaux, from des Côteaux, apparently derived from Les Côteaux, a placename in France. —Amer. **Decato, Decoteaux, Decota, Decoto, Hill**.

— Ange Lefebvre dit **Descôteaux**, son of Pierre from Sceaux in Hauts-de-Seine (Île-de-France), m. Marie-Madeleine Cusson (Jean and Marie Foubert) in Québec c. 1680.

Deselle, Deselles, see **Decelle**.

Deserre, from *de Serre* 'from Serre', a placename in France. —Amer. **Desair, Desaire.**

— *Antoine **Deserre** (François and Antoinette Ruby) from Saint-Amant-de-Boixe in Charente (Poitou-Charentes) m. Mathurine Bélanger (François and Marie Guyon) in Château-Richer, QC in 1674.*

Desforges, from *des Forges*, derived from *Les Forges*, a placename in France. —Amer. **Desforge.**

— *Robert **Desforges** dit Picard (Nicolas and Marie Lemoine) from Athies-sous-Laon in Aisne (Picardie) m. Marie Malboeuf (Jean-Baptiste and Marie-Madeleine Simard) in Sainte-Anne-de-Beaupré, QC in 1758.*

Desgroseilliers, from *des Groseilliers*, apparently derived from *Les Groseilliers* or *Les Groseillers*, placenames in France. — Amer. **Gooseberry, Grozelle.**

— *Jean-Baptiste Bouchard dit Dorval, sieur **Desgroseilliers**, grandson of Claude from Montigny-Lengrain in Aisne (Picardie), m. Marie-Josèphe (de) Chavigny (François and Geneviève Guyon) in Beauport, QC in 1734.*

Deshaies, alteration *des Hayes*, derived from *Les Hayes*, a placename in France. — Amer. **Daha, Dehais.**

— *Pierre **Deshayes** dit Saint-Cyr from France m. Marguerite Guillet (Pierre and Jeanne Saint-Père) in Québec c. 1677.*

Deshane, see **Deschênes.**

Deshautelle, see **Desautels.**

Deshaw, Deshon, Deshong, see **Deschamps.**

Deshetler, see **Deschâtelets.**

Deshotel, Deshotels, see **Desautels.**

Desjardins, either from *des Jardins*, derived from *Les Jardins*, a placename in France, or from *des jardins* 'from the gardens', a soldier's nickname. — Amer. **Desjarden, Desjardine, Gardiner, Gardner.**

— *Claude **Desjardins** dit Charbonnier (Marin and Marguerite Gabrielle) from Isle-et-Bardais in Allier (Auvergne) m. Marguerite Cardillon (Noël and Marie Dubois) in Québec, QC in 1666.*

— *Antoine Roy dit **Desjardins** (Olivier and Catherine Bodard) from Joigny in Yonne (Bourgogne) m. Marie Major (Jean and Marguerite Le Pelé) in Québec, QC in 1668.*

Desjarlais, alteration of *de Gerlache* 'from Gerlache' via *de Gerlaise*, a placename in Belgium. — Amer. **Dejarlais, Desjarlis.**

— *Jean-Jacques (de) **Gerlaise** dit/sieur de Saint-Amand (Ferdinand and Dorothée Cona) from Liège in Belgium m. Jeanne Trudel (Jean and Marguerite Thomas) in L'Ange-Gardien, QC in 1667.*

Deslauriers, from *des Lauriers*, derived from *Les Lauriers*, a placename in France. — Amer. **Delorey, Deloria, Delorier, Deloriers, Delory.**

— *Thomas Jacquet dit **Deslauriers** (Jean and Marie-Catherine Gonfray) from Rouans in Loire-Atlantique (Pays de la Loire) m. Marguerite Sigouin (Germain and Louise Quay) in Lavaltrie, QC in 1752.*

— *Jean-Baptiste Renaud/Arnaud dit **Deslauriers** (Jean and Marie Forget) from Astaillac in Corrèze (Limousin) m. Marie-Anne Provost (René and Anne Daudelin) in Varennes, QC in 1705.*

Desloges, from *des Loges*, derived from *Les Loges*, a placename in France. — Amer. **Delorge.**

— *Joseph Poirier dit* **Desloges** *(Jacques and Françoise Brunet) from Lathus-Saint-Ré-my in Vienne (Poitou-Charentes) m. Marie Gauthier (Pierre and Charlotte Roussel) in Montréal, QC in 1709.*

Desmarais, from *des Marais,* derived from *Les Marais,* a placename in France. — Amer. **Demar, Demara, Demarie, Demarr, Demarre, Demera, Demerais, Demore.**

— *Paul* **Desmarais**/*Marais (Jacques and Marie-Marthe Laporte) from Paris (Île-de-France) m. Marie Tétreau (Louis and Noëlle Landeau) in Champlain, QC in 1681.*

— *René Abraham dit* **Desmarais** *(Jean and Jeanne Brassard) from Secondigné-sur-Belle in Deux-Sèvres (Poitou-Charentes) m. Marguerite Girard in Saint-François-du-Lac, QC in 1690.*

Desnoyers, from *des Noyers,* derived from *Les Noyers,* a placename in France. — Amer. **Denoya, Denoyer, Hickory.**

— *Jean* **Desnoyers** *dit Desmarais from France m. Thérèse Ménard (Jacques and Catherine Forestier) in Longueuil, QC in 1709.*

Deso, see **Dussault.**

Desonia, Desonie, see **Desaulniers.**

Desorcy, from *de Sorcy* 'from Sorcy', a placename in France. — Amer. **Desorcie, Zercie.**

— *Michel* **Desorcy** *(François and Marie *Souvegnac) from Sceaux in Hauts-de-Seine (Île-de-France) m. Françoise de La Barre (Jean and Andrée Bertin) in La Rochelle in Charente-Maritime (Poitou-Charentes) in 1656.*

Desormeaux, from *des Ormeaux,* derived from *Les Ormeaux,* a placename in France. — Amer. **Desarmeau, Desarmeaux.**

— *Pierre Monteau/Monceaux/Monciau dit* **Desormeaux** *(Gencien and Marie Oudet) from Boulay-les-Barres or Bricy in Loiret (Centre) m. Marguerite Auger (Jean-Baptiste and Marie-Françoise Bon) in Montréal, QC in 1716.*

Desotell, Desotelle, see **Desautels.**

Dépatie, alteration of *Despatis,* from *des Patis,* derived from *Les Patis,* a placename in France. — Amer. **Departie, Depotie, Depotsie.**

— *Nicolas Forget dit* **Despatis** *(Paul and Nicole Chevalier) from Alençon in Orne (Basse-Normandie) m. Madeleine Martin (Abraham and Marguerite Langlois) in Québec, QC in 1653.*

Despaw, see **Dépault.**

Despins, from *des Pins,* apparently derived from *Les Pins,* a placename in France. — Amer. **Dupaw.**

— *Antoine Lefebvre dit* **Despins,** *son of Gabriel from Paris (Île-de-France), m. Marie-Anne Morand (Jean-Baptiste and Élisabeth Dubois) in La Pérade, QC in 1731.*

Desranleau, alteration of *Déranlot,* from Old French *dorenlot* 'spoiled child, pet'. — Amer. **Deraleau, Deranleau.**

— *Jean* **Desranleau** *dit Châteauneuf (Jacques and Jeanne *Durinost) from Chaunay in Vienne (Poitou-Charentes) m. Marie-Madeleine Trottier (Jean-Baptiste and Geneviève Lafond) in Batiscan, QC in 1698.*

Desrochers, from *des Rochers,* derived from *Les Rochers,* a placename in France. — Amer. **Derocha, Deroche, Derochea, Derochier, Derouche, Derusha, Derushia.**

— *Louis Brien dit* **Desrochers** *(Élie and Jeanne Liou) from Plaine-en-l'Isle in Ille-et-Vilaine (Bretagne) m. Suzanne Bouvier (Michel and Mathurine Desbordes) in Mont-*

réal, QC in 1681.

Desroches, from *des Roches,* derived from *Les Roches,* a placename in France. — Amer. **Deresh, Deroch, Derush, Stone.**

— *Jean* **Desroches** *(... and Antoinette ...) from Lucy-le-Bois in Yonne (Bourgogne) m. Françoise Godé (Nicolas and Françoise Gadois) in Montréal, QC in 1647.*

— *Louis* **Desroches** *(Georges and Jacqueline Huault) from Carolles in Manche (Basse-Normandie) m. Marguerite Arseneau (Pierre and Marie-Anne Boudrot) in Prince Edward Island c. 1731.*

Desrosiers, alteration of *de Ronzier* 'from Ronzier', a placename in France. — Amer. **Derose, Derosia, Derosie, Rosebush.**

— *Antoine Deronzier/***Desrosiers** *(Jean and ...) from Noailly or Renaison in Loire (Rhône-Alpes) m. Anne Leneuf (Michel and ...) in Québec in 1647.*

Desruisseaux, from *des Ruisseaux,* apparently derived from *Les Ruisseaux,* a placename in France. — Amer. **Derousseau, Deruso.**

— *Jacques Houde dit* **Desruisseaux,** *son of Louis from Manou in Eure-et-Loir (Centre), m. Marie-Louise Beaudet (Jean and Marie Grandin) in Québec in 1686.*

Desseau, see **Dussault.**

Desselle, Desselles, see **Decelle.**

Desso, see **Dussault.**

Destrempes, alteration of *d'Estrampes* 'from Estrampes', a placename in Ariège (Midi-Pyrénées). — Amer. **Destromp.**

— *Jean-Baptiste* **Destrempes** *(Pierre and Bertrande Saillant) from Bordes-de-Rivière in Haute-Garonne (Midi-Pyrénées) m. Geneviève Buron (Noël and Marie-Catherine Michelon) in Québec, QC in 1752.*

Destroismaisons, from *des Trois Maisons,* derived from *Les Trois Maisons,* a placename in Pas-de-Calais (Nord-Pas-de-Calais). — Amer. **Threehouse.**

— *Philippe* **Destroismaisons** *dit Picard (Adrien and Antoinette Leroux) from Montreuil in Pas-de-Calais (Nord-Pas-de-Calais) m. Martine Crosnier (Pierre and Jeanne Rotreau) in Château-Richer, QC in 1669.*

Destromp, see **Destrempes.**

Deszell, see **Déziel.**

Deuby, see **Dubé.**

Deugaw, see **Dugas.**

Deuso, see **Dussault.**

Devaux, from *de Vaux* 'from Vaux', a placename in France. — Amer. **Deview, Devoe.**

— *Michel* **Devaux**/*Deveau from France m. Marie-Madeleine Martin (Pierre and Joachine Lafleur) in Acadia c. 1693.*

Deveneau, Devenow, see **Davignon.**

Deview, see **Devaux.**

Devino, see **Davignon.**

Devoe, see **Devaux.**

Devoid, see **Daviau.**

Dewey, Dewyea, see **Duguay.**

Deyette, see **Guillet(te).**

Deyo, see **Dion.**

Dezalia, see **Desalliers.**

Déziel, alteration of *Delguel,* from *de Le Guel* 'from Le Guel', a placename in France. — Amer. **Deszell.**

— Pierre Delguel dit Labrèche (Pierre and Jeanne Dunien) from Doissat in Dordogne (Aquitaine) m. Marie-Anne Baron (Nicolas and Marie Chauvin) in Trois-Rivières, QC in 1709.

Dezotell, Dezotelle, see **Desautels.**

Dicaire, alteration of the English name *Dicker,* from Old English *dicere* 'ditchdigger'. — Amer. **Decaire, Decare.**

— John Dicker/Jean-Louis Dicaire (John and Sarah Teckel) from Newfoundland m. Marie-Suzanne Lorrain (Pierre and Marie Matou) in Rivière-des-Prairies, QC in 1720.

Diette, see **Guillet(te).**

Digue, see **Daigle.**

Diguette, Dillette, see **Guillet(te).**

Dion, alteration of *Guyon,* derived from *Guy,* from the Germanic name *Wido,* derived from *wid* 'wood'. — Amer. **Deo, Deon, Deyo, Young.**

— Jean Guyon (Jacques and Marie Huet) from Tourouvre in Orne (Basse-Normandie) m. Mathurine Robin (Eustache and Madeleine Avrard) in Mortagne-au-Perche in Orne in 1615.

Dionne, alteration of *d'Yonne* 'from Yonne', the nickname of an individual from that region in Burgundy. — Amer. **Deon, Young.**

— Antoine Dionne from France m. Catherine Ivory in France c. 1660.

Dishaw, see **Deschamps.**

Dishneau, Dishno, see **Deschenaux.**

Dishon, Dishong, Dishongh, see **Deschamps.**

Disotell, Disotelle, see **Desautels.**

Doaner, see **Daunais.**

Dodelin, see **Daudelin.**

Doe, see **Daoust.**

Doiron, from *d'Oiron* 'from Oiron', a placename in Deux-Sèvres (Poitou-Charentes). — Amer. **Durant, Gould.**

— Jean Doiron/Douaron from Oiron in Deux-Sèvres (Poitou-Charentes) m. Marie-Anne Canol in Acadia c. 1671.

Dolan, Dolen, see **Daudelin.**

Domay, alteration of *Daumé,* origin undetermined. — Amer. **Doma, Dome, Domer, Domey, Domin, Domy.**

— Pierre-Sébastien Daumé/Domay dit Laviolette (Louis and Marguerite Ricau) from Paris (Île-de-France) m. Marie-Félicité Marié (Jacques and Angélique Desroches) in Saint-Charles-sur-Richelieu, QC in 1760.

Dominé, from Latin *domine* 'lord!', the nickname of a cantor. — Amer. **Domina.**

— Pierre-Henri Dominé dit Saint-Sauveur from Vitry-le-François in Marne (Champagne-Ardenne) m. Marie-Madeleine Laforest (Joseph and Marie-Anne Girouard) in Acadia c. 1752.

Domingue, from the Latin name *Dominicus,* derived from *dominus* 'master'. — Amer. **Doming.**

— Dominique Ostiguy dit Domingue (Jean and Catherine Chevery) from Arcangues in Pyrénées-Atlantiques (Aquitaine) m. Marie-Marguerite Parent (Pierre and Marie-Ca-

therine James) in Chambly, QC in 1754.

Dompierre, from *Dompierre,* a placename in France. — Amer. **Dompier.**

— *Charles **Dompierre** dit Saint-Martin (Rémi and Catherine Forget) from Cany-Bar-ville in Seine-Maritime (Haute-Normandie) m. Marie-Agnès Destouches (Pierre and Marie Gulet) in Sainte-Famille, Île d'Orléans, QC in 1669.*

Domy, see **Domay.**

Donah, see **Daunais.**

Donat, from the Latin name *Donatus,* from *donatus* 'given (to God)'. — Amer. **Danette.**

— *Martial **Donat** dit Laverdure (Jacques and Françoise ...) from Montpellier in Hé-rault (Languedoc-Roussillon) m. Marie-Élisabeth Parent (Pierre and Marie-Catherine Langlois) in Saint-Mathias, QC in 1762.*

Doner, Doney, see **Daunais.**

Donna, see **Danis.**

Donner, Donor, see **Daunais.**

Doré, from *doré* 'golden', the nickname of a gilder or a goldsmith. — Amer. **Dora, Do-rey.**

— *Louis **Doré** (Louis and Anne Sylvestre) from Versailles in Yvelines (Île-de-France) m. Marie-Catherine Roussel (Pierre and Marie-Catherine Morand) in Saint-Sulpice, QC in 1760.*

Dostie, origin undetermined. — Amer. **Dustin, Dusty.**

— *Pierre Bellot dit **Dostie** (Marc and Toinette Casse) from Monflanquin in Lot-et-Ga-ronne (Aquitaine) m. Marie-Rose Raté (André and Marie-Jeanne Martel) in Saint-Pi-erre, Île d'Orléans, QC in 1754.*

Doucet(te), either from *(Le) Doucet,* a placename in France, or derived from *doux* 'mild-mannered, gentle'. — Amer. **Doucett, Dousay, Dousett, Dousette, Ducette.**

— *Germain **Doucet**, sieur de Laverdure from Conflans-sur-Seine in Marne (Champa-gne-Ardenne) or Coupru in Aisne (Picardie) m. an unknown spouse in France or Aca-dia c. 1620.*

Douglas, see **Daudelin.**

Douillet, either from *Douillet,* a placename in France, or derived from Old French *doille* 'soft, tender'. — Amer. **Doyea.**

— *Jean-Baptiste **Douillet** (François and Jeanne Charpentier) from France m. Marie-Anne Lemerle (Louis and Marie-Anne Chesne) in Forges du Saint-Maurice, QC in 1749.*

Dousay, Dousett, Dousette, see **Doucet(te)**.

Dow, see **Daoust.**

Downey, see **Danis.**

Doyea, see **Douillet.**

Doyon, probably from *Doyon,* a placename in Gironde (Aquitaine). — Amer. **Dyer.**

— *Jean **Doyon** (Jacques and Françoise Couturier) from Périgny in Charente-Maritime (Poitou-Charentes) m. Marthe Gagnon (Mathurin and Vincente Gaultier) in Québec, QC in 1650.*

Dragon, see **Daragon.**

Drainville, alteration of *de Rainville* 'from Rainville', a placename in Orne (Basse-Nor-mandie). — Amer. **Drinville.**

— *Paul **de Rainville** (Jean and Jeanne Brechet) from Touques in Calvados (Basse-Nor-*

mandie) m. Roline Poète/Poite in Touques c. 1638.

Drewior, Drewyor, see **Drouillard.**

Drinkwine, see **Boivin.**

Drinville, see **Drainville.**

Drolet, alteration of *de Rolet* 'from Rolet', a placename in France. — Amer. **Drolett, Drolette, Drollett, Drollette, Droulette.**

— *Christophe Drolet from Paris (Île-de-France) m. Jeanne Levasseur (Noël and Geneviève Gaugé) in Paris c. 1653.*

Drouillard, from *Drouillard,* a placename in France. — Amer. **Drewior, Drewyor, Droullard.**

— *Simon Drouillard dit Argencourt (Jean and Jeanne Chevreau) from Marennes in Charente-Maritime (Poitou-Charentes) m. Marguerite Ferré (Pierre and Marie Lasnon) in Québec, QC in 1698.*

Drouin, derived from the Germanic name *Drogo,* apparently from *drog* 'battle'. — Amer. **Delaware, Deroin, Derouen, Derway, Derwin.**

— *Robert Drouin (Robert and Marie Dubois) from Le Pin-la-Garenne in Orne (Basse-Normandie) m. Marie Chapelier (Jean and Marguerite Dodier) in Québec, QC in 1649.*

Droulette, see **Drolet.**

Droullard, see **Drouillard.**

Drury, see **Duguay.**

Duaime, see **Duhaime.**

Dubé, from *du Bé,* derived from *Le Bé,* a placename in France. — Amer. **Deuby, Duba, Dubay, Dubie, Duby.**

— *Mathurin Dubé (Jean and Renée Suzanne) from Chapelle-Thémer in Vendée (Pays de la Loire) m. Marie Campion (Pierre and Marguerite Hénaut) in Sainte-Famille, Île d'Orléans, QC in 1670.*

Dubeau, from *du Beau,* derived from *Le Beau,* a placename in France. — Amer. **Debo.**

— *Toussaint Dubeau from Paris (Île-de-France) m. Anne Jousselot (Pierre and Ozanne Drapeau) in Québec, QC in 1678.*

Dubie, see **Dubé.**

Dubois, from *du Bois,* derived from *Le Bois,* a placename in France. — Amer. **Wood, Woods.**

— *François Dubois dit Lafrance (François and Claude Fayel) from Saint-Pôtan in Côtes-d'Armor (Bretagne) m. Anne Guillaume (Michel and Germaine *Ermolin) in Québec, QC in 1671.*

— *François Dubois dit Jolicoeur (Jean and Catherine Dumas) from Saint-Yrieix-la-Perche in Haute-Vienne (Limousin) m. Marguerite Charles (Étienne and Madeleine Niel) in Boucherville, QC in 1700.*

Dubourg, from *du Bourg,* derived from *Le Bourg,* a placename in France. — Amer. **Dubour.**

— *François Dubourg (Étienne and Marie Durand) from Granville in Manche (Basse-Normandie) m. Marie-Gertrude Thériault (Guy and Marie-Anne Poulin) in Québec, QC in 1737.*

Dubreuil, from *du Breuil,* derived from *Le Breuil,* a placename in France. — Amer. **Dubray.**

— *Jean Dubreuil/Dubreul dit Marin (Jacques and Marie *Turtonde/*Jurtonde) from*

Lacapelle-Biron in Lot-et-Garonne (Aquitaine) m. Marie-Josèphe Lapointe in Montréal, QC in 1729.

Duby, see **Dubé.**

Ducate, Ducatte, see **Duquet(te).**

Ducèdre, from *du Cèdre,* derived from *le cèdre* 'the cedar', a nickname apparently from the site of an estate or property. — Amer. **Cedar.**

— *Antoine Leboeuf dit **Ducèdre**, descendant of Jacques from Ciré-d'Aunis in Charente-Maritime (Poitou-Charentes), m. Marie Jax/Yacks (Jean-Baptiste-Guillaume and Marie-Judith Huyet) in Grosse Pointe, MI in 1781.*

Ducette, see **Doucet(te).**

Duchaine, see **Duchesne.**

Duchano, see **Duchesneau.**

Ducharme, from *du Charme,* derived from *Le Charme,* a placename in France. — Amer. **Ducharm, Dusharm, Dusharme.**

— *Pierre Charron dit **Ducharme** (Pierre and Judith Martin) from Meaux in Seine-et-Marne (Île-de-France) m. Catherine Pillard (Pierre and Marguerite Moulinet) in Montréal, QC in 1665.*

Duchen, see **Deschamps.**

Ducheney, see **Duchesny.**

Duchesne, from *du Chesne,* derived from *Le Chesne,* a placename in France. — Amer. **Duchaine, Duschene, Dushane.**

— *Pierre **Duchesne** dit Lapierre (Jean and Catherine Poullet) from Mesnil-Saint-Georges in Somme (Picardie) m. Catherine Rivet (Pierre and Marie *Sorgeaut) in Québec in 1666.*

Duchesneau, from *du Chesneau,* derived from *Le Chesneau,* a placename in France. — Amer. **Duchano.**

— *René **Duchesneau** dit Sansregret (Pierre and Marie-Charlotte Roy) from Fleuré in Vienne (Poitou-Charentes) m. Jeanne Guérin (Clément and Perrine Coirier) in Charlesbourg, QC in 1695.*

Duchesny, from *du Chesny,* apparently derived from *Le Chesney* or *Le Chesnay,* placenames in France. — Amer. **Ducheney, Duchesney.**

— *Jean Baril dit **Duchesny**, son of Jean from Charente-Maritime (Poitou-Charentes), m. Jeanne-Judith Blanchet (René and Marie Sédilot) in Batiscan, QC in 1704.*

Duclos, from *du Clos,* derived from *Le Clos,* a placename in France. — Amer. **Declue, Ducklo.**

— *Gabriel Celle/Decelle dit **Duclos** (Jean and Colette Roquet) from Nonant in Calvados (Basse-Normandie) m. Barbe Poisson (Jean and Barbe Broust) in Montréal, QC in 1651.*

Dudley, see **Daudelin.**

Duegaw, see **Dugas.**

Dueso, see **Dussault.**

Dufault, probable alteration of *du Faou,* derived from *Châteauneuf-du-Faou,* a placename in Finistère (Bretagne). — Amer. **Default, Defoe, Dufoe.**

— *Gilles **Dufault** (Pierre and Marie *Riont) from Châteauneuf-du-Faou in Finistère (Bretagne) m. Françoise Siméon (Pierre and Marie Gervaise) in Québec, QC in 1678.*

Duffany, Duffiney, Duffiny, Duffney, see **Dauphinais.**

Dufoe, see **Dufault.**

Dufore, see **Dufour.**

Dufort, from *du Fort*, derived from *Le Fort*, a placename in France. — Amer. **Deford, Dufore, Strong.**

— *Prudent Bougret dit **Dufort** (Pierre and Catherine Guérin) from Mantes-la-Jolie in Yvelines (Île-de-France) m. Marie-Charlotte Étienne (Philippe and Marie Vien) in Trois-Rivières, QC in 1673.*

Dufour, from *du Four*, derived from *Le Four*, a placename in France. — Amer. **Defore, Dufore, Oven.**

— *Pierre **Dufour** dit Latour (Michel and Hélène Neveu) from Arras in Pas-de-Calais (Nord-Pas-de-Calais) m. Geneviève Guignard (Pierre and Geneviève Vanier) in Montréal, QC in 1722.*

Dufresne, from *du Fresne*, derived from *Le Fresne*, a placename in France. — Amer. **Ash, Ashe, Defrain, Defraine, Defresne, Dufrain, Dufrane.**

— *Antoine **Dufresne** dit Saint-Antoine (Nicolas and Catherine Domin) from Saint-Omer in Pas-de-Calais (Nord-Pas-de-Calais) m. Jeanne Fauconnier (Antoine and Jeanne Perlin) in Montréal, QC in 1668.*

Dugas, from *du Gas*, derived from *Le Gas*, a placename in France. — Amer. **Degon, Deugaw, Duegaw, Duga, Dugar, Dugaw.**

— *Abraham **Dugas** from France m. Marguerite Doucet (Germain and ...) in Acadia c. 1647.*

Dugré, alteration of *de Lugré* 'from Lugré', a placename in Maine-et-Loire (Pays de la Loire). — Amer. **Degree.**

— *Charles Delugré dit **Dugré**, grandson of Jacques from La Rochelle in Charente-Maritime (Poitou-Charentes), m. Madeleine-Judith Duret (Jacques and Catherine Jamin) in Québec, QC in 1727.*

Dugrenier, from *du Grenier*, derived from *Le Grenier*, a placename in France. — Amer. **Degreenia, Degrenier.**

— *Joseph **Dugrenier** dit Perron (Pierre and Thérèse Grenet) from Rouen in Seine-Maritime (Haute-Normandie) m. Marie-Anne Jacques (Pierre and Marie-Ambroise Chalifou) in Saint-Joseph-de-Beauce, QC in 1742.*

Duguay, from *du Guay* or an alteration of *du Gay*, derived from *Le Guay* or *Le Gay*, placenames in France. — Amer. **Dewey, Dewyea, Drury.**

— *Jean **Duguay** (Bernard and Jeanne Julien) from Saint-Sulpice-sur-Lèze in Haute-Garonne (Midi-Pyrénées) m. Jeanne Thomas (François and Claudine Graillard) in Yamachiche, QC in 1749.*

Duhaime, apparently an alteration of *du Hem*, derived from *Le Hem*, a placename in France. — Amer. **Duaime, Duhame.**

— *François Lemaître dit **Duhaime**, grandson of François from Flers in Orne (Basse-Normandie), m. Marie-Charlotte Gignard (Pierre and Marie-Madeleine Banliac) in Louiseville, QC in 1733.*

Duhamel, from *du Hamel*, derived from *Le Hamel*, a placename in France. — Amer. **Campbell, Duhamell, Youmell.**

— *Thomas **Duhamel** dit Sansfaçon (Jacques and Marie-Anne Tranchard) from Bolbec in Seine-Maritime (Haute-Normandie) m. Angélique Besnier (Massé and Michelle Charlier) in Champlain, QC in 1698.*

— *François Brasseur dit* **Duhamel** *(François and Geneviève Villet) from Le Hamel in Somme (Picardie) m. Marie-Angélique Jérome (Jean-Mathias and Marie-Louise Leduc) in Pierrefonds, QC in 1765.*

Duket, Dukett, Dukette, see **Duquet(te)**.

Dulude, from *du Lude*, derived from *Le Lude*, a placename in Sarthe (Pays de la Loire). — Amer. **Delude**.

— *Joseph Huet dit* **Dulude** *(Michel and Jeanne Jacquelin) from Le Lude in Sarthe (Pays de la Loire) m. Catherine Sicot (Jean and Marguerite Maclin) in Montréal, QC in 1679.*

Dumas, from *du Mas*, derived from *Le Mas*, a placename in France. — Amer. **Demas**.

— *François* **Dumas** *(François and Anne Rollin) from Nanteuil-en-Vallée in Charente (Poitou-Charentes) m. Marguerite Foy (Pierre and Catherine Blanchard) in Québec in 1667.*

Dumont, from *du Mont*, derived from *Le Mont*, a placename in France. — Amer. **Demoe, Demont, Dumo, Dumore, Jimmo**.

— *Julien* **Dumont** *dit Lafleur (Jacques and Marie Maubert) from Bernières-le-Patry in Calvados (Basse-Normandie) m. (1) Catherine Topsan (Charles and Marie Clémence) in Québec, QC in 1667; (2) Marie-Madeleine Tourneroche (Robert and Marie Targer) in Saint-Jean, Île d'Orléans, QC in 1694.*

— *Jacques Guéret dit* **Dumont** *(René and Madeleine Vigoureux) from Canchy in Calvados (Basse-Normandie) m. Anne Tardif (Jacques and Barbe d'Orange) in Beauport, QC in 1694.*

Dumoulin, alteration of *des Moulins*, derived from *Les Moulins*, a placename in France. — Amer. **Miller**.

— *André Renaud dit* **Desmoulins** *(Gabriel and Françoise *Ladresse) from Poiré-sur-Vie in Vendée (Pays de la Loire) m. Marie Brault (Henri and Marie-Ursule Bolduc) in Québec, QC in 1710.*

Dupaw, see **Despins**.

Dupee, see **Dupuis**.

Dupell, Dupelle, see **Riopel**.

Dupéré, from *du Péré*, derived from *Le Péré*, a placename in France. — Amer. **Duperry**.

— *Michel* **Dupéré** *dit Larivière (Jacques and Renée Badeau) from Luynes in Indre-et-Loire (Centre) m. Marie Chrétien (Michel and Marie Meunier) in Charlesbourg, QC in 1686.*

Dupey, see **Dupuis**.

Duphiney, see **Dauphinais**.

Dupil, probable alteration of *du Pile*, derived from *Le Pile*, a placename in Nord (Nord-Pas-de-Calais). — Amer. **Dupile, Dupill, Dupille**.

— *Rémi* **Dupil** *(Martin and Françoise Le Mercier) from Ponchon in Oise (Picardie) m. Anne Lagoue (Pierre and Marie *Boiscochin) in Neuville, QC in 1682.*

Duplacy, see **Duplessis**.

Duplanty, from *du Planty*, derived from *Le Planty*, a placename in France. — Amer. **Deplanty, Deplaunty, Duplanti**.

— *Jacques Héry dit* **Duplanty** *(Pierre and Marthe Chapiot) from Saint-Jean-d'Angély in Charente-Maritime (Poitou-Charentes) m. Marie-Renée Lamoureux (Pierre and Marguerite Pigarouiche) in Montréal, QC in 1693.*

Duplessis, from *du Plessis,* derived from *Le Plessis,* a placename in France. — Amer. **Duplacy, Duplease, Duplessie, Duplessy, Duplisea, Duplissa, Duplisse, Duplissea, Duplissey, Duplissie, Duplissis.**

— *François Sirois dit* **Duplessis** *(Jean and Marie-Angélique Dumond) from Saint-Germain-en-Laye in Yvelines (Île-de-France) m. Marie-Françoise Roy (Pierre and Marie-Anne Martin) in Québec in 1721.*

Dupperon, see **Perron.**

Dupra, see **Dupré.**

Duprat, from *du Prat,* derived from *Le Prat,* a placename in France. — Amer. **Dupraw.**

— *Jean-Robert Duprac/***Duprat** *(Jacques and Françoise Lamoureux) from Poitiers in Vienne (Poitou-Charentes) m. Marguerite Vachon (Paul and Marguerite Langlois) in Québec in 1675.*

Dupré, from *du Pré,* derived from *Le Pré,* a placename in France. — Amer. **Dupra, Dupray, Dupree, Duprey.**

— *Antoine* **Dupré** *dit Rochefort (Jean and Claudine de la Haye) from Saint-Sorlin in Rhône (Rhône-Alpes) m. Élisabeth Valiquet (Jean and Renée Loppé) in Boucherville, QC in 1681.*

Dupuis, alteration of *du Puits,* derived from *Le Puits,* a placename in France. — Amer. **Dupee, Dupey, Dupree, Duprie, Dupris, Wells.**

— *François* **Dupuis** *(François and Marguerite Resneau) from Saint-Laurent-sur-Gorre in Haute-Vienne (Limousin) m. Georgette Richer (Jean and Léonarde Bornay) in Québec, QC in 1670.*

—ᴸ *François* **Dupuis** *dit Jolicoeur (François and Philippe David) from Saint-Astier in Dordogne (Aquitaine) m. Marguerite Banliac (François and Marie-Angélique Pelletier) in Champlain, QC in 1698.*

— *Louis* **Dupuis** *dit Parisien (Guillaume and Marie* *Maudemé*) from Paris (Île-de-France) m. Barbe Dubeau (Toussaint and Marguerite Damy) in Québec, QC in 1688.*

— *Michel* **Dupuis** *from France m. Marie Gautrot (François and Marie ...) in Acadia c. 1664.*

— *Régis Dubeau dit* **Dupuis,** *descendant of Toussaint from Paris (Île-de-France), m. Hélène-Angélique Lévesque (Martin and Marie* *Nappe*) probably in Penetanguishene, ON c. 1850.*

Duquet(te), either from *du Quet,* derived from *Le Quet,* a placename in France, or derived from *duc* 'duke', an ironic nickname. — Amer. **Dekett, Ducate, Ducatte, Duket, Dukett, Dukette.**

— *Denis* **Duquet** *from France m. Catherine Gauthier (Philippe and Marie Pichon) in Québec, QC in 1638.*

Duranceau, derived from *Durand,* either from *(Le) Durand,* a placename in France, or from the Latin name *Durandus,* apparently derived from *durare* 'to last, endure'. — Amer. **Duranso.**

— *Pierre* **Duranceau** *dit Brindamour (Jean and Élisabeth Marsillac) from Niort in Deux-Sèvres (Poitou-Charentes) m. Marie-Jeanne Frappier (Hilaire and Marie-Rose Petit) in Québec, QC in 1696.*

Durand, see **Ladurantaye.**

Duranso, see **Duranceau.**

Durant, see **Doiron** and **Ladurantaye.**

Durepos, from *du Repos,* derived from *Le Repos,* a placename in France. — Amer. **Hoskins.**

— *Gabriel* **Durepos** *(Nicolas and Marie Boissel) from Genets in Manche (Basse-Normandie) m. Marie-Marguerite Côté (Louis and Louise-Angélique Thibierge) in Montmagny, QC in 1753.*

Duret(te), either from *(Le) Duret* or *du Ret,* derived from *Le Ret,* placenames in France. — Amer. **Durett.**

— *Jacques* **Duret** *(Antoine and Marguerite Renaud) from Bournezeau in Vendée (Pays de la Loire) m. Catherine Jamin (Julien and Marie Ripoche) in Québec, QC in 1687.*

Durocher, from *du Rocher,* derived from *Le Rocher,* a placename in France. — Amer. **Derochie, Derouchie, Deruchie, Derusha, Derushe.**

— *François Lafleur dit* **Durocher** *(Pierre and Catherine Roche) from Saint-Romain-de-Benet in Charente-Maritime (Poitou-Charentes) m. Geneviève Renaud (Jean and Marguerite Charbonneau) in Montréal, QC in 1729.*

Duschene, Dushane, see **Duchesne.**

Dusharm, Dusharme, see **Ducharme.**

Duso, Dusoe, see **Dussault.**

Dusome, see **Jusseaume.**

Dussault, alteration of *du Sault,* derived from *Le Sault,* a placename in France. — Amer. **Desaw, Deso, Desseau, Desso, Deuso, Dueso, Duso, Dusoe, Dusseau.**

— *Jean-Baptiste Toupin dit* **Du Sault,** *son of Toussaint from France, m. (1) Marie Gloria (Jean and Marie Bourdon) in Québec, QC in 1669; (2) Marie-Madeleine Mézeray (Jean and Madeleine Masse) in Neuville, QC in 1688.*

Dussia, see **Lussier.**

Dustin, Dusty, see **Dostie.**

Duval, from *du Val,* derived from *Le Val,* a placename in France. — Amer. **Duvall.**

— *Pierre-Edmé Thuot dit* **Duval** *(Pierre-Edmé and Marie-Louise Duval) from Tonnerre in Yonne (Bourgogne) m. Marie Fournier (Antoine and Marie Ronceray) in Montréal, QC in 1712.*

Dyer, see **Doyon.**

E

Eber, Ebert, see **Hébert.**

Édouin, alteration of *Hédouin,* from the Germanic name *Haidwin* composed of *haid* 'kind' and *win* 'friend'. — Amer. **Edwin.**

— *Jacques **Hédouin** dit Laforge (Romain and Marguerite Bachelin) from Orival in Seine-Maritime (Haute-Normandie) m. Jeanne Brassard (Antoine and Françoise Méry) in Québec, QC in 1656.*

Eggsware, see **Isoir.**

Eithier, see **Éthier.**

Émard, from the Germanic name *Haimhard* composed of *haim* 'home' and *hard* 'hard, strong'. — Amer. **Amore, Emore.**

— *Pierre **Émard**/Aymard dit Poitevin (Pierre and Marie Aubineau) from Melle in Deux-Sèvres (Poitou-Charentes) m. Jeanne-Marguerite Beloy (Julien and Marguerite Leclerc) in Longueuil, QC in 1702.*

Emeott, see **Amiotte.**

Emlaw, see **Hamelin.**

Émond, from the Germanic name *Haimo,* derived from *haim* 'house'. — Amer. **Amo, Emmonds, Emmons.**

— *Pierre **Émond** (Isaac and Marie Garineau) from Rochefort in Charente-Maritime (Poitou-Charentes) m. Marie-Agnès Grondin (Jean and Sainte Mignault) in Rivière-Ouelle, QC in 1690.*

Emore, see **Émard.**

Eno, see **Hénault.**

Erno, see **Renaud.**

Eschete, see **Jetté.**

Eslin, see **Asselin.**

Éthier, from the Germanic name *Asthari* composed of *ast* 'spear' and *hari* 'army'. — Amer. **Aikey, Akey, Eithier, Etie, Etier, Hakey.**

— *Léonard **Éthier** (Étienne and Marguerite Sabelle) from Manot in Charente (Poitou-Charentes) m. Élisabeth Godillon (Nicolas and Marie Boulay) in Montréal, QC in 1670.*

Etu, Etue, see **Hétu.**

Eubar, Euber, see **Hubert.**

Eugair, see **Giguère.**

Eurto, see **Hurteau.**

Evon, see **Yvon.**

Exware, see **Isoir.**

F

Facteau, Facto, see **Fecteau.**

Fafard, probably derived from Old French *fafelu* 'plump, chubby'. — Amer. **Faufau.**
— *Bertrand **Fafard** dit Laframboise (Jean and Antoinette Leverdier) from Hotot-en-Auge in Calvados (Basse-Normandie) m. Marie Sédilot (Louis and Marie Challe) in Québec in 1640.*

Faguy, alteration of *Faye* via *Failly*, a placename in France. — Amer. **Fagga.**
— *Pierre **Faye/Failly** dit Villefagnan (Jacques and Isabelle Béguin) from Villefagnan in Charente (Poitou-Charentes) m. Marie Chauvet/Quinquenel (Jacques and Marie Michelette) in Québec, QC in 1668.*

Faille, alteration of *(La) Faye*, a placename in France. — Amer. **Fayette, Foy.**
— *Claude **Faye/Faille** from Saint-Jean d'Aubrigoux in Haute-Loire (Auvergne) m. Jeanne Perras (Pierre and Denise Lemaître) in Laprairie, QC in 1688.*

Fairfield, see **Beauchamp.**

Faneuf, Faneuff, see **Phaneuf.**

Farland, see **Ferland.**

Farmer, see **Therrien.**

Faubert, from the Germanic name *Falcberht* composed of *falc* 'falcon' and *berht* 'bright'. — Amer. **Ferguson, Fobair, Fobare, Fober, Fobert.**
— *Jean-Baptiste **Faubert** dit Lecocq from Paris (Île-de-France) m. Marie-Geneviève Durocher (François and Marie-Geneviève Renaud) in Oka, QC in 1753.*

Faucher, alteration of *Foucher*, from the Germanic name *Folchari* composed of *folc* 'people' and *hari* 'army'. — Amer. **Foshia, Fouchea, Fouchia, Fushey, Moen.**
— *Jean **Foucher** (Pierre and Jeanne *Tropslonge) from Cressac-Saint-Génis in Charente (Poitou-Charentes) m. Jeanne (de) Richecourt/Malteau (Paul and Marie Gaubert) in Québec, QC in 1659.*

Faufau, see **Fafard.**

Favreau, either an alteration of *Favereau*, derived from Old French *favier* 'producer/seller of beans', or derived from *favre*, a regional variant of Old French *fèvre* 'blacksmith'. — Amer. **Favero, Favro, Fevreau.**
— *Pierre **Favreau**/Favereau dit Deslauriers from France m. Marie Benoît in Québec c. 1668.*

Fayette, see **Faille.**

Fecteau, alteration of *Filteau*, a variant of *Filleteau*, derived from Old French *fillet* 'small child', probably the nickname of the youngest son. — Amer. **Facteau, Facto, Fecto.**
— *Pierre **Filteau**/Feuilleteau (Robert and Marguerite Brochet) from Saint-Georges-de-Montaigu in Vendée (Pays de la Loire) m. Gillette Savard (François and Jeanne Moran) in Québec, QC in 1666.*

Fefee, see **Fyfe.**

Felio, Felion, see **Filion.**

Félix, from the Latin name *Felix,* from *felix* 'happy'. — Amer. **Phelix.**

— *François Péloquin dit **Félix,** grandson of François from Niort in Deux-Sèvres (Poitou-Charentes), m. Marie-Antoinette Lavallée (Jean and Jeanne-Catherine Hus) in Sorel, QC in 1745.*

Fellion, see **Filion.**

Fenoff, see **Phaneuf.**

Fercy, see **Forcier.**

Ferguson, see **Faubert.**

Ferland, alteration of *Freland,* from the Germanic name *Fridland* composed of *frid* 'peace' and *land* 'land'. — Amer. **Farland, Furlong.**

— *François **Ferland** (André and Marguerite Bariteau) from Saint-Vincent-Sterlanges in Vendée (Pays de la Loire) m. Jeanne-Françoise Milloir (Jean and Jeanne Roy) in Sainte-Famille, Île d'Orléans, QC in 1679.*

Fernet, alteration of *Ferronnet,* derived from Old French *ferron* 'blacksmith, ironware merchant'. — Amer. **Fernette.**

— *Michel Frenet/**Fernet** (Michel and Christine Juneau) from Sainte-Marguerite-del'Autel in Eure (Haute-Normandie) m. Marie-Olive Lavoie (Pierre and Jacquette Grenon) in Neuville, QC in 1684.*

Fevreau, see **Favreau.**

Fields, see **Deschamps.**

Filie, see **Philie.**

Filion, from Old French *fillon* 'little boy', probably the nickname of the youngest in a family. — Amer. **Felio, Felion, Fellion.**

— *Antoine **Filion** (André and Gabrielle Senlet) from Paris (Île-de-France) m. Anne (d')Anneville (Brice and Marguerite Roy) in Paris c. 1656.*

Firkey, see **Fortier.**

Fish, Fisher, see **Poissant** and **Poisson.**

Flagg, see **Papillon.**

Flamand, from *Flamand* 'Fleming', the nickname of an inhabitant of Flanders. — Amer. **Flamond, Flammond, Fleming.**

— *Joseph Ladrière dit **Flamand** (Pierre and Marie-Josèphe Bertun) from Mons in Belgium m. Marie-Anne Lemieux (Michel et Marguerite Samson) in Lauzon, QC in 1742.*

Fleury, from *Fleury,* a placename in France. — Amer. **Fluery.**

— *André **Fleury** (Richard-Nicolas and Marie-Louise *Lahaudes/*Lohandes) from La Ronde-Haye in Manche (Basse-Normandie) m. Marie-Josèphe Tanguay (Jacques and Geneviève Mercier) in Saint-Vallier, QC in 1760.*

Fobair, Fobare, Fober, Fobert, see **Faubert.**

Foco, see **Foucault.**

Foisy, from Old French *foisil* 'gunflint', the nickname of a maker or seller. — Amer. **Foisie, Freeman.**

— *Martin **Foisy** (Pierre and Marguerite Froment) from Bossus-lès-Rumigny in Ardennes (Champagne-Ardenne) m. Marie-Madeleine Beaudoin (Jean and Noëlle Landeau) in Québec in 1679.*

Fontaine, from *Fontaine,* a placename in France. — Amer. **Fountain, Fountaine.**

— *Pierre **Fontaine** dit Bienvenu (Jacques and Claude Giron) from Orléans in Loiret*

(Centre) m. (1) Marguerite Anthiaume (Michel and Marie Dubois) in Québec in 1692; (2) Marguerite Gentès (Étienne and Catherine Messier) in Varennes, QC in 1700.

Fontaine, see **Lafontaine.**

Foote, see **Frappier.**

Footer, see **Fortin.**

Forand, probable alteration of Old French *forain* 'stranger'. — Amer. **Forend, Forrant, Forrend.**

— *André* **Forand** *from La Rochelle in Charente-Maritime (Poitou-Charentes) m. Marie Boyer (Charles and Marguerite Ténard) in Laprairie, QC in 1684.*

Forcier, apparently from Old French *forcier* 'violent'. — Amer. **Fercy, Forcia.**

— *Pierre* **Forcier** *(Guillaume and Sébastienne Gaultier) from Nantes in Loire-Atlantique (Pays de la Loire) m. Marguerite Girard in Québec c. 1674.*

Forend, see **Forand.**

Forest, either from *(La) Forest*, a placename in France, or from Old French *forest* 'forest', the nickname of a park ranger. — Amer. **Fuller.**

— *Marin-Paul* **Forest** *(Marin and Marguerite Dreux) from Orléans in Loiret (Centre) m. Marie-Anne Riquet (François and Marie-Anne Renaud) in Terrebonne, QC in 1738.*

Forget, either derived from the Latin name *Ferreolus*, from *ferrum* 'iron', or an alteration of *Froget*, from the Germanic name *Frodgari* composed of *frod* 'wise, prudent' and *gari* 'spear'. — Amer. **Forga, Forgett.**

— *Antoine Latour dit* **Forget,** *son of Pierre from France, m. Marie-Louise Plouf (Louis and Marie Truchon) in Québec in 1737.*

Forkey, see **Fortier.**

Forney, see **Fournier.**

Forrant, Forrend, see **Forand.**

Fortain, see **Fortin.**

Fortier, variant of *Foretier*, derived from *forêt* 'forest', the nickname of a park ranger. — Amer. **Firkey, Forkey, Furkey.**

— *Noël* **Fortier** *(Antoine and ...) from Dieppe in Seine-Maritime (Haute-Normandie) m. Marthe Golle in Dieppe in 1638.*

Fortin, derived from the Latin name *Fortis*, from *fortis* 'strong'. — Amer. **Footer, Fortain, Fortine, Fortune, Foster, Fotter, Furtaw.**

— *Julien* **Fortin** *dit Bellefontaine (Julien and Marie Lavye) from Saint-Cosme-en-Vairais in Sarthe (Pays de la Loire) m. Geneviève Gamache (Nicolas and Jacqueline Cadot) in Québec, QC in 1652.*

Foshia, see **Faucher.**

Foster, Fotter, see **Fortin.**

Foucault, alteration of *Fouquereau*, derived from *Fouquier*, from the Germanic name *Folchari* composed of *folc* 'people' and *hari* 'army'. — Amer. **Foco.**

— *Urbain* **Fouquereau** *(Jean and Renée Bataille) from Continvoir in Indre-et-Loir (Centre) m. Jeanne Rossignol (Martin and Renée Desjardins) in Québec, QC in 1676.*

Fouchea, Fouchia, see **Faucher.**

Fougère, from *(La) Fougère*, a placename in France. — Amer. **Fraser.**

— *Jean* **Fougère** *(Jean and Marie Barré) from Poupry in Eure-et-Loir (Centre) m. Marie Bourg (Abraham and Marie Brun) in Port-Royal, NS in 1713.*

Fountain, Fountaine, see **Fontaine.**

Fournier, either from *(Le) Fournier*, a placename in France, or from Old French *fo(u)r-nier* 'baker'. — Amer. **Forney, Fournet, Fournia, Fuller, Furnia.**

— *Guillaume Fournier (Gilles and Noëlle *Gageut) from Coulmer in Orne (Basse-Normandie) m. Françoise Hébert (Guillaume and Hélène Desportes) in Québec, QC in 1651.*

— *Nicolas Fournier (Hugues and Jeanne Huguette) from Marans in Charente-Maritime (Poitou-Charentes) m. Marie Hubert (Pierre and Bonne Brie) in Québec, QC in 1670.*

— *Pierre Fournier, sieur de Belleval (Jacques and Ursule Gaucher) from Orléans in Loiret (Centre) m. Marie Ancelin (René and Marie Juin) in Québec, QC in 1693.*

Foy, see **Faille.**

Francoeur, alteration of *franc coeur* 'brave heart', a soldier's nickname. — Amer. **Francouer, Francour, Franker, Hart.**

— *Claude Charland dit Francoeur (Jean and Catherine Mavile) from Châteauroux in Indre (Centre) m. Jeanne Pelletier (Simon and Marie Large) in Québec, QC in 1661.*

— *Jean Leclerc dit Francoeur (Jean and Perrine Merceron) from Nantes in Loire-Atlantique (Pays de la Loire) m. Marie-Madeleine Langlois (Jean and Charlotte-Françoise Bélanger) in Saint-Pierre, Île d'Orléans, QC in 1691.*

— *François Ravary dit Francoeur (René and Marie Lancelin) from Laval in Mayenne (Pays de la Loire) m. Catherine Marot (Jean-Baptiste and Catherine-Agathe Chevalier) in La Pérade, QC in 1761.*

Frane, see **Fresne.**

Franker, see **Francoeur.**

Fransway, see **Lefrançois.**

Frappier, either from *(Le) Frappier*, a placename in France, or a variant of Old French *frepier* 'secondhand clothes dealer'. — Amer. **Foote, Frappiea.**

— *Hilaire Frappier (Hilaire and Renée Dugué) from La Rochelle in Charente-Maritime (Poitou-Charentes) m. Marie-Rose Petit (Jean and Jeanne Guéribout) in Québec, QC in 1668.*

Fraser, see **Fougère.**

Frazho, Frazier, see **Frégeau.**

Freehart, Freeheart, see **Généreux.**

Freeman, see **Foisy** and **Laliberté.**

Frégeau, probably derived from the Latin name *Ferreolus*, from *ferrum* 'iron'. — Amer. **Frazho, Frazier.**

— *Daniel Frégeau dit Laplanche (Daniel and Marie Mergot) from Poitiers in Vienne (Poitou-Charentes) m. Anne Pauzé (Jacques and Marie Jobidon) in Montmagny, QC in 1699.*

Frego, Fregoe, see **Frigon.**

Frémault, probably from the Germanic name **Framwald* composed of *fram* 'valiant' and *wald* 'power, authority'. — Amer. **Fremeau.**

— *Jean-Baptiste Frémault dit Champagne and Latendresse (Nicolas and Nicole Arnoux) from Reims in Marne (Champagne-Ardenne) m. Marie-Marguerite Groinier (Augustin and Marie-Françoise Pépin) in Montréal, QC in 1757.*

Frenière, apparently from *La Fresnière* or *La Frenière*, placenames in France. — Amer. **Frenia, Frenier, Frenya, Frenyea.**

— *Antoine Daunay dit Fresnière/**Frenière**, son of Antoine from Luçon in Vendée (Pays de la Loire), m. Marie Robert (Louis and Marie Bourgery) in Boucherville, QC in 1702.*

Fresne, from *(Le) Fresne,* a placename in France. — Amer. **Frane.**

— *Léonard **Fresne** dit Sanscartier (François and Élisabeth Marmont) from Venon in Isère (Rhône-Alpes) m. Cécile Dubé (Pierre and Marguerite Sigouin) in Montréal, QC in 1756.*

Frigon, apparently derived from the Germanic name *Frigo,* from *fric* 'greedy, grasping'.

— Amer. **Frego, Fregoe.**

— *François **Frigon** from France m. Marie-Claude Chamois (Honoré and Jacqueline Girard) in Québec c. 1673.*

Fuller, see **Forest** and **Fournier.**

Furkey, see **Fortier.**

Furlong, see **Ferland.**

Furnia, see **Fournier.**

Furtaw, see **Fortin.**

Fushey, see **Faucher.**

Fyfe, alteration of the German name *Pfeiffer,* from Middle High German *phifer* 'piper'.

— Amer. **Fefee.**

— *Peter **Pfeiffer** m. Catherine Marx probably in Germany c. 1782.*

G

Gabaree, see **Gaboury.**

Gaboriault, alteration of *Gaboriau,* derived from *Gabory,* same origin as **Gaboury.** — Amer. **Gabrio.**

— *Jean **Gaboriau** dit Lapalme (Pierre and Marguerite Michel) from Saint-Jérôme in Gironde (Aquitaine) m. Marguerite-Françoise Boileau (Pierre and Marguerite Ménard) in Chambly, QC in 1732.*

Gaboury, variant of *Gabory,* derived from Old French *gabeor* 'joker, scoffer'. — Amer. **Gabaree, Gabourie, Gabree, Gabrey.**

— *Antoine **Gaboury**/Gabory (Jacques and Jeanne Beaudoin) from La Rochelle in Charente-Maritime (Poitou-Charentes) m. Jeanne Mignault (Jean and Louise Cloutier) in Québec in 1678.*

Gabrio, see **Gaboriault.**

Gadbois, alteration of *gâte bois* 'spoils wood', the nickname of a carpenter or woodworker. — Amer. **Gadbaw, Gadwood, Godbois, Goodway, Gudbaur, Wood, Woods.**

— *Joseph Van Den Dyke/Vandandaigue dit Gatebois/**Gadbois** (Josse and Madeleine Dubois) from Brussels in Belgium m. Louise Chalifou (Paul and Jacquette Archambault) in Québec, QC in 1678.*

Gadouas, alteration of *Gadois,* origin uncertain. — Amer. **Gadwa, Gadwaw, Gadway.**

— *Pierre **Gadois** from Igé in Orne (Basse-Normandie) m. Louise Mauger in Igé c. 1627.*

Gadwood, see **Gadbois.**

Gagné, either a variant of *Gagn(i)er,* probably from Old French *ga(a)igneor* 'farmer, plowman', or from *Gasnier,* a variant of *Garnier,* from the Germanic name *Warinhari* composed of *warin* 'protection' and *hari* 'army'. — Amer. **Gaunya, Gaynier, Gonia, Goniea, Gonier, Gonya, Gonye, Gonyea, Gonyar, Gonyer.**

— *Louis **Gagné**/Gasnier (Louis and Marie Launay) from Igé in Orne (Basse-Normandie) m. Marie Michel (Pierre and Louise Gory) in France c. 1638.*

Gagnon, probably derived from Old French *ga(a)igneor* 'farmer, plowman'. — Amer. **Ganyo, Ganyon, Gonion, Gonyaw, Gonyeau, Gonyo, Gonyon, Gonyou.**

— *Mathurin **Gagnon** (Pierre and Renée Roger) from Tourouvre in Orne (Basse-Normandie) m. Françoise Godeau (François and Jeanne Jahan) in Québec, QC in 1647.*

— *Pierre **Gagnon** (Pierre and Renée Roger) from Tourouvre in Orne (Basse-Normandie) m. Vincente Desvarieux (Jean and Marie Chevalier) in Québec, QC in 1642.*

— *Robert **Gagnon**/Gaignon (Jean and Marie Geffray) from La Ventrouze in Orne (Basse-Normandie) m. Marie Parenteau (Antoine and Anne Brisson) in Québec, QC in 1657.*

Gaillard, from *(Le) Gaillard,* a placename in France. — Amer. **Guyor.**

— *Hippolyte **Gaillard** dit Lyonnais (Léonard and Marguerite Massot) from Lyon in*

Rhône (Rhône-Alpes) m. Marie-Josèphe Debien (Étienne and Marie Campeau) in Montréal, QC in 1729.

Gailloux, alteration of *(Le) Gaillou,* a placename in France. — Amer. **Gayou.**

— *Nicolas **Gaillou**, sieur de La Taille from Marans in Charente-Maritime (Poitou-Charentes) m. Vivienne Godet in France c. 1640.*

Galarneau, alteration of *Galerneau,* derived from *Galerne,* the nickname of an individual from this region in Loire-Atlantique (Pays de la Loire). — Amer. **Galarneault, Galarno, Galerno, Galineau, Gallarno, Gallerno, Gallineau, Galorneau, Garno.**

— *Jacques **Galarneau**/Galerneau (Pierre and Élisabeth Goujat) from La Rochelle in Charente-Maritime (Poitou-Charentes) m. Jacqueline Héron/Néron (Pierre and Cécile Dupont) in Québec, QC in 1665.*

Galipeau, either from *Galipeau,* a placename in Loir-et-Cher (Centre), or derived from *La Galipe* or *La Galippe,* placenames in France. — Amer. **Galipo, Gallipo.**

— *Antoine **Galipeau** (Antoine and Perrine Raineau) from Dissay in Vienne (Poitou-Charentes) m. Marie-Françoise Cambin (Laurent and Françoise ...) in Pointe-aux-Trembles, QC in 1688.*

Gallarno, Gallerno, Gallineau, see **Galarneau.**

Gallipeau, see **Galipeau.**

Galorneau, see **Galarneau.**

Gamache, from *(La) Gamache,* a placename in France. — Amer. **Gamash.**

— *Nicolas **Gamache** (Nicolas and Jacqueline Cadot) from Saint-Illiers-la-Ville in Yvelines (Île-de-France) m. Élisabeth-Ursule Cloutier (Charles and Louise Morin) in Château-Richer, QC in 1676.*

Gamelin, derived from the Germanic name *Gamelo,* from *gamal* 'old, aged'. — Amer. **Gumlaw.**

— *Michel **Gamelin** dit/sieur de La Fontaine (Michel and Françoise Bélanger) from Blois in Loir-et-Cher (Centre) m. Marguerite Crevier (Christophe and Jeanne Évard) in Québec in 1661.*

Gandron, Gandrow, see **Gendron.**

Ganyo, Ganyon, see **Gagnon.**

Garand, probably derived from a Germanic name containing the element *warin* 'protection'. — Amer. **Garrand, Garrant, Garrow.**

— *Pierre **Garand** (Charles and Anne Maillet) from Rouen in Seine-Maritime (Basse-Normandie) m. (1) Renée Chanfrain (Vincent and Marguerite Le Breton) in Sainte-Famille, Île d'Orléans, QC in 1669; (2) Catherine Labrecque (Pierre and Jeanne Chotard) in Saint-Laurent, Île d'Orléans, QC in 1684.*

Garceau, derived from Old French *gars* 'valet, servant'. — Amer. **Garso.**

— *Jean **Garceau** dit Tranchemontagne (Pierre and Jacquette Soulard) from Saint-René in Vienne (Poitou-Charentes) m. Marie Levron (François and Catherine Savoie) in Port-Royal, NS in 1703.*

Gardapee, see **Gariépy.**

Gardiner, see **Desjardins.**

Gardipee, see **Gariépy.**

Gardner, see **Desjardins.**

Gareau, variant of *Garaud,* from the Germanic name *Garwald* composed of *gari* 'spear' and *wald* 'power, authority'. — Amer. **Garrow, Gorrow.**

— *Jean **Gareau** dit Saint-Onge (Dominique and Marie Pinard) from La Rochelle in Charente-Maritime (Poitou-Charentes) m. Anne Talbot (Eustache/Isaac and Marie de Lalonde) in Boucherville, QC in 1670.*

— *Pierre **Gareau** (Dominique and Marie Pinard) from La Rochelle in Charente-Maritime (Poitou-Charentes) m. Barbe (de) Montreau (Léonard and Marguerite Levaigneur) in Boucherville, QC in 1684.*

Gariépy, apparently an alteration of *Garibay,* a placename in the Spanish Basque country. — Amer. **Gardapee, Gardipee, Garypie, Guardipee.**

— *François **Gariépy** (Jean and Jeanne Daragon) from Montfort-en-Chalosse in Landes (Aquitaine) m. Marie Oudin (Antoine and Madeleine *de la Russière) in Québec, QC in 1657.*

Garneau, alteration of *Garnaud,* from the Germanic name *Warinwald* composed of *warin* 'protection' and *wald* 'power, authority'. — Amer. **Garno.**

— *Louis **Garneau** (Pierre and Jeanne Barault) from La Grimaudière in (Poitou-Charentes) m. Marie Mazoue (Étienne and Marie Mérand) in Québec, QC in 1663.*

Garno, see **Galarneau.**

Garrand, Garrant, see **Garand.**

Garrett, see **Grenier** and **Guérette.**

Garrow, see **Garand** and **Gareau.**

Garso, see **Garceau.**

Garypie, see **Gariépy.**

Gates, see **Barrière.**

Gaudet(te), derived from the Germanic name *Waldo,* from *wald* 'power, authority'. — Amer. **Gaudett, Goddard, Goddette, Godett, Godette, Goudette.**

— *Jean **Gaudet** from France m. (1) an unknown spouse in France c. 1622; (2) Nicole Colleson in Acadia c. 1652.*

Gaudry, from the Germanic name *Waldric* composed of *wald* 'power, authority' and *ric* 'powerful'. — Amer. **Goodrie.**

— *Joseph Beaudry dit **Gaudry,** descendant of Toussaint from Velluire in Vendée (Pays de la Loire), m. Suzanne Nabestiwayan probably in the Northwest Territories c. 1803.*

Gaulin, origin uncertain. — Amer. **Golen.**

— *François **Gaulin** (Vincent and Marie Bonnemer) from Saint-Martin-du-Vieux-Bellême in Orne (Basse-Normandie) m. Marie Rocheron (Julien and Martine Lemoyne) in Québec, QC in 1657.*

Gaulthier, see **Gauthier.**

Gaumond, from the Germanic name *Gautmund* composed of *Gaut,* the name of the Gothic people, and *mund* 'protection'. — Amer. **Goman, Gomo, Gomon, Gorman.**

— *Robert **Gaumond**/Gaumont (René and Jeanne Dallaine) from Charenton-le-Pont in Val-de-Marne (Île-de-France) m. Louise Robin (Étienne and Éléonore Maucuit) in Québec, QC in 1671.*

Gaunya, see **Gagné.**

Gauslin, Gausline, Gausselin, see **Gosselin.**

Gauthier, from the Germanic name *Waldhari* composed of *wald* 'power, authority' and *hari* 'army'. — Amer. **Gaulthier, Gilmore, Gocha, Gochee, Gochie, Goka, Gokey, Gokie, Gosha, Gotchey, Gotchy, Gothier, Gouchie, Gouthier.**

— *Germain **Gauthier** dit Saint-Germain (Germain and Louise Veillard) from Beaubec-*

la-Rosière in Seine-Maritime (Haute-Normandie) m. Jeanne Beauchamp (Jacques and Marie Dardenne) in Pointe-aux-Trembles, QC in 1677.

— *Jacques* **Gauthier** *(Simon and Marie Aubé) from Rouen in Seine-Maritime (Haute-Normandie) m. Élisabeth-Ursule Denevers (Étienne and Anne Hayot) in Québec in 1672.*

— *Jean* **Gauthier** *dit Larouche (Mathurin and Catherine Loumeaux) from Échillais in Charente-Maritime (Poitou-Charentes) m. Angélique Lefebvre (Louis and Suzanne de Bure) in Québec, QC in 1675.*

— *Pierre* **Gauthier** *dit Saguingoira (Jacques and Marie Boucher) from Surgères or Échillais in Charente-Maritime (Poitou-Charentes) m. Charlotte Roussel (Thomas and Barbe Poisson) in Montréal, QC in 1668.*

— *Pierre* **Gauthier** *dit Poitevin (Charles and Catherine Arnaud) from Le Poiré-sur-Vie in Vendée (Pays de la Loire) m. Marguerite Arcand (Simon and Marie-Anne Inard) in Deschambault, QC in 1723.*

Gautreau, derived from **Gauthier.** — Amer. **Gauthreaux, Gautreaux, Gouthreau.**

— *François* **Gautreau**/*Gotreau*/*Gautrot from France m. (1) Marie ... in Acadia c. 1635; (2) Edmée/Aimée Lejeune in Acadia c. 1644.*

Gauvreau, probably derived from *Gauvin,* from the Welsh name *Gwalchgwyn* composed of *gwalch* 'falcon' and *gwyn* 'white'. — Amer. **Gover, Govero, Govreau, Govro.**

— *Étienne* **Gauvreau** *(Pierre and Anne Arrivé) from La Roche-sur-Yon in Vendée (Pays de la Loire) m. Marguerite-Françoise Legris (Adrien and Marie-Françoise Branche) in Québec, QC in 1712.*

Gaynier, see **Gagné.**

Gayou, see **Gailloux.**

Gebeau, Gebeault, Gebo, Gebow, see **Gibeau.**

Geddry, see **Guédry.**

Gegare, see **Giguère.**

Gehue, see **Guilbault.**

Gelbar, see **Jalbert.**

Gélinas, same origin as **Gélineau.** — Amer. **Genaw, Geno, Genow.**

— *Étienne* **Gélinas** *from Pons or Saintes in Charente-Maritime (Poitou-Charentes) m. Huguette Robert in Saintes in 1645.*

Gélineau, derived from *Gélin,* a variant of *Geslin,* from the Germanic name *Giselo,* from *gisal* 'hostage'. — Amer. **Gelino, Gellineau, Leno.**

— *François* **Gélineau** *dit Lachapelle (Jehan and Marguerite Boucq) from La Chapelle-des-Pots in Charente-Maritime (Poitou-Charentes) m. Marie-Marguerite Ménard (Pierre and Marguerite Deshayes) in Contrecoeur, QC in 1687.*

Genaw, see **Gélinas.**

Gendreau, same origin as **Gendron.** — Amer. **Gendrow, Jandreau, Jerdo, Johndrow.**

— *Pierre* **Gendreau** *dit Lapoussière (Georges and Jeanne Coulon) from Saint-Denis-d'Oléron in Charente-Maritime (Poitou-Charentes) m. Jeanne Garnier (Sébastien and Marie Roux) in Château-Richer, QC in 1663.*

Gendron, derived from *gendre* 'son-in-law'. — Amer. **Gandron, Gandrow, Gendro, Gendrow, Jandrew, Jandro, Jeandron, Jendro, Johndro, Johndrow, Johnroe, Jondro, Jondrow.**

— *Nicolas* **Gendron** *dit Lafontaine (Pierre and Marie Renaud) from Le Château-d'O-*

léron in Charente-Maritime (Poitou-Charentes) m. Marie-Marthe Hubert (Toussaint and Catherine Champagne) in Québec, QC in 1656.

Gendrow, see **Gendreau**.

Généreux, from the Latin name *Generosus*, from *generosus* 'distinguished, noble'. — Amer. **Freehart, Freeheart, Genereau, Genereaux, Generous, Generoux.**

— Pierre Généreux from Limoges in Haute-Vienne (Limousin) m. Françoise Dessureaux (François and Marie Bouart) in Champlain, QC in 1699.

Genett, Genette, Gennett, see **Jeannotte**.

Gennette, see **Guénet(te)** and **Jeannotte**.

Geno, see **Gélinas**.

Genore, see **Guinard**.

Genot, see **Jeannotte**.

Genow, see **Gélinas**.

Geoffrion, derived from **Geoffroy**. — Amer. **Jefferson, Joffrion.**

— Pierre Geoffrion from Fontenay-le-Comte in Vendée (Pays de la Loire) m. Marie Priault in Québec c. 1669.

Geoffroy, from the Germanic name *Gautfrid* composed of *Gaut*, the name of the Gothic people, and *frid* 'peace'. — Amer. **Jeffrey.**

— Étienne Geoffroy (Louis and Anne Flamand) from La Flotte in Charente-Maritime (Poitou-Charentes) m. Marie-Charlotte Lecomte (Pierre and Marie-Charlotte Fournier) in Montréal, QC in 1743.

Geor, see **Giard**.

Gerard, Geraw, see **Girard**.

Gereau, Gereaux, Gerew, see **Giroux**.

Germain, from the Latin name *Germanus*, from *germanus* 'natural, real, authentic'. — Amer. **Germaine.**

— Robert Germain (Julien and Julienne *Bevais) from Lonlay-l'Abbaye in Orne (Basse-Normandie) m. Marie Coignard (François and Françoise Petit) in Québec, QC in 1669.

Germaine, see **St-Germain**.

Gernon, see **Guernon**.

Gero, see **Giroux**.

Geromette, see **Auger**.

Geror, see **Girard**.

Gerou, Geroux, Gerow, see **Giroux**.

Gerrior, Gerroir, see **Girouard**.

Gerue, see **Giroux**.

Gervais, from the Latin name *Gervasius*. — Amer. **Jarvais, Jarvey, Jarvis, Jerva, Jervah, Jervais.**

— Jean-Baptiste Gervais dit Saint-Martin (Charles and Jacquette Rosé) from Rennes in Ille-et-Vilaine (Bretagne) m. Marie-Jeanne Tessier (Mathurin and Élisabeth Létourneau) in La Pérade, QC in 1700.

— Mathieu Gervais dit Parisien (Pierre and Catherine Saillard) from Saint-Maur-des-Fossés in Val-de-Marne (Île-de-France) m. Michelle Picard (Hugues and Antoinette de Liercourt) in Montréal, QC in 1676.

— Jean-Jacques Talbot dit Gervais (Nicolas and Marie Duchesne) from Rouen in Sei-

ne-Maritime (Haute-Normandie) m. (1) Charlotte Sommereux (Noël and Jeanne Goguet) in Québec in 1698; (2) Catherine Lamarre (Pierre and Marie Paulet) in Montmagny, QC in 1710.

Gervaise, same origin as **Gervais.** — Amer. **Jarvis.**

— Jean **Gervaise** (Urbain and Jeanne Hérisse) from Souvigné in Indre-et-Loire (Centre) m. Anne Archambault (Jacques and Françoise Tourault) in Montréal, QC in 1654.

Gévry, alteration of *Givry,* a placename in France. — Amer. **Javery.**

— Jean-Baptiste Givry/**Gévry** dit Saint-François (Philibert and Marie-Pierre Bosseron) from Chalon-sur-Saône in Saône-et-Loire (Bourgogne) m. Marie-Josèphe Ledoux (Joseph and Marie-Josèphe Bousquet) in Saint-Denis-sur-Richelieu, QC in 1760.

Ghostlaw, see **Gosselin.**

Giard, probable variant of *Gillard,* from the Germanic name *Gislehard* composed of *gisal* 'hostage' and *hard* 'hard, strong'. — Amer. **Geor, Joure, Shor, Shore.**

— Nicolas **Giard** dit Saint-Martin (Louis and Michelle David) from Melleran in Deux-Sèvres (Pays de la Loire) m. Claude Prat (Jean and Agnès Le Jeune) in Montréal, QC in 1665.

Gibeau, alteration of *Gibault,* from the Germanic name *Gibwald* composed of *gib* 'gift' and *wald* 'power, authority'. — Amer. **Gebeau, Gebeault, Gebo, Gebow, Gibaut, Gibbo, Gibo, Jebo.**

— Gabriel **Gibault** dit Poitevin (Pierre and Renée Lorillière) from Lusignan in Vienne (Poitou-Charentes) m. Suzanne Durand (Étienne and Geneviève de la Mare) in Québec, QC in 1667.

Giguère, probably derived from Old French *giguer* 'to leap, to prance, to wriggle', the nickname of a restless or cheerful individual. — Amer. **Eugair, Gegare, Gigger, Jiguere.**

— Robert **Giguère** (Jean and Michelle Journel) from Tourouvre in Orne (Basse-Normandie) m. Aimée Miville (Pierre and Charlotte Maugis) in Québec, QC in 1652.

Gilbar, see **Jalbert.**

Gilbault, Gilbeau, Gilbeault, see **Guilbault.**

Gilbert, from the Germanic name *Gislebert* composed of *gisal* 'hostage' and *berht* 'bright'. — Amer. **Gilblair.**

— Charles Dupuis dit **Gilbert** (Gilbert and Françoise Petitjean) from Rosnay in Indre (Centre) m. Marie-Jeanne Brunet (Jean and Angélique Sédilot) in Sainte-Foy, QC in 1741.

Gilbo, Gilboe, see **Guilbault.**

Gilcott, see **Turcot(te).**

Gilmet, Gilmette, see **Guilmette.**

Gilmore, see **Gauthier.**

Gingras, variant of *Gingreau,* probably derived from Old French *ginguer* 'to move, to fidget', the nickname of a restless or playful individual. — Amer. **Gingrass, Jangraw, Shangraw.**

— Charles **Gingras**/Gingreau (Hilaire and Françoise Saint-Lo) from Saint-Michel-le-Cloucq in Vendée (Pays de la Loire) m. Françoise Amiot (Mathieu and Marie Miville) in Québec, QC in 1675.

Girard, from the Germanic name *Gerhard* composed of *gari* 'spear' and *hard* 'hard, strong'. — Amer. **Gerard, Geraw, Geror.**

— Jean **Girard** dit Deraine (Jean and Élisabeth *Planteson) from Haarlem in the Netherlands m. Dorothée Rancin (Charles and Françoise Conflans) in Québec, QC in 1694.
— Pierre **Girard** from Les Sables-d'Olonne in Vendée (Pays de la Loire) m. Suzanne Lavoie (Pierre and Jacquette Grinon) in Québec in 1669.

Girouard, from the Germanic name Gerward composed of gari 'spear' and ward 'guard'. — Amer. **Gerrior, Gerroir, Giroir, Girrior, Girroir.**
— François **Girouard** dit Lavaranne from France m. Jeanne Aucoin in Acadia c. 1647.

Giroux, from the Germanic name Gerwulf composed of gari 'spear' and wulf 'wolf'. — Amer. **Gereau, Gereaux, Gerew, Gero, Gerou, Geroux, Gerow, Gerue, Jareo, Jero, Jerue.**
— Toussaint **Giroux** (Jean and Marguerite Quilleron) from Réveillon in Orne (Basse-Normandie) m. Marie Godard in Québec, QC in 1654.

Girrior, Girroir, see **Girouard.**

Glad, Gladd, see **Contant.**

Gladu, origin uncertain. — Amer. **Callihoo, Clodgo, Gladeau, Gladue.**
— Jean **Gladu** dit Cognac (François and Claude Baudri) from Cognac in Charente (Poitou-Charentes) m. Marie Langlois (Pierre and Jeanne Thoret) in Québec in 1665.

Gocha, Gochee, Gochie, see **Gauthier.**

Godair, Godare, see **Godère.**

Godbois, see **Gadbois.**

Godda, see **Godin.**

Goddard, see **Gaudet(te).**

Goddeau, see **Godin.**

Goddette, see **Gaudet(te).**

Goddin, see **Godin.**

Godère, alteration of Coderre, from (Le) Coderc, a placename in France. — Amer. **Godair, Godare.**
— Pierre **Coderre** dit Lacaillade from Sarrazac in Dordogne (Aquitaine) m. Marie-Louise Ferron (Jean and Élisabeth Patenaude) in Kingston, ON in 1732.

Godett, Godette, see **Gaudet(te).**

Godhue, alteration of Godu, origin undetermined. — Amer. **Goodhue.**
— Yves-Pierre **Godu**/Goddu dit Sansoucy (Pierre and Jeanne Persy) from Poitiers in Vienne (Poitou-Charentes) m. Jeanne Choquet (Nicolas and Anne Julien) in Varennes, QC in 1698.

Godin, derived either from the Germanic name Godo, from god 'god', or Waldo, from wald 'power, authority'. — Amer. **Godda, Goddeau, Goddin, Goodin, Goodine, Gordon.**
— Charles **Godin**/Gaudin (Jacques and Marguerite *Nieule/*Nyeulle) from Aubermesnil-Beaumais in Seine-Maritime (Haute-Normandie) m. Marie Boucher (Marin and Perrine Mallet) in Québec, QC in 1656.
— Pierre **Godin** dit Châtillon (Claude and Marie Bardin) from Châtillon-sur-Seine in Côte-d'Or (Bourgogne) m. Jeanne Rousselière (Louis and Isabelle Parisé) in Montréal, QC in 1654.

Goguen, alteration of Guéguen, from Old Breton Uuicon, derived from uuic 'combat'. — Amer. **Gogan.**
— Joseph **Guéguen** (Jacques and Anne-Françoise Hamonez) from Plougonver in

Côtes-d'Armor (Bretagne) m. (1) Anne Arsenault (François and Anne Bourgeois) in Baie-Sainte-Anne, NB in 1760; (2) Anne Surette (Joseph and Isabelle Babineau) in Cocagne, NB in 1808.

Goka, Gokey, Gokie, see **Gauthier.**

Golen, see **Gaulin.**

Goman, Gomo, Gomon, see **Gaumond.**

Gonia, Goniea, Gonier, see **Gagné.**

Gonion, see **Gagnon.**

Gonneville, apparently from *Gonneville,* a placename in France. — Amer. **Gonville, Gunville.**

*— René Lemire dit **Gonneville**, grandson of Jean from Rouen in Seine-Maritime (Haute-Normandie), m. Marie-Madeleine Gélinas (Pierre and Marie-Madeleine Bourbeau) in Yamachiche, QC in 1736.*

Gonya, Gonye, Gonyea, Gonyar, see **Gagné.**

Gonyaw, Gonyeau, see **Gagnon.**

Gonyer, see **Gagné.**

Gonyo, Gonyon, Gonyou, see **Gagnon.**

Goodblood, see **Bonsang.**

Goodchild, see **Bonenfant.**

Goodfriend, see **Bonami.**

Goodheart, see **Vadeboncoeur.**

Goodhue, see **Godhue.**

Goodin, Goodine, see **Godin.**

Goodnature, see **Belhumeur.**

Goodness, Goodniss, see **Labonté.**

Goodreau, see **Goudreau.**

Goodrie, see **Gaudry.**

Goodro, see **Goudreau.**

Goodroad, Goodrode, see **Beauchemin.**

Goodroe, Goodrow, see **Goudreau.**

Goodwater, see **Bonneau.**

Goodway, see **Gadbois.**

Goodwill, see **Bonvouloir.**

Gooler, Gooley, see **Goulet.**

Gooseberry, see **Desgroseilliers.**

Gooshaw, see **Gougeon.**

Gordon, see **Godin.**

Gore, see **Gour.**

Gorman, see **Gaumond.**

Gorrow, see **Gareau.**

Gosha, see **Gauthier.**

Gosselin, derived from the Germanic name *Gosso,* from *Gaut,* the name of a Germanic people. — Amer. **Gauslin, Gausline, Gausselin, Ghostlaw, Goslant, Gosley, Goslin, Gosline, Goslyn, Gosseline, Gouslin, Gushlaw, Joslyn.**

*— Gabriel **Gosselin** (Nicolas and Marguerite *Dubréal) from Combray in Calvados (Basse-Normandie) m. (1) Françoise Lelièvre (Christophe and Georgette Clément) in*

Québec, QC in 1653; (2) Louise Guillot (Geoffroy and Marie d'Abancourt) in Sainte-Famille, Île d'Orléans, QC in 1677.

Gotchey, Gotchy, Gothier, Gouchie, see **Gauthier**.

Goudette, see **Gaudet(te)**.

Goudreau, alteration of *Gaudreau*, derived from *Gaudier*, same origin as **Gauthier**. — Amer. **Goodreau, Goodro, Goodroe, Goodrow, Gudroe**.
— *Jean Gaudreau/Gotreau (Jean and Marie Rouer) from La Flotte in Charente-Maritime (Poitou-Charentes) m. Marie Roy (Nicolas and Jeanne Lelièvre) in Québec, QC in 1679.*

Gougeon, probably derived from Old French *gouge* 'servant, messenger'. — Amer. **Gooshaw**.
— *Pierre Gougeon (Pierre and Marie Bougron) from Aubigny in Vendée (Pays de la Loire) m. Catherine Danis (Honoré and Perrine Lapierre) in Montréal, QC in 1686.*

Gouin, either from the Germanic name *Godwin* composed of *god* 'god' and *win* 'friend', or the same origin as **Godin**. — Amer. **Gouine, Guire**.
— *Sébastien Gouin dit Champagne (Pierre and Marie Bonneau) from Saintes in Charente-Maritime (Poitou-Charentes) m. Louise Rainville (Jean and Élisabeth *de La Guéripière) in Montréal, QC in 1703.*

Goulah, Goulais, Goulay, see **Goulet**.

Gould, see **Doiron**.

Goulet, from *(Le) Goulet*, a placename in France. — Amer. **Gooler, Gooley, Goulah, Goulais, Goulay**.
— *Jacques Goulet (Thomas and Antoinette Feuillard) from Normandel in Orne (Basse-Normandie) m. Marguerite Mulier (Jean and Marguerite Chauvin) in La Poterie in Orne in 1645.*

Goupil, from Old French *goupil* 'fox', the nickname of a wily, crafty individual. — Amer. **Coopee**.
— *Antoine Goupil dit Laviolette (Jean and Marie *Chusson) from Cornil in Corrèze (Limousin) m. Marie Gaboury (Louis and Nicole Souillard) in La Durantaye, QC in 1698.*

Gour, from Breton *gour* 'man'. — Amer. **Gore, Goure**.
— *Pierre Gour dit Lavigne (Julien and Marie Gomet) from Lamballe in Côtes-d'Armor (Bretagne) m. Catherine Richaume (Jacques and Marguerite Gratiot) in Saint-Sulpice, QC in 1713.*

Gourneau, see **Grenon**.

Gouslin, see **Gosselin**.

Gouthier, see **Gauthier**.

Gouthreau, see **Gautreau**.

Gover, Govero, Govreau, Govro, see **Gauvreau**.

Goyer, from the Germanic name *Godhari* composed of *god* 'god' and *hari* 'army'. — Amer. **Guyer**.
— *Mathurin Goyer dit Laviolette (Jacques and Mathurine Sauvage) from Tourouvre in Orne (Basse-Normandie) m. Barbe Lefebvre (Jacques and Barbe Thieulin) in Montréal, QC in 1669.*

Goyet(te), alteration of *Goguet*, derived from Old French *gogue* 'merry, happy'. — Amer. **Goyett, Guyet, Guyett, Guyette**.

— Pierre **Goguet** *(Michel and Marie Jounot) from Marans in Charente-Maritime (Poitou-Charentes) m. Louise Garnier in Marans c. 1656.*

Grandaw, see **Grondin**.

Grandbois, from *Grandbois, (Le) Grand-Bois* or *(Le) Grand Bois*, placenames in France. — Amer. **Grumbo, Grumbois**.

— *Louis Guibault dit* **Grandbois** *(Antoine and Marie Motel) from Nieul-sur-l'Autise in Vendée (Pays de la Loire) m. Marie Lefebvre (Pierre and Michelle Jovet) in Québec, QC in 1670.*

Grandchamp, from *(Le) Grandchamp, (Le) Grand-Champ* or *(Le) Grand Champ*, placenames in France. — Amer. **Grashaw**.

— *Pierre Cornellier dit* **Grandchamp** *from Tierceville in Calvados (Basse-Normandie) m. Catherine Certain in France c. 1684.*

Grandeau, see **Grondin**.

Grandmaison, from *(La) Grand'maison, (La) Grand-Maison* or *(La) Grand Maison*, placenames in France. — Amer. **Grandmason**.

— *Pierre Barbary dit* **Grandmaison** *(Pierre and Marguerite Beloy) from Thiviers in Dordogne (Aquitaine) m. Marie Lebrun (Jacques and Marie Michel) in Montréal, QC in 1668.*

Grandow, see **Grondin**.

Grant, see **Lagrandeur**.

Grashaw, see **Grandchamp**.

Gravel, alteration of *(La) Gravelle*, a placename in France. — Amer. **Gravell**.

— *Joseph-Massé* **Gravel** *dit Brindelière from Orne (Basse-Normandie) m. Marguerite Tavernier (Éloi and Marguerite Gagnon) in Québec, QC in 1644.*

Graveline, alteration of *(Les) Gravelines*, a placename in France. — Amer. **Gravelin, Gravlin**.

— *Urbain Baudreau dit* **Graveline** *(Jean and Marie Chauveau) from Clermont-Créans in Sarthe (Pays de la Loire) m. Mathurine Juillet (Blaise and Antoinette de Liercourt) in Montréal, QC in 1664.*

Greania, Greanya, see **Grenier**.

Greemore, see **Grimard**.

Green, Greeney, Greenia, Greenier, see **Grenier**.

Greenleaf, see **Vertefeuille**.

Greeno, Greenough, see **Grignon**.

Greenwood, see **Boisvert**.

Greenya, see **Grenier**.

Greffard, origin uncertain. — Amer. **Griffore**.

— *Louis* **Greffard**/*Griffard dit Le Coq (Jean and Louise Roy) from Chaillé-sous-les-Ormeaux in Vendée (Pays de la Loire) m. Louise Gauthier (Élie and Marguerite Moitié) in Sainte-Famille, Île d'Orléans, QC in 1684.*

Grégoire, from the Greek name *Gregorios*, derived from *gregoros* 'vigilant'. — Amer. **Gregory, Gregware**.

— *François* **Grégoire** *(Théophile and Madeleine *Clénance/*Clémance) from Montpellier in Hérault (Languedoc-Roussillon) m. (1) Mathurine Bélanger (François and Marie Guyon) in Neuville, QC in 1688; (2) Marie-Anne Liénard (Sébastien and Françoise Pelletier) in Sainte-Foy, QC in 1701.*

— Jean-Pierre **Grégoire** dit *Nantais (Pierre and Marie-Anne Léveillé) from Lyon in Rhône (Rhône-Alpes) m. Marie-Anne Apert (Jacques and Marie-Anne Daniau) in Montréal, QC in 1765.*

— Joseph Deblois dit **Grégoire**, *son of Grégoire from Champagne-Mouton in Charente (Poitou-Charentes), m. Marguerite Rousseau (Symphorien and Jeanne *Sinallon/*Sinnalon) in Sainte-Famille, Île d'Orléans, QC in 1686.*

Gremar, Gremard, Gremore, see **Grimard**.

Grenier, alteration of *Garnier*, from the Germanic name *Warinhari* composed of *warin* 'protection' and *hari* 'army'. — Amer. **Garrett, Greania, Greanya, Green, Greeney, Greenia, Greenier, Greenya**.

— Charles **Garnier** *(Guillaume and Françoise *Deschallais) from Tournebu in Calvados (Basse-Normandie) m. Louise Vézina (Jacques and Marie Boisdon) in Québec, QC in 1664.*

— François **Garnier** *(François and Antoinette Boulay) from Saint-Cosme-en-Vairais in Sarthe (Pays de la Loire) m. Jacqueline Freslon (René and Renée Armange) in Québec, QC in 1663.*

Greno, see **Grignon**.

Grenon, from *Grenon*, a placename in France. — Amer. **Gourneau, Gurneau, Gurno, Gurnoe**.

— Pierre **Grenon** *(Pierre and Marie Sauzeau) from Marsais in Charente-Maritime (Poitou-Charentes) m. Marie Lavoie (Pierre and Jacquette Grinon) in Québec, QC in 1676.*

Grenough, see **Grignon**.

Grew, see **Groulx**.

Griffore, see **Greffard**.

Grignon, from *(Le) Grignon*, a placename in France. — Amer. **Greeno, Greenough, Greno, Grenough**.

— Jacques **Grignon** *(Jacques and Jeanne Tessier) from Saint-Philbert du Pont Charrault in Vendée (Pays de la Loire) m. Marie-Thérèse Richer (Pierre and Dorothée Brassard) in Batiscan, QC in 1692.*

Grimard, from the Germanic name *Grimhard* composed of *grim* 'cruel' and *hard* 'hard, strong'. — Amer. **Greemore, Gremar, Gremard, Gremore**.

— Jean-Baptiste Morand dit **Grimard**, *son of Pierre from Thiolières in Puy-de-Dôme (Auvergne), m. Élisabeth Dubois (Jean and Anne Mailloux) in Québec, QC in 1707.*

Grondin, either from *Grondin*, a placename in France, or from Old French *grondin* 'growling animal', the nickname of a grumbling, irascible individual. — Amer. **Grandaw, Grandeau, Grandow, Groder, Grodi**.

— Jean **Grondin** *(Pierre and Marie Rigoulet) from Brouage in Charente-Maritime (Poitou-Charentes) m. Sainte Mignault (Jean and Louise Cloutier) in Québec, QC in 1669.*

Groulx, alteration of *Grou*, from the Germanic name *Gerwulf* composed of *gari* 'spear' and *wulf* 'wolf'. — Amer. **Grew, Lagrew, Lagrou**.

— Jean **Grou**/*Groust/Guéroult (Étienne and Judith Lefer) from Rouen in Seine-Maritime (Haute-Normandie) m. Marie-Anne Goguet (Pierre and Louise Garnier) in Montréal, QC in 1671.*

Grozelle, see **Desgroseilliers**.

Grumbo, Grumbois, see **Grandbois.**

Guardipee, see **Gariépy.**

Gudbaur, see **Gadbois.**

Gudroe, see **Goudreau.**

Guédry, from the Germanic name *Widric* composed of *wid* 'wood' and *ric* 'powerful'.
— Amer. **Geddry, Guidry, Jeddry.**

— *Claude* **Guédry** *dit Grivois and Laverdure from France m. Marguerite Petitpas (Claude and Catherine Bugaret) in Acadia c. 1681.*

Guénet(te), derived from the Germanic name *Wano*, from *wan* 'hope, expectation'. — Amer. **Gennette.**

— *Pierre* **Guénet** *(Jacques and Marie de Saint-Lô) from Soissons in Aisne (Picardie) m. Élisabeth Paquet (Isaac and Élisabeth Meunier) in Saint-Laurent, Île d'Orléans, QC in 1689.*

Guérette, alteration of *Guéret*, probably derived from *Guérard*, from the Germanic name *Gerhard* composed of *gari* 'spear' and *hard* 'hard, strong'. — Amer. **Garrett.**

— *Jacques* **Guéret** *dit Dumont (René and Madeleine Vigoureux) from Canchy in Calvados (Basse-Normandie) m. Anne Tardif (Jacques and Barbe d'Orange) in Beauport, QC in 1694.*

Guérin, from the Germanic name *Warino*, derived from *warin* 'protection'. — Amer. **Jerry, Ward.**

— *Claude* **Guérin** *dit Lafontaine (Michel and Jeanne Veron) from Lusignan in Vienne (Poitou-Charentes) m. Jeanne Cusson (Jean and Marie Foubert) in Montréal, QC in 1696.*

— *Guillaume* **Guérin** *dit Saint-Hilaire (Léonard and Marie Paignon) from Saint-Symphorien-des-Monts in Manche (Basse-Normandie) m. Anne Guillot (Vincent and Élisabeth Blais) in Saint-Pierre, Île d'Orléans, QC in 1704.*

Guernon, probably derived from **Guérin.** — Amer. **Gernon, Yarneau, Yarno.**

— *François* **Guernon** *dit Belleville (François and Marie-Michelle Coulon) from Paris (Île-de-France) m. Marie-Marguerite Delpêche (Jean-Baptiste and Marguerite Robillard) in Saint-Sulpice, QC in 1761.*

Guertin, alteration of *Guéretin*, probably derived from *Guérard* via *Guéret*, from the Germanic name *Gerhard* composed of *gari* 'spear' and *hard* 'hard, strong'. — Amer. **Yarter, Yartin, Yatta, Yattaw, Yatter, Yettaw, Yetter, Yetto.**

— *Louis* **Guertin**/*Guéretin dit Le Sabotier (Louis and Georginne Leduc) from Daumeray in Maine-et-Loire (Pays de la Loire) m. Élisabeth Camus (Pierre and Jeanne Charas/Charles) in Montréal, QC in 1659.*

Guidry, see **Guédry.**

Guiette, see **Guillet(te).**

Guilbault, from the Germanic name *Wilbald* composed of *wil* 'will' and *bald* 'bold'. — Amer. **Gehue, Gilbault, Gilbeau, Gilbeault, Gilbo, Gilboe, Guilbeaux.**

— *Pierre* **Guilbault**/*Guilbeau from France m. Catherine Thériot (Jean and Perrine Rau) in Acadia c. 1668.*

Guillet(te), derived either from *Guillaume*, from the Germanic name *Wilhelm* composed of *wil* 'will' and *helm* 'helmet', or from *Guy*, from the Germanic name *Wido*, from *wid* 'wood'. — Amer. **Deaett, Deaette, Deitte, Deyette, Diette, Diguette, Dillette, Guiette.**

— Pierre **Guillet** dit Lajeunesse *(François and Perrine Ménard) from La Rochelle in Charente-Maritime (Poitou-Charentes) m. Jeanne Saint-Père (Étienne and Madeleine Couteau) in Québec c. 1648.*

Guilmain, alteration of *Guillemin*, derived from *Guillaume*, from the Germanic name *Wilhelm* composed of *wil* 'will' and *helm* 'helmet'. — Amer. **Guilman**.

— Charles *Guillimin/**Guillemin** (Guillaume and Marguerite Moreau) from Concarneau in Finistère (Bretagne) m. Françoise Lemaître (François and Marguerite Poulin) in Montréal, QC in 1710.*

Guilmette, alteration of *Guillemet*, derived from *Guillaume*, from the Germanic name *Wilhelm* composed of *wil* 'will' and *helm* 'helmet'. — Amer. **Gilmet, Gilmette**.

— Nicolas **Guillemet**/*Guilmet (Nicolas and Jeanne Souhaité) from Nesles-la-Montagne in Aisne (Picardie) m. Marie Selle (Guillaume and Marguerite Dormesnil) in Québec, QC in 1667.*

Guimond, from the Germanic name *Wigmund* composed of *wig* 'combat' and *mund* 'protection'. — Amer. **Demo, Guymon**.

— Louis **Guimond**/*Guimont (François and Jeanne Delaunay) from Champs in Orne (Basse-Normandie) m. Jeanne Bitouset (Antoine and Nicole Duport/Lecerf) in Québec, QC in 1653.*

Guinard, alteration of *Guignard*, from the Germanic name *Winhard* composed of *win* 'friend' and *hard* 'hard, strong'. — Amer. **Genore**.

— Pierre **Guignard** *(Nicolas and Isabelle Laisné) from Chavagnes-en-Paillers in Vendée (Pays de la Loire) m. Jeanne Guillemet (Nicolas and Marie Sel) in Saint-Jean, Île d'Orléans, QC in 1683.*

Guindon, probable alteration of *Guédon*, apparently derived from the Germanic name *Wido*, from *wid* 'wood'. — Amer. **Yaddow, Yandon, Yandow**.

— Pierre **Guindon**/*Guédon (François and Marie Mollé) from Loudun in Vienne (Poitou-Charentes) m. Catherine Barsa (André and Françoise Pilois) in Montréal, QC in 1706.*

Guire, see **Gouin**.

Gumlaw, see **Gamelin**.

Gunville, see **Gonneville**.

Gurneau, Gurno, Gurnoe, see **Grenon**.

Gushlaw, see **Gosselin**.

Gutchell, see **Bonenfant**.

Guyer, see **Goyer**.

Guyet, Guyett, Guyette, see **Goyet(te)**.

Guymon, see **Guimond**.

Guyon, derived from *Guy*, from the Germanic name *Wido*, from *wid* 'wood'. — Amer. **Yon, Young, Youngs**.

— Jean **Guyon** *(Jacques and Marie Huet) from Tourouvre in Orne (Basse-Normandie) m. Mathurine Robin (Eustache and Madeleine Avrard) in Mortagne-au-Perche in Orne in 1615.*

Guyor, see **Gaillard**.

H

Haché, probable alteration of *Aché*, from the Germanic name *Achari* composed of *ac* 'blade' and *hari* 'army'. — Amer. **Achee, Achey.**

— *Michel **Haché** dit Gallant from France m. Anne Cormier (Thomas and Marie-Madeleine Girouard) in Acadia c. 1690.*

Hakey, see **Éthier.**

Hall, see **Houle.**

Halo, see **Hélot.**

Hamann, alteration of the German name *Hamann*, either from *Hahne*, derived from *Johannes* 'John', or *Hamm*, a placename in Germany, and Middle High German *mann* 'man'. — Amer. **Amans.**

— *Nikolaus **Hamann** (Johann and Anna Katharina Müller) from Dudenhofen in Germany m. Isabelle Fontaine (Jean-Baptiste and Marie-Françoise Fortier) in Québec, QC in 1786.*

Hamel, from *(Le) Hamel*, a placename in France. — Amer. **Amell, Ammell, Hamill.**

— *Jean **Hamel** (François and ...) from Avremesnil in Seine-Maritime (Haute-Normandie) m. Marie Auvray in France c. 1660.*

Hamelin, from the Germanic name *Amalin*, derived from *amal* 'labor'. — Amer. **Amlaw, Amlin, Emlaw, Hamlin.**

— *François **Hamelin** (Nicolas and Jeanne Levasseur/Vasseur) from La Daguenière or Saint-Mathurin-sur-Loire in Maine-et-Loire (Pays de la Loire) m. Marie-Madeleine Aubert (Jacques and Antoinette Meunier) in Grondines, QC in 1685.*

— *Jacques **Hamelin** (Nicolas and Marie Dubois) from Saint-Planchers in Manche (Basse-Normandie) m. Marie-Barbe Sullière (Jean and Marie-Louise Lesage) in L'Assomption, QC in 1749.*

Hamill, see **Hamel.**

Hamlin, see **Hamelin.**

Hance, Hanks, see **Hinse.**

Happy, see **L'Heureux.**

Harel, from Old French *harel* 'shout, riot, commotion', the nickname of a rowdy, quarrelsome individual. — Amer. **Ariel, Rell, Relle.**

— *Jean **Harel** from France m. Marie Pescher in Québec c. 1671.*

Harper, see **Arpin.**

Hart, see **Francoeur, Jolicoeur** and **Vadeboncoeur.**

Harteau, see **Hertault.**

Harvieux, see **Hervieux.**

Heald, see **Talon.**

Hébert, alteration of *Herbert*, from the Germanic name *Haribert* composed of *hari* 'army' and *berht* 'bright'. — Amer. **Abair, Abaire, Abar, Abare, Abear, Aber, Eber, Ebert.**

— *Antoine **Hébert** from France m. Geneviève Lefranc in France or Acadia c. 1648.*
— *Augustin **Hébert** dit Jolicoeur (Jean and Isabeau Troussart) from Paris (Île-de-France) m. Adrienne Duvivier (Antoine and Catherine Journé) in France c. 1646.*
Hélot, alteration of the Breton name *Hello,* from *hael* 'generous'. — Amer. **Halo.**
— *Julien **Hélot**/Hellot (Mathurin and Guillemette Durant) from Saint-Jouan-des-Guérets in Ille-et-Vilaine (Bretagne) m. Marie-Josèphe Deguise (Guillaume and Marie-Anne Morin) in Québec, QC in 1721.*
Hénault, alteration of *Hunault,* from the Germanic name *Hunwald* composed of *hun* 'bear cub' and *wald* 'power, authority'. — Amer. **Ano, Anoe, Eno.**
— *Toussaint **Hunault** dit Deschamps (Nicolas and Marie Benoist) from Saint-Pierre-ès-Champs in Oise (Picardie) m. Marie Lorgueil (Pierre and Marie Bruyère) in Montréal, QC in 1654.*
Hermès, from the Greek name *Hermes.* — Amer. **Armey.**
— ***Hermès** Émond, descendant of Pierre from Rochefort in Charente-Maritime (Poitou-Charentes), m. Théotiste Théroux (André and Marie-Louise Condrat) in Yamaska, QC in 1831.*
Héroux, variant of *Hérou,* from the Germanic name *Hariwulf* composed of *hari* 'army' and *wulf* 'wolf'. — Amer. **Ero, Hero.**
— *Jean **Hérou**/Héroux dit Bourgainville (Jean and Marie Royer) from Blonville-sur-Mer in Calvados (Basse-Normandie) m. Jeanne Pépin (Guillaume and Jeanne Méchin) in Trois-Rivières, QC in 1674.*
Hertault, from the Germanic name *Hartwald* composed of *hard* 'hard, strong' and *wald* 'power, authority'. — Amer. **Harteau.**
— *Jacques **Hertault**/Artault dit Saint-Pierre (Jacques and Françoise Godard) from Dieppe in Seine-Maritime (Haute-Normandie) m. Marguerite Rousseau (Antoine and Marie Roinay) in Québec in 1700.*
Hervieux, derived from *Hervé,* either from the Breton name *Hoiearnviu* composed of *hoiarn* 'iron' and *biu* 'quick', or from the Germanic name *Hariwig* composed of *hari* 'army' and *wig* 'combat'. — Amer. **Harvieux.**
— *Isaac **Hervieux** (Jacques and Jeanne Moussard) from Lonlay-l'Abbaye in Orne (Basse-Normandie) m. Marie-Anne Pinguet (Pierre and Anne Chevalier) in Québec, QC in 1676.*
Hétu, alteration of *Estur,* from the Old Norse name *Styrr* via Latin *Sturus.* — Amer. **Atchue, Etu, Etue, Hetue, Hickey, Itchue.**
— *Georges Estur/**Hétu** dit Lafleur (Jean and Claire Lecordier) from Le Havre in Seine-Maritime (Haute-Normandie) m. Marie Loiseau (Lucas and Françoise Curé) in Boucherville, QC in 1699.*
Hévey, alteration of *Devé* via *Hévé,* from Old French *desvé* 'crazy, furious', the nickname of an irascible individual. — Amer. **Avery, Avey.**
— *Nicolas **Hévé**/Devé (Nicolas and Anne Leballeur/Lebailleur) from Saint-Valéry-en-Caux in Seine-Maritime (Haute-Normandie) m. Jeanne Chalut (Pierre and Marie Bonin) in Québec, QC in 1672.*
Hickey, see **Hétu.**
Hickory, see **Desnoyers.**
Hill, see **Descôteaux.**
Hinse, alteration of the English name *Haynes,* derived from *Hain,* from the Germanic

name *Hagano*. — Amer. **Ance, Hance, Hanks.**

— *Joseph* **Haynes** *(John and Sarah Moulton) from Newbury, MA m. Marguerite Marois (Guillaume and Catherine Laberge) in L'Ange-Gardien, QC in 1710.*

— *Jonathan* **Haynes** *(John and Sarah Moulton) from Newbury, MA m. Marie Pauzé (Jacques and Marie Jobidon) in Montmagny, QC in 1712.*

Hoague, see **Hogue.**

Hobart, see **Aubertin.**

Hogue, alteration of *La Hogue*, a placename in France. — Amer. **Hoague, Hogg.**

— *Pierre* **Hogue** *(Jean and Nicole Dubus) from Bellifontaine in Somme (Picardie) m. Jeanne Théodore (Michel and Jacqueline Lagrange) in Montréal, QC in 1676.*

Hood, see **Houde.**

Hool, see **Houle.**

Hope, see **Lespérance.**

Hoskins, see **Durepos.**

Houde, from either the Germanic name *Hildo*, derived from *hild* 'combat', or *Audo*, derived from *aud* 'riches, prosperity'. — Amer. **Hood, Wood.**

— *Louis* **Houde** *(Noël and Anne Lefebvre) from Manou in Eure-et-Loir (Centre) m. Madeleine Boucher (Marin and Perrine Mallet) in Québec, QC in 1655.*

Houle, alteration of **Houde.** — Amer. **Hall, Hool.**

— *Jean-Baptiste Houde/**Houle**, descendant of Louis from Manou in Eure-et-Loir (Centre), m. Marie-Jeanne Vanasse (Étienne and Marie-Charlotte Dubois) in Saint-François-du-Lac, QC in 1748.*

Huard, derived from the Germanic name *Hugo*, from *hug* 'mind'. — Amer. **Loon.**

— *Jean* **Huard** *(Marin and Julienne Bouillet) from Courson-Monteloup in Essonne (Île-de-France) m. Anne-Marie Amiot (Mathieu and Marie Miville) in Québec, QC in 1670.*

Hubert, from the Germanic name *Hugberht* composed of *hug* 'mind' and *berht* 'bright'. — Amer. **Eubar, Euber, Hurbert.**

— *René* **Hubert** *(René and Anne Horry/Orry) from Paris (Île-de-France) m. Françoise (de) Lacroix (Antoine and Barbe Cassin) in Québec, QC in 1669.*

— *Pierre Leber dit* **Hubert** *(Pierre and Madeleine Tavernier) from Château-du-Loir in Sarthe (Pays de la Loire) m. Anne Charbonneau (Jean and Élisabeth Boire) in Montréal in 1721.*

Hughto, see **Hurteau.**

Hunter, see **Chassé.**

Huot, same origin as **Huard.** — Amer. **Hyott, Hyotte, Yott, Youtt.**

— *Mathurin* **Huot** *(René and Renée Poirier) from Segré in Maine-et-Loire (Pays de la Loire) m. Marie Letartre (René and Louise Goulet) in L'Ange-Gardien, QC in 1671.*

Hurbert, see **Hubert.**

Hurteau, alteration of *Hurtault*, either from *(Le) Hurtault*, a placename in France, or derived from Old French *hurt* 'bump, shock', the nickname of a rowdy, quarrelsome individual. — Amer. **Eurto, Hughto, Hurto, Huto.**

— *Jean* **Hurtault** *dit Dragon (Jean and Marie Christy) from Nanterre in Hauts-de-Seine (Île-de-France) m. Marie-Madeleine Dubeau (Jacques and Catherine Bédard) in Québec, QC in 1734.*

Hyott, Hyotte, see **Huot.**

I

Imbault, from the Germanic name *Imbald* composed of *irmin* (> *im*) and *bald* 'bold'. — Amer. **Ambeau.**

— *Guillaume **Imbault**/Raimbault dit Matha (Pierre and Marie Reault) from Saint-Hérie in Charente-Maritime (Poitou-Charentes) m. Louise-Marie Chorau (Charles and Jacqueline Bonnin) in Montréal, QC in 1703.*

Imbleau, variant of *Imblot*, a probable alteration of *Humblot*, derived from the Germanic name *Hunbald* composed of *hun* 'bear cub' and *bald* 'bold'. — Amer. **Amblo.**

— *Luc **Imbleau** (Victor and Élisabeth Petitot) from Moloy in Côte-d'Or (Bourgogne) m. Marie-Geneviève Content (André and Marie-Anne Sylvestre) in Champlain, QC in 1751.*

Iott, see **Ayotte.**

Isoir, from the Germanic name *Isoward* composed of *is(an)* 'iron' and *ward* 'guard'. — Amer. **Eggsware, Exware.**

— *Antoine **Isoir** dit Provençal (Blaise and Françoise *Sarbacan) from Aix-en-Provence in Bouches-du-Rhône (Provence-Alpes-Côte-d'Azur) m. Marie-Thérèse (de) Rainville (Jean and Élisabeth *de La Guéripière) in Beauport, QC in 1699.*

Itchue, see **Hétu.**

J

Jabotte, see **Chabot**.

Jacob, from the Hebrew name *Ya'aqobh* 'one that takes by the heel'. — Amer. **Jacobs**.
— *Étienne Jacob (Edmé and Jeanne Bellejambe) from Paris (Île-de-France) m. Jeanne Fressel/Fresel (André and Marie Avice) in Québec, QC in 1670.*

Jacques, from the Hebrew name *Ya'aqobh* 'one that takes by the heel' via Latin *Jacobus*. — Amer. **Jock**.
— *Louis Jacques (Nicolas and Marie Soyer) from Amiens in Somme (Picardie) m. Antoinette Leroux (François and Marie Renaud) in Québec, QC in 1688.*

Jalbert, alteration of *Gerbert*, from the Germanic name *Gariberht* composed of *gari* 'spear' and *berht* 'bright'. — Amer. **Gelbar, Gilbar**.
— *Mathurin Gerbert dit Lafontaine (Jean and Perrine Pelé) from Saint-Sulpice-des-Landes in Loire-Atlantique (Pays de la Loire) m. Isabelle Targer (Daniel and Louise Martin) in Québec, QC in 1659.*

Jandreau, see **Gendreau**.

Jandrew, Jandro, see **Gendron**.

Jangraw, see **Gingras**.

Jareo, see **Giroux**.

Jarret, from *(Le) Jarret*, a placename in France. — Amer. **Sharai, Sharrai**.
— *André Jarret, sieur de Beauregard (Jean and Perrette Sermet) from Vignieu in Isère (Rhône-Alpes) m. Marguerite Anthiaume (Michel and Marie Dubois) in Montréal, QC in 1676.*

Jarvais, Jarvey, see **Gervais**.

Jarvis, see **Gervais** and **Gervaise**.

Jasmin, from Persian *yasemin* 'jasmine'. — Amer. **Jasman, Jasmer, Jasmine, Jesmer, Jessmer**.
— *Louis-Laurent Duhault dit Jasmin (Louis-Laurent and Antoinette Joachim) from Poitiers in Vienne (Poitou-Charentes) m. Marie-Madeleine Ducorps (Nicolas and Marie-Marguerite Bisaillon) in Montréal, QC in 1769.*

Javery, see **Gévry**.

Jeandron, see **Gendron**.

Jeannotte, alteration of *Janot*, derived from *Jean*, from the Hebrew name *Yohanan* 'the Lord is gracious' via Latin *Jo(h)annes*. — Amer. **Genett, Genette, Gennett, Gennette, Genot, Jenette, Jennette**.
— *Jean-Baptiste Chiasson/Giasson dit Janot, grandson of Guyon from La Rochelle in Charente-Maritime (Poitou-Charentes), m. Marie Pitre (Claude and Marie Comeau) in Port-Royal, NS in 1722.*

Jeanpierre, from the given names *Jean* 'John' and *Pierre* 'Peter'. — Amer. **Johnpeer, Johnpier**.
— *Jean Girard dit Jeanpierre (Pierre and Claire Dufresne) from La Flèche in Sarthe*

(Pays de la Loire) m. *Marie-Madeleine Chanluc/Chalut (François and Marie Amaury) in Québec, QC in 1715.*

Jeanvenne, from the given name *Jean* 'John' and **Venne.** — Amer. **Johnvin.**
— *Jean Venne/Voyne from France m. Françoise Manseau in France c. 1645.*

Jebo, see **Gibeau.**

Jeddry, see **Guédry.**

Jefferson, see **Geoffrion.**

Jeffrey, see **Geoffroy.**

Jendro, see **Gendron.**

Jenette, Jennette, see **Jeannotte.**

Jerdo, see **Gendreau.**

Jero, see **Giroux.**

Jerry, see **Guérin.**

Jerue, see **Giroux.**

Jerva, Jervah, Jervais, see **Gervais.**

Jesmer, Jessmer, see **Jasmin.**

Jetté, origin undetermined. — Amer. **Eschete, Staie, Stay.**
— *Urbain Jetté (Mathurin and Barbe Hulin/Heulin) from La Flèche in Sarthe (Pays de la Loire) m. Catherine Charles (Samuel and Françoise Cochet) in Montréal, QC in 1659.*

Jewtraw, see **Jutras.**

Jiguere, see **Giguère.**

Jimmo, see **Dumont.**

Jock, see **Jacques.**

Jodoin, from the Germanic name *Gaudwin* composed of *Gaut*, the name of the Gothic people, and *win* 'friend'. — Amer. **Jodway, Judware.**
— *Claude Jodoin (Barnabé and Michelle Gremillon) from Poitiers in Vienne (Poitou-Charentes) m. Anne Thomas (Jean and Madeleine Platon) in Montréal, QC in 1666.*

Joffrion, see **Geoffrion.**

Johndro, see **Gendron.**

Johndrow, see **Gendreau** and **Gendron.**

Johnpeer, Johnpier, see **Jeanpierre.**

Johnroe, see **Gendron.**

Johnvin, see **Jeanvenne.**

Joler, see **Jolin.**

Jolicoeur, from *joli coeur* 'tender heart', a soldier's nickname. — Amer. **Hart.**
— *Claude Devault dit Jolicoeur (Jean and Marguerite Calus) from Saint-Martin-d'Auxigny in Cher (Centre) m. Catherine Quintin (Jean and Jeanne Delpé) in Repentigny, QC in 1730.*

Jolin, derived from Old French *joli(f)* 'happy, cheerful'. — Amer. **Joler, Sholan.**
— *Jean Jolin from Saint-Martin-de-Ré in Charente-Maritime (Poitou-Charentes) m. Marie Boileau (René and Joachine Serrant) in Saint-François, Île d'Orléans, QC in 1690.*

Joly, from Old French *joli(f)* 'happy, cheerful'. — Amer. **Jolly, Nice.**
— *Nicolas Joly (Jean and Marguerite Duquesne) from Bosc-Guérard-Saint-Adrien in Seine-Maritime (Haute-Normandie) m. Françoise Hunault (Toussaint and Marie Lor-*

gueil) in Montréal, QC in 1681.

Joncas, from *(Le) Joncas,* a placename in France. — Amer. **Junco.**

— *Pierre* **Joncas**/*Junqua dit Lapierre (Antoine and Arnaude Garlin) from Maurens in Gers (Midi-Pyrénées) m. Jacqueline Boulay (Robert and Françoise Grenier) in Sainte-Famille, Île d'Orléans, QC in 1672.*

Jondro, Jondrow, see **Gendron.**

Joslyn, see **Gosselin.**

Joubert, from the Germanic name *Gautberht* composed of *Gaut,* the name of the Gothic people, and *berht* 'bright'. — Amer. **Juber, Jubert.**

— *Jean* **Joubert** *(François and Jeanne Maillet) from Saint-Aubin-la-Plaine in Vendée (Pays de la Loire) m. Madeleine Têtu (Edmé and Élisabeth de La Cour) in Québec, QC in 1669.*

Joure, see **Giard.**

Joyal, alteration of *Joyel,* probably from Old French *joiel* 'cheerful'. — Amer. **Lively, Playful.**

— *Jacques* **Joyal**/*Joyel dit Bergerac (Étienne and Suzanne Masseau) from Bergerac in Dordogne (Aquitaine) m. Gertrude Moral (Quentin and Marie Marguerie) in Trois-Rivières, QC in 1676.*

Jubenville, see **Jubinville.**

Juber, Jubert, see **Joubert.**

Jubinville, alteration of *Jubainville,* a placename in France. — Amer. **Jubenville.**

— *Michel* **Jubinville** *dit Saint-Michel (Pierre and Marguerite *Belinville) from Paris (Île-de-France) m. Marguerite Barbeau (François and Marguerite Hédouin) in Montréal, QC in 1706.*

Judware, see **Jodoin.**

Junco, see **Joncas.**

Juneau, alteration of *Jouineau* via *Juineau,* derived from *Jouin,* from the Latin name *Jovinus,* derived from *Jovis* 'Jupiter'. — Amer. **Juno.**

— *Pierre Jouineau/**Juineau** from Angoulins in Charente-Maritime (Poitou-Charentes) m. Anne Rousseau in Québec c. 1666.*

Jusseaume, from the Germanic name *Gauzhelm* composed of *Gaut,* the name of a Germanic people, and *helm* 'helmet'. — Amer. **Dusome.**

— *Alexandre* **Jusseaume** *(François and Catherine Langelier) from Duras in Lot-et-Garonne (Aquitaine) m. Marie-Madeleine Audet (Innocent and Geneviève Lemelin) in Boucherville, QC in 1749.*

Jutras, probable variant of *Jutreau,* deriver from *Jutier,* origin uncertain. — Amer. **Jewtraw.**

— *Dominique* **Jutras** *dit Desrosiers (Pierre and Claude Boucher) from Paris (Île-de-France) m. Marie Niquet (Pierre and Françoise Lemoine) in Sorel, QC in 1684.*

K

Kentile, see **Quintal**.
Kenville, see **Quenneville**.
Kiah, see **Cadieux**.
King, see **Roy**.
Kinville, see **Quenneville**.
Kirby, see **Corbeil**.
Kirkey, see **Cartier**.
Kérouac, alteration of *Kervoac*, a placename in Finistère (Bretagne). — Amer. **Curwick**.
  *— Urbain-François Le Bihan, sieur de **Kervoac** (François-Joachim and Catherine Bi-*
  zien) from Huelgoat in Finistère (Bretagne) m. Louise Bernier (Jean and Geneviève Ca-
  ron) in Cap-Saint-Ignace, QC in 1732.

L

Labadie, from *Labadie* or *L'Abadie*, placenames in France. — Amer. **Laberdee, Laberdie.**

— *François **Labadie** (François and Marie Renoux) from Saint-Léger in Charente-Maritime (Poitou-Charentes) m. Jeanne Hébert (François and Anne Fauconnier) in L'Ange-Gardien, QC in 1671.*

Labaff, see **Leboeuf.**

Labare, see **Labarre.**

Labarge, see **Laberge.**

Labarre, either from *Labarre* or *La Barre*, placenames in France. — Amer. **Labare, Labor, Labore.**

— *Jacques Genest dit **Labarre** from France m. Catherine Doribeau in France c. 1670.*

Labbé, from *l'abbé* 'the abbott', an ironic nickname. — Amer. **Labay, Labby, Libby.**

— *Pierre **Labbé** dit Lacroix (François and Marie Forest) from La Ferté-Bernard in Sarthe (Pays de la Loire) m. Marguerite Meunier (Mathurin and Françoise Fafard) in Beaupré, QC in 1674.*

Labeaf, see **Leboeuf.**

Labean, see **Labine.**

Labeau, see **Lebeau.**

Labeef, Labeff, see **Leboeuf.**

Labelle, from *la belle* 'the beautiful one'. — Amer. **Labell, Lebelle.**

— *Guillaume **Labelle** (Jean and Marie Loué) from Saint-Benoît-d'Hébertot in Calvados (Basse-Normandie) m. Anne Charbonneau (Olivier and Marie Garnier) in Montréal, QC in 1671.*

Labeouf, see **Leboeuf.**

Laberdee, Laberdie, see **Labadie.**

Laberge, from *La Berge*, a placename in France. — Amer. **Labarge, Lebarge, Leberge.**

— *Robert **Laberge** (Jacques and Marie Poitevin) from Colomby-sur-Thaon in Calvados (Basse-Normandie) m. Françoise Gausse (Maurice and Marguerite Blée) in Château-Richer, QC in 1663.*

Labier, see **Lebire.**

Labine, origin undetermined. — Amer. **Labean, Lebean, Lebine.**

— *Claude Guédry dit Laverdure and **Labine** from France m. Marguerite Petitpas (Claude and Catherine Bugaret) in Acadia c. 1681.*

Lablanc, see **Leblanc.**

Lablue, see **Lebleu.**

Labo, Laboe, see **Lebeau.**

Laboeuf, see **Leboeuf.**

Labombarde, from *la bombarde* 'the bombard', the nickname of an artilleryman. — Amer. **Bombard, Labombard, Labonbard.**

— *André Bombardier dit* **Labombarde** *and Passepartout (Jean and Marie-Françoise Guillin) from Lille in Nord (Nord-Pas-de-Calais) m. Marguerite Demers (Jean-Baptiste and Cunégonde Masta) in Montréal, QC in 1706.*

Labonté, from *la bonté* '(the) goodness', a soldier's nickname. — Amer. **Goodness, Goodniss, Labonty, Labounty, Lebonte.**

— *Antoine Boudriau dit* **Labonté** *(Jean and Françoise Vau) from Sainte-Fortunade in Corrèze (Limousin) m. Jeanne Poutré (André and Jeanne Burel) in Pointe-aux-Trembles, QC in 1712.*

— *Jean Marot dit* **Labonté** *(Jean and Madeleine Travers) from Augé in Deux-Sèvres (Poitou-Charentes) m. Geneviève Boutin (Antoine and Geneviève Gandin) in Beauport, QC in 1690.*

Labor, Labore, see **Labarre.**

Labouff, see **Leboeuf.**

Labounty, see **Labonté.**

Labow, see **Lebeau.**

Labrec, see **Labrecque.**

Labrèche, from *La Brèche*, a placename in France. — Amer. **Labrash.**

— *Jean Dugas dit* **Labrèche** *(Jean and Marie Deshayes) from Pau in Pyrénées-Atlantiques (Aquitaine) m. Marie-Charlotte Vandandaigue (Joseph and Louise Chalifou) in Beauport, QC in 1708.*

Labrecque, variant of *La Brèque*, a placename in Seine-Maritime (Haute-Normandie). — Amer. **Labrack, Labrake, Labrec, Labreck, Lebreck.**

— *Pierre* **Labrecque** *(Jacques and Jeanne Baron) from Dieppe in Seine-Maritime (Haute-Normandie) m. Jeanne Chotard (Jacques and Suzanne Gabaret) in Château-Richer, QC in 1663.*

Labrie, from *La Brie*, a region situated to the east of the Parisian basin. — Amer. **Labree.**

— *Jean Mignault dit* **Labrie** *(Louis and Jeanne Chaillou) from Saint-Germain-Laxis in Seine-et-Marne (Île-de-France) m. Marie Boucher (Pierre and Marie-Anne Saint-Denis) in Château-Richer, QC in 1689.*

Labrière, from *La Brière*, a placename in France. — Amer. **Labrier, Labruyere, Labryer.**

— *Pierre Normand dit* **Labrière** *(Pierre and Marie Guillemain) from Saint-Martin-du-Vieux-Bellême in Orne (Basse-Normandie) m. Catherine Normand (Jean-Baptiste and Catherine Pajot) in Québec, QC in 1665.*

Labrue, see **Lebreux.**

Labrun, see **Lebrun.**

Labruyere, Labryer, see **Labrière.**

Labuff, see **Leboeuf.**

Labutte, apparently from *La Butte*, a placename in France. — Amer. **Labute.**

— *Pierre Chesne dit* **Labutte,** *son of Pierre from Reignac in Charente (Poitou-Charentes), m. Marie-Madeleine Roy (Pierre and Margurite Ouabankekoué) in Detroit, MI in 1728.*

Lacaillade, from *La Caillade*, a placename in France. — Amer. **Lackyard.**

— *Pierre Coderre dit* **Lacaillade** *from Sarrazac in Dordogne (Aquitaine) m. Marie-Louise Ferron (Jean and Élisabeth Patenaude) in Kingston, ON in 1732.*

Lacaille, from *La Caille,* a placename in France. — Amer. **Lacoy.**

— *Nicolas **Lacaille** (Nicolas and Anne Morlon) from Favières in Meurthe-et-Moselle (Lorraine) m. Brigitte Petit (Étienne and Élisabeth Favreau) in Boucherville, QC in 1762.*

Lacasse, from *(La) Casse,* a placename in France. — Amer. **Lacoss, Lacosse.**

— *Antoine Cassé/**Lacasse** (Noël and Michelle Durant) from Doué-la-Fontaine in Maine-et-Loire (Pays de la Loire) m. Françoise Pilois (François and Claudine Poullet) in Château-Richer, QC in 1665.*

Lacerte, probable alteration of *La Serte,* a placename in Deux-Sèvres (Poitou-Charentes). — Amer. **Lasarte.**

— *Jean-Guy Vacher dit **Lacerte** (Guillaume and Guillemine Vinsonneau) from Angers in Maine-et-Loire (Pays de la Loire) m. Marguerite Benoît (Gabriel and Marie-Anne Guédon) in Trois-Rivières, QC in 1685.*

Lachance, from *la chance* '(the) luck', apparently the nickname of a lucky individual. — Amer. **Lashon, Lashus, Lechance, Luck.**

— *Antoine Pépin dit **Lachance** (André and Jeanne Chevalier) from Le Havre in Seine-Maritime (Haute-Normandie) m. Marie Teste (Jean and Louise Talonneau) in Québec, QC in 1659.*

Lachesnaye, from *(La) Chesnaye,* a placename in France. — Amer. **Lacheney, Lachney.**

— *Charles Aubert, sieur de **La Chesnaye** (Jacques and Marie Goupy) from Amiens in Somme (Picardie) m. Marie-Louise Juchereau (Jean and Marie-Françoise Giffard) in Québec, QC in 1668.*

Lackyard, see **Lacaillade.**

Laclair, Laclaire, Laclare, Laclear, see **Leclerc.**

Lacombe, from *Lacombe* or *La Combe,* placenames in France. — Amer. **Lacomb.**

— *Pierre Balan dit **Lacombe** (Pierre and Perrine Courier) from Cantillac in Dordogne (Aquitaine) m. Renée Biret (Jean and Simone Périne) in Québec, QC in 1672.*

Lacoss, Lacosse, see **Lacasse.**

Lacount, see **Lecompte.**

Lacoy, see **Lacaille.**

Lacroix, from *Lacroix* or *La Croix,* placenames in France. — Amer. **Cross, Lacross, Lacrosse, Lecroix.**

— *Joseph/David **Lacroix** (Jacques and Antoinette Chambon) from Confolens in Charente (Poitou-Charentes) m. Barthélemie Maillou (Michel and Jeanne Mercier) in Québec, QC in 1681.*

— *Louis Quévillon dit **Lacroix,** descendant of Adrien from Saint-Ouen-le-Mauger in Seine-Maritime (Haute-Normandie), m. Catherine Benoit (Antoine and Véronique Nault) in Sorel, QC in 1803.*

Ladabauche, Ladabouche, Ladderbush, see **Ladébauche.**

Ladeau, see **Ledoux.**

Ladébauche, from *la débauche* '(the) debauchery', a nickname presumably referring to someone's lifestyle. — Amer. **Ladabauche, Ladabouche, Ladderbush.**

— *Jean Casavant dit **Ladébauche** (Jean and Marie Guignière) from Auch in Gers (Midi-Pyrénées) m. Jeanne Charpentier (Jean and Barbe Renaud) in Contrecoeur, QC in 1681.*

Ladieu, see **Ledoux.**

Ladouceur, from *la douceur* '(the) gentleness', a soldier's nickname. — Amer. **Ladoucer, Laducer.**

— *Pierre Martin dit* **Ladouceur** *(Jean and Anne Desmoulins) from Bergerac in Dordogne (Aquitaine) m. Marie-Anne Limousin (Hilaire and Antoinette Lefebvre) in Montréal, QC in 1696.*

Ladoux, see **Ledoux.**

Laduc, see **Leduc.**

Laducer, see **Ladouceur.**

Ladue, see **Ledoux.**

Laduke, see **Leduc.**

Ladurantaye, alteration of *La Durantaie* or *La Durantais*, placenames in France. — Amer. **Durand, Durant.**

— *Olivier Morel, sieur de* **Ladurantaye** *(Thomas and Alliette du Houssay) from Le Gâvre in Loire-Atlantique (Pays de la Loire) m. Françoise Duquet (Denis and Catherine Gauthier) in Québec, QC in 1670.*

Lafaire, see **Laferrière.**

Lafaive, see **Lefebvre.**

Lafalier, see **Laferrière.**

Lafar, see **Laforest.**

Lafarier, see **Laferrière.**

Lafarr, Lafarrer, see **Laforest.**

Lafave, Lafavor, Lafavre, see **Lefebvre.**

Lafayette, see **Lafeuillade.**

Laferier, see **Laferrière.**

Lafernier, see **Lafrenière.**

Laferrière, from *La Ferrière*, a placename in France. — Amer. **Lafaire, Lafalier, Lafarier, Laferier, Laferrier.**

— *Pierre Ferrière dit* **Laferrière** *(Jean and Suzanne Lacombe) from Sumène in Gard (Languedoc-Roussillon) m. Félicité Gibault (Gabriel and Félicité Dupuis) in Saint-Philippe, QC in 1778.*

Lafeuillade, from *La Feuillade*, a placename in France. — Amer. **Lafayette.**

— *Louis Javillon dit* **Lafeuillade** *from Limoges in Haute-Vienne (Limousin) m. Marie-Anne Fafard (Jean and Marguerite Couc) in Québec c. 1722.*

Laffond, see **Lafond.**

Laffra, Laffrey, see **Laforest.**

Laflair, see **Lafleur.**

Laflamme, from *la flamme* 'the flame', a soldier's nickname. — Amer. **Laflam.**

— *François Quemeneur dit* **Laflamme** *(Hervé and Françoise Joseph) from Ploudaniel in Finistère (Bretagne) m. Marie-Madeleine Chamberland (Simon and Marie Boileau) in Saint-François, Île d'Orléans, QC in 1700.*

Laflèche, from *La Flèche*, a placename in France. — Amer. **Laflesh.**

— *Pierre Richer dit* **Laflèche** *(Jean and Marie *Galardé) from Thouarcé in Maine-et-Loire (Pays de la Loire) m. Dorothée Brassard (Antoine and Françoise Méry) in Québec, QC in 1671.*

Lafleur, from *la fleur* 'the flower', a soldier's nickname. — Amer. **Laflair, Laflower,**

Lefleur, Leflour.

— *André Barsa dit **Lafleur** (Étienne and Léonarde *Choseau) from Auriat in Creuse (Limousin) m. Françoise Pilois (Gervais and Hélène Tellier) in Montréal, QC in 1669.*

Lafond, from *Lafond* or *La Fond*, placenames in France. — Amer. **Laffond, Lafoe.**

— *Étienne (de) **Lafond** (Pierre and Françoise Prieur) from Saint-Laurent-de-la-Barrière in Charente-Maritime (Poitou-Charentes) m. Marie Boucher (Gaspard and Nicole Lemaire) in Québec, QC in 1645.*

Lafontaine, either from *La Fontaine*, a placename in France, or from *la fontaine* 'the fountain', a soldier's nickname. — Amer. **Fontaine, Lafountain, Lafountaine.**

— *Jean-François Lariou dit **Lafontaine** (Jean and Catherine Brusquet) from Le Mas-d'Agenais in Lot-et-Garonne (Aquitaine) m. Catherine Mongeau (Pierre and Louise Dubois) in Québec, QC in 1674.*

— *Louis Robert dit **Lafontaine** (André and Catherine Bonin) from La Rochelle in Charente-Maritime (Poitou-Charentes) m. Marie Bourgery (Jean-Baptiste and Marie Gendre) in Trois-Rivières, QC in 1666.*

Laford, Lafore, see **Lefort.**

Laforest, from *Laforest* or *La Forest*, placenames in France. — Amer. **Lafar, Lafarr, Lafarrer, Laffra, Laffrey, Laforrest.**

— *Julien Joly dit **Laforest** from France m. Catherine Vanet (Charles and Catherine Magnan) in Québec c. 1698.*

— *François Tiriac dit **Laforest** (Jacques and Marie-Agnès Monigon) from Paris (Île-de-France) m. Marie-Madeleine Bénard (Jean and Marie-Madeleine Périllard) in Montréal, QC in 1748.*

Lafort, see **Lefort.**

Lafountain, Lafountaine, see **Lafontaine.**

Laframboise, from *la framboise* 'the strawberry', a soldier's nickname. — Amer. **Berry, Laframbois, Lafrombois, Lafromboise, Rasberry, Raspberry.**

— *Pierre Devoyau dit **Laframboise** (Léonard and Anne Letay) from Poitiers in Vienne (Poitou-Charentes) m. Marie-Jeanne Prévost (Jean and Françoise Leblanc) in Montréal, QC in 1706.*

— *Jean-Baptiste Lafoy dit **Laframboise** (Jean and Suzanne Michaud) from Amiens in Somme (Picardie) m. Marie-Charlotte Liénard (François-de-Sales and Marie-Agnès Bonhomme) in Beauharnois, QC in 1742.*

Lafrancis, Lafrancois, see **Lefrançois.**

Lafrenière, apparently from *La Frenière* or an alteration of *La Fresnière*, placenames in France. — Amer. **Ashley, Lafernier, Lafrania, Lafranier, Lafraniere, Lafrenere, Lafrenier, Lafrinier, Lafriniere.**

— *Joseph Baron dit Lupien and **Lafrenière**, son of Nicolas from Villenauxe-la-Grande in Aube (Champagne-Ardenne), m. (1) Marie-Anne Lemire (Jean-François and Françoise Foucault) in Québec in 1721; (2) Marie-Madeleine Sicard (Jean and Geneviève Raté) in Québec in 1741.*

— *Antoine Desrosiers dit **Lafresnière**, son of Antoine from Renaison in Loire (Rhône-Alpes), m. Marie-Renée Lepellé (Jean and Jeanne Isabel) in Champlain, QC in 1696.*

Lafrombois, Lafromboise, see **Laframboise.**

Lagacé, from *l'agacé* 'the excited one', a soldier's nickname. — Amer. **Lagassey, Lagassie, Legacy, Legassey.**

— *André Mignier dit* **Lagacé** *(Michel and Catherine Masson) from Le Bois-Plage-en-Ré in Charente-Maritime (Poitou-Charentes) m. Jacquette Michel (Jacques and Jeanne Dupont) in Québec, QC in 1668.*

Lagarry, Lagary, see **Légaré.**

Lagassey, Lagassie, see **Lagacé.**

Lagesse, Lagest, see **Dagesse.**

Lago, Lagoe, see **Legault.**

Lagoy, see **Lécuyer.**

Lagrandeur, from *la grandeur* '(the) height, tallness', a soldier's nickname. — Amer. **Grant.**

— *Joseph Grasset dit* **Lagrandeur** *(Jean and Dauphine Rouche) from Aramon in Gard (Languedoc-Roussillon) m. Françoise Boissel (Charles and Thérèse Daudelin) in Verchères, QC in 1761.*

Lagray, Lagree, see **Legris.**

Lagrenade, from *la grenade* 'the grenade', a soldier's nickname. — Amer. **Legnard.**

— *Jean-Baptiste Plantier dit* **Lagrenade** *(François and Jeanne Rivel) from Rivel in Aude (Languedoc-Roussillon) m. Marie-Josèphe Choquet (Nicolas and Marie-Anne Casavant) in Varennes, QC in 1760.*

Lagrew, see **Groulx.**

Lagro, see **Legros.**

Lagrou, see **Groulx.**

Lagrow, see **Legros.**

Lagüe, from *(La) Lagüe*, a placename in France. — Amer. **Lahue, Layaou, Layou.**

— *Michel* **Lagüe** *dit Sanscartier (Claude and Marie Merrain) from Orléans in Loiret (Centre) m. Catherine Leclerc (Guillaume and Marie-Thérèse Hunault) in Boucherville, QC in 1710.*

Lahaie, either from *La Haie*, a placename in France, or an alteration of *Lahey*, an anglicization of the Irish name *Ó Lathaigh*. — Amer. **Laha, Lahay, Lahie.**

— *Jacques-Charles (de)* **Lahaie** *dit Lajeunesse (Charles and Jeanne *Acolare) from Dunkerque in Nord (Nord-Pas-de-Calais) m. Marie-Claire Garand (Pierre and Marie-Josèphe Masson) in Saint-François-de-la-Rivière-du-Sud, QC in 1760.*

— *John Lahey/Jean* **Lahaie** *dit Hibernois (Thomas and Catherine Williams) from Tullow in Ireland m. Mary Swarton (John and Hannah Hibbard) in Québec, QC in 1697.*

Lahaye, from *La Haye*, a placename in France. — Amer. **Lahay, Lehay.**

— *Pierre Lepellé/Lepelé dit/sieur de* **Lahaye** *(Pierre and Jeanne Girardeau) from Hiers-Brouage in Charente-Maritime (Poitou-Charentes) m. Catherine Dodier (Sébastien and Marie Belhomme) in Trois-Rivières, QC in 1653.*

Lahie, see **Lahaie.**

Lahue, see **Lagüe.**

Laiguille, from *L'Aiguille*, a placename in France. — Amer. **Legue, Neadle, Needle.**

— *Jean Louismet dit* **Laiguille** *(Gilles and Cécile Dupuy) from Dunkerque in Nord (Nord-Pas-de-Calais) m. Marie-Catherine Marquet (François and Marie-Louise Galarneau) in Québec, QC in 1757.*

Lainé, alteration of *l'aîné* 'the eldest'. — Amer. **Laney.**

— *Bernard* **Lainé**/*Laisné dit Laliberté (Gilles and Luce Léonard) from Châtelaudren in Côtes-d'Armor (Bretagne) m. Anne Dionne (Antoine and Catherine Ivory) in Île d'Or-*

léans, QC c. 1679.

Lajambe, from *la jambe* 'the leg', a nickname of undetermined connotation. — Amer. **Lashomb, Lashombe, Lashum, Shum.**

— *Jean-Baptiste Pitre dit Lajambe, descendant of Jean from France, m. Élisabeth Vandandaigue (Joseph and Marie-Catherine Laliberté) in Saint-Régis, QC in 1824.*

Lajesse, see **Dagesse.**

Lajeunesse, from *la jeunesse* '(the) youth', a soldier's nickname. — Amer. **Lisherness, Young.**

— *Étienne Charles dit Lajeunesse (François and Colombe Regnault) from Villejuif in Val-de-Marne (Île-de-France) m. Madeleine Niel (Robert and Anne Lambert) in Trois-Rivières, QC in 1667.*

Lajoie, from *la joie* '(the) joy', the nickname of a cheerful individual. — Amer. **Lajoice, Lajoy, Lajoye, Lashaway, Lashua, Lashuay, Lashway, Laushway.**

— *Pierre Bernard dit Lajoie (Daniel and Marie Bertrand) from Pons in Charente-Maritime (Poitou-Charentes) m. Marguerite Durand (Pierre and Marie-Thérèse Mondin) in Montréal, QC in 1726.*

— *Jean-Baptiste Drogue dit Lajoie (Jean-Baptiste and Françoise Gros) from Tarascon in Bouches-du-Rhône (Provence-Alpes-Côte-d'Azur) m. Marie-Josèphe Lemoine (Noël and Jeanne Chauvin) in Saint-Charles-sur-Richelieu, QC in 1758.*

— *Mathias Masselot dit Lajoie (Claude and Barbe Merlin) from Châtenois in Vosges (Lorraine) m. Marie-Gertrude-Amable Demers (Joseph and Marie-Josèphe Poirier) in Chambly, QC in 1760.*

Lalancette, from *la lancette* 'the (small) lance', a soldier's nickname. — Amer. **Delancett, Delancette, Lancette.**

— *Pierre-Henri Lebreton dit Dubois and Lalancette (Jean-François and Marie-Jeanne Samson) from Rennes in Ille-et-Vilaine (Bretagne) m. Louise-Agnès Larchevêque (Jean and Angélique (de) Rainville) in Québec, QC in 1741.*

Laliberté, from *la liberté* '(the) freedom', a soldier's nickname. — Amer. **Freeman, Lalibert, Laliberty, Liberty.**

— *Pierre Alexandre dit Laliberté (Bernard and Perronne Desfaux) from Saint-Michel-Loubéjou in Lot (Midi-Pyrénées) m. Marie-Louise Leprince (Jean-Baptiste and Marie-Anne Blais) in Saint-François-du-Lac, QC in 1762.*

— *Gaspard Roireau/Roirou dit Laliberté from France m. Marguerite Hébert (Michel and Anne Galet) in Lotbinière, QC c. 1695.*

— *Nicolas Senet dit Laliberté (Pierre and Suzanne Varnier) from Vitry-le-François in Marne (Champagne-Ardenne) m. Marie-Gertrude Daunay (Antoine and Marie Richard) in Boucherville, QC in 1689.*

Lalonde, from *La Londe,* a placename in Normandie. — Amer. **Delane, Lalone.**

— *Jean (de) Lalonde dit Lespérance (Philippe and Jeanne Duval) from Le Havre in Seine-Maritime (Haute-Normandie) m. Marie Barbant (Alexandre and Marie Le Noble) in Québec in 1669.*

Lalumandière, alteration of *La Limandière,* a placename in Charente-Maritime. — Amer. **Lalumondiere.**

— *François Lalumandière/Lalumaudière dit Lafleur (François and Renée Frérot) from Saint-Jean-d'Angély in Charente-Maritime (Poitou-Charentes) m. Marie-Anne Morand (Antoine and Marie-Madeleine Poutré) in Montréal, QC in 1713.*

Lamar, see **Lamarre.**

Lamarche, from *la marche* 'the walk', a soldier's nickname. — Amer. **Walker.**

— *Jean Bricault dit **Lamarche** (Julien and Perrine Roussel) from Vay in Loire-Atlantique (Pays de la Loire) m. Marie Chénier (Jean and Jacqueline Sédilot) in Montréal, QC in 1674.*

Lamarre, alteration of *La Mare,* a placename in France. — Amer. **Lamar, Lamoore, Lamore.**

— *Louis (de) **Lamarre** dit Gasion (Adrien and Marie Lebec) from Pîtres in Eure (Haute-Normandie) m. Jeanne Garnier (Sébastien and Marie Roux) in Québec, QC in 1659.*

Lamay, see **Lemay.**

Lambert, from the Germanic name *Landberht* composed of *land* 'land' and *berht* 'bright'. — Amer. **Lumbra.**

— *Pierre **Lambert** (Jacques and Pierrette Bachelet) from Fourmetot in Eure (Haute-Normandie) m. Marie Normand (Jean and Anne Lelaboureur) in Québec, QC in 1680.*

Lamear, see **Lemire.**

Lamerand, see **Lamirande.**

Lamere, see **Lemire.**

Lamey, Lamie, see **Lamy.**

Lamica, see **Lamitié.**

Lamier, see **Lemire.**

Lamirande, from *La Mirande,* a placename in France. —Amer. **Lamerand, Lamirand, Lemerand, Lemerond, Lemirande.**

— *Pierre Dulignon, sieur de **La Mirande** (Théodore and Marthe Pasquet) from La Rochefoucaud in Charente (Poitou-Charentes) m. Marguerite (de) Gerlaise (Jean and Jeanne Trudel) in Louiseville, QC in 1703.*

Lamire, see **Lemire.**

Lamitié, from *l'amitié* '(the) friendship', probably a soldier's nickname. —Amer. **Lamica.**

— *Louis-Rémi Delief/Deliège/Liège dit **Lamitié** (Henri and Madeleine Labrosse) from Fismes in Marne (Champagne-Ardenne) m. Marie-Anne Perron (Nicolas and Marie-Françoise Arcand) in La-Baie-du-Febvre, QC in 1761.*

Lamoine, see **Lemoine.**

Lamonda, Lamonday, Lamondia, Lamondie, see **Normandin.**

Lamont, see **Lamothe.**

Lamontagne, from *la montagne* 'the mountain', a soldier's nickname. — Amer. **Lamountain.**

— *Joseph Rauch dit **Lamontagne** (Joseph and Catherine *Opermont) from Innsbruck in Austria m. Madeleine Giguère (Pierre and Madeleine Brouillard) in Yamaska, QC in 1789.*

Lamoore, see **Lamarre.**

Lamora, see **Lamoureux.**

Lamore, see **Lamarre.**

Lamoreaux, Lamoreux, Lamorey, Lamorie, see **Lamoureux.**

Lamothe, from *Lamothe* or *La Mothe,* placenames in France. — Amer. **Lamont, Lamott.**

— *Jacques Cauchon dit **Lamothe** (Jean and Jeanne Abraham) from Dieppe in Seine-*

Maritime (Haute-Normandie) m. Barbe-Delphine Tardif (Olivier and Barbe Émard) in Château-Richer, QC in 1661.

*— Alexis Lepellé dit **Lamothe**, grandson of Pierre from Hiers-Brouage in Charente-Maritime (Poitou-Charentes), m. Marie-Jeanne Bigot (François and Marie Bouchard) in Champlain, QC in 1710.*

Lamountain, see **Lamontagne.**

Lamoureux, from Old French *l'amoureux* 'the kindly one'. — Amer. **Lamora, Lamoreaux, Lamoreux, Lamorey, Lamorie, Lamoureaux, Lamouria, Lamourie, Lemorie.**

*— Louis **Lamoureux** from France m. Françoise Boivin in Québec c. 1668.*

Lamoy, see **Lemoy.**

Lamoyne, see **Lemoine.**

Lampron, alteration of *Laspron,* a probable variant of *Lapron,* a placename in Allier (Auvergne). — Amer. **Lamphron, Lampro, Lamproe.**

*— Jean Laspron/**Lampron** dit Lacharité (Jean and Marguerite Delaby) from La Charité-sur-Loire in Nièvre (Bourgogne) m. Anne-Michelle Renaud (Jean and Catherine de Saint-Amour) in Québec, QC in 1669.*

Lamudge, see **Limoges.**

Lamy, from Old French *l'amy* 'the trusted friend, lover, parent'. — Amer. **Lamey, Lamie.**

*— Pierre **Lamy** (Clément and Anne Tillant) from Ourville-en-Caux in Seine-Maritime (Haute-Normandie) m. Renée Suard (René and Jeanne ...) in L'Islet, QC in 1680.*

Lanaville, see **Laneuville.**

Lanaway, see **Lanoix.**

Lancette, see **Lalancette.**

Lancor, Lancour, Lancourt, see **Lincourt.**

Lanctôt, either an alteration of *Lanquetot,* a placename in Seine-Maritime (Haute-Normandie), or of *l'Anqueteau,* derived from *Anquetil,* from the Germanic name *Ansketill* composed of *Ans,* the name of a god, and *ketill* '(sacrificial) cauldron'. — Amer. **Lancto, Loncto, Longto, Longtoe, Lonto.**

*— Jean **Lanctôt**/Lanqueteau from France m. Marie Vien (Étienne and Marie Denot) in Québec c. 1652.*

Lander, see **Therrien.**

Landreville, from *Landreville,* a placename in France. — Amer. **Landerville, Launderville, Lunderville.**

*— Mathurin Gauthier dit **Landreville** (Pierre and Anne Lemaistre) from Legé in Loire-Atlantique (Pays de la Loire) m. Nicole Philippeau in Québec c. 1671.*

Landry, from the Germanic name *Landric* composed of *land* 'land' and *ric* 'powerful'. — Amer. **Landrey, Landrie, Laundra, Laundre, Laundrie, Laundry, Londeree, Londrie, Londry.**

*— Guillaume **Landry** (Mathurin and Damiane Desavis) from La Ventrouze in Orne (Basse-Normandie) m. Gabrielle Barré (Jacques and Judith Dusault/Dubeau) in Québec, QC in 1659.*

*— René **Landry** dit L'Aîné (Étienne and Catherine Goulet) from La Chaussée in Vienne (Poitou-Charentes) m. Perrine Bourg in Acadia c. 1645.*

*— René **Landry** dit Le Jeune from France m. Marie Bernard (... and Andrée Guyon) in*

Acadia c. 1659.

Laneau, see **Lanoue.**

Laneuville, from *Laneuville* or *La Neuville,* placenames in France. — Amer. **Lanaville, Naneville.**

— *Jacques Dehornay dit **Laneuville** (Jacques and Catherine Duval) from Dieppe in Seine-Maritime (Haute-Normandie) m. Marie Sivadier/Civadier (Louis and Agnès Olivier) in Saint-Laurent, Île d'Orléans, QC in 1702.*

Laney, see **Lainé.**

Langdeau, alteration of *Languedoc,* a former province in France. — Amer. **Langdo, Londo, Longdo.**

— *Alexandre Lacoste dit **Languedoc** (Olivier and Jeanne Bastide) from Saint-Julien-de-Cassagnas in Gard (Languedoc-Roussillon) m. Marguerite Deniau (Jean and Hélène Dodin) in Boucherville, QC in 1690.*

Lange, from *l'Ange,* from the Latin name *Angelus,* from Greek *angelos* 'messenger'. — Amer. **Longe.**

— *Ange Ossant dit **Lange,** grandson of Antoine from La Rochelle in Charente-Maritime (Poitou-Charentes), m. Marie-Anne Bonin (André and Marie-Angélique Pinard) in Sorel, QC in 1731.*

Langelier, from *l'Angelier,* from the Germanic name *Angilhari* composed of *Angil,* the name of a Germanic people, and *hari* 'army'. — Amer. **Langellier, Layaw, Layo.**

— *Sébastien **Langelier** (Michel and Catherine Bideau) from Fresquienne in Seine-Maritime (Haute-Normandie) m. Marie (de) Beauregard (Olivier and Philippe Ardouin) in Québec, QC in 1665.*

Langevin, from *l'Angevin,* the nickname of a native of Anjou, a former province in France. — Amer. **Langeway, Langway, Longevin, Longever, Longeway, Longver, Longway, Lonsway.**

— *Michel **Langevin** (Michel and Marguerite Hélie/Samson) from Paris (Île-de-France) m. Marguerite Guertin (Louis and Marie-Madeleine Chicoine) in Contrecoeur, QC in 1714.*

— *Jean Bergevin dit **Langevin** (Mathurin and Marie Tesnier) from Angers in Maine-et-Loire (Pays de la Loire) m. Marie Piton (Rémi and Marie *Poilen) in Québec, QC in 1668.*

— *René Bodinaud dit **Langevin** (André and Marie Trigory) from Chavagnes in Maine-et-Loire (Pays de la Loire) m. Geneviève Raymond (Joseph and Geneviève Landry) in Chambly, QC in 1784.*

— *Charles Citoleux/Sitoleux dit **Langevin** (Jean and Perrine *Baudissau) from Chambellay in Maine-et-Loire (Pays de la Loire) m. Marie-Louise Harel (Jean-François and Marie-Madeleine Brunet) in Montréal, QC in 1739.*

Langlade, apparently from *L'Anglade,* a placename in France. — Amer. **Longlade.**

— *Augustin Mouet, sieur de **Langlade,** grandson of Pierre from Castelsarrasin in Tarn-et-Garonne (Midi-Pyrénées), m. Domitilde Lafourche in Michillimackinac (Mackinaw City), MI c. 1723.*

Langlais, from *l'Anglais* 'the Englishman', the nickname of an individual from the United States. — Amer. **Langlay, Langley.**

— *Daniel Sargent/Louis-Philippe **Langlais** dit Sérien (Digory and Mary Oben) from Worcester, MA m. Marguerite Lavoie (Jean and Marie-Madeleine Boucher) in Rivière-*

Ouelle, QC in 1718.

Langlois, from Old French *l'Anglois* 'the Englishman'. — Amer. **Longley, Longua, Longway.**

— *Nicolas **Langlois** (Charles and Marie Cordier) from Yvetot in Seine-Maritime (Haute-Normandie) m. Élisabeth Cretel (Guillaume and Jeanne Godefroy) in Québec, QC in 1671.*

Langway, see **Langevin.**

Lanier, alteration of *Lasnier,* from Old French *l'asnier* 'the donkey driver'. — Amer. **Longey.**

— *Louis **Lasnier** dit Belhumeur (Pierre and Marie Robert) from Avignon in Vaucluse (Provence-Alpes-Côte-d'Azur) m. Marie-Anne Vêtu (Jacques-Philippe and Marie-Anne Laroche) in Chambly, QC in 1757.*

Lanoix, from *la noix* 'the nut', a soldier's nickname. — Amer. **Lanaway, Lanway, Lenaway, Leneway, Lenway.**

— *Louis Énouille/Dautrèpe dit **Lanoix**/Lanoie (Guillaume and Marie Ledoux) from Paris (Île-de-France) m. Marie-Madeleine Delaunay (Henri and Françoise Crête) in Québec, QC in 1712.*

Lanoue, from *La Noue,* a placename in France. — Amer. **Laneau, Lanoux, Lenoue.**

— *Pierre **Lanoue** from Brittany m. Jeanne Gautrot (François and Edmée Lejeune) in Acadia c. 1682.*

Lanthier, from the Germanic name *Landhari* composed of *land* 'land' and *hari* 'army'. — Amer. **Lonkey.**

— *Jacques **Lanthier** (Jacques and Catherine Picard) from Brûlain in Deux-Sèvres (Pays de la Loire) m. Catherine-Angélique Matou (Philippe and Marguerite Doucinet) in Montréal, QC in 1694.*

Lanway, see **Lanoix.**

Lapage, see **Lepage.**

Lapalme, from *La Palme,* a placename in France. — Amer. **Lapan, Lapanne, Lapham, Lappan.**

— *Pierre Janson dit **Lapalme** (Barthélemi and Jeanne Duvoisin) from Paris (Île-de-France) m. Ursule Rancin (Charles and Françoise Conflans) in Québec, QC in 1689.*

Laparch, Laparche, see **Laperche.**

Lapatra, see **Lapoterie.**

Lapean, see **Lépine.**

Lapearl, see **Laperle.**

Lapeer, see **Lapierre.**

Lapell, Lapelle, see **Lepellé.**

Lapensée, from *la pensée* 'the pansy', a soldier's nickname. — Amer. **Laponse, Laponsee, Laponsey, Laponsie.**

— *François Clauzier dit **Lapensée** (Marc and Françoise Dessaudes) from Moncontour in Côtes-d'Armor (Bretagne) m. Marie-Anne Desforges (Pierre and Marie Cardinal) in Pointe-Claire, QC in 1776.*

Laperche, from *Laperche* or *La Perche,* placenames in France. — Amer. **Laparch, Laparche.**

— *Jean-Baptiste **Laperche** dit Saint-Jean (Jean-Baptiste and Marguerite Cousineau) from Saint-Martin-de-Goyne in Gers (Midi-Pyrénées) m. Françoise Émery (Antoine* *and Marie Devault) in Boucherville, QC in 1700.*

Laperle, from *La Perle,* a placename in France. — Amer. **Lapearl.**

— *Mathurin Banlier dit **Laperle** from Poitiers in Vienne (Poitou-Charentes) m. Françoise Vernin (Jacques and ...) in Québec c. 1678.*

Lapete, see **Lepitre.**

Lapham, see **Lapalme.**

Lapierre, either from *Lapierre* or *La Pierre,* placenames in France, or from *la pierre* 'the stone', a soldier's nickname or derived from the name *Pierre.* — Amer. **Lapeer, Lapier, Stone.**

— *Pierre Mazuret dit **Lapierre** from France m. Angélique Végeard (Raymond and Marie-Charlotte Charron) in Verchères, QC in 1714.*

— *Pierre Marsan/Mersan dit **Lapierre** (Jean and Jacqueline de Vincent) from Rouen in Seine-Maritime (Haute-Normandie) m. Françoise Baiselat (Benjamin and Claude Prou) in Québec, QC in 1670.*

— *Pierre Meunier dit **Lapierre** (Bertrand and Madeleine Guibourg) from Rennes in Ille-et-Vilaine (Bretagne) m. Barbe Richaume (Pierre and Marthe Arnu) in Québec in 1675.*

Lapine, see **Lépine.**

Laplante, from *la plante* 'the plant', a soldier's nickname. — Amer. **Laplant, Planty, Plonty.**

— *Louis Badaillac dit **Laplante** from Périgueux in Dordogne (Aquitaine) m. Catherine Lawlor (Charles and Catherine Després) in Québec c. 1672.*

— *Jean-Baptiste (de) Labourlière dit **Laplante** (Jacques and Françoise Ferrande) from Niort in Deux-Sèvres (Poitou-Charentes) m. Catherine-Françoise Martin (Joachim and Anne-Charlotte Petit) in Saint-Pierre, Île d'Orléans, QC in 1697.*

— *Clément Lériger, sieur de **Laplante** (Paul and Mauricette du Souchet) from Gourville in Charente (Poitou-Charentes) m. Marie Roy (Pierre and Catherine Ducharme) in Laprairie, QC in 1700.*

Lapointe, either from *La Pointe,* a placename in France, or from *la pointe* 'the point', a soldier's nickname. — Amer. **Lapoint, Lepoint, Lepointe.**

— *Nicolas Audet dit **Lapointe** (Innocent and Vincente Roy) from Maulais in Deux-Sèvres (Poitou-Charentes) m. Madeleine Després (François and Madeleine Le Grand) in Sainte-Famille, Île d'Orléans, QC in 1670.*

— *Pierre Desautels dit **Lapointe** (Thomas and Marie Buisson) from Malicorne-sur-Sarthe in Sarthe (Pays de la Loire) m. (1) Marie Rémy (Nicolas and Marie *Vener) in Montréal, QC in 1666; (2) Catherine Lorion (Mathurin and Françoise Morinet) in Montréal, QC in 1676.*

— *Étienne Godard dit **Lapointe** (François and Louise Leriche) from Senlis in Oise (Picardie) m. Marie-Madeleine Lavoie (René and Anne Godin) in Beaupré, QC in 1687.*

Laponse, Laponsee, Laponsey, Laponsie, see **Lapensée.**

Laporte, from *Laporte* or *La Porte,* a placename in France. — Amer. **Laport.**

— *Jacques (de) **Laporte** dit Saint-Georges (Jacques and Marie Hamelin) from Nocé in Orne (Basse-Normandie) m. Nicole Duchesne (François and Marie Rolet) in Montréal, QC in 1657.*

Lapoterie, from *La Poterie,* a placename in France. — Amer. **Lapatra.**

— *Nicolas Godin/Gaudin dit **Lapoterie** (Nicolas and Catherine Allier) from Brest in Fi-*

nistère (Bretagne) m. Marie-Madeleine Gilbert (Étienne and Marguerite Thibault) in Québec, QC in 1723.

Lappan, see **Lapalme.**

Laprade, from *la prade* 'the meadow', a soldier's nickname. — Amer. **Laprad, Lapratt.**

— *Jean Régeas/Réjasse dit **Laprade** (Gilles and Marguerite Blanchet) from Maisonnais-sur-Tardoire in Haute-Vienne (Limousin) m. Marie Jamin (Julien and Marie Repoche) in Contrecoeur, QC in 1683.*

Laprel, see **April.**

Laprise, from *La Prise*, a placename in France. — Amer. **Lapress.**

— *Jean Daniau dit **Laprise** (Jean and Renée Brunet) from Niort in Deux-Sèvres (Poitou-Charentes) m. Françoise Rondeau (Pierre and Catherine Verrier) in Saint-Jean, Île d'Orléans, QC in 1686.*

Laquee, see **Lécuyer.**

Laquerre, from *La Querre*, a placename in France. — Amer. **Laquier, Laquiere, Laquire.**

— *Jean **Laquerre** dit Rencontre (Joseph and Marguerite Dubois) from Chavagnes-lès-Redoux in Vendée (Pays de la Loire) m. Marie Croiset (Pierre and Marie Brouard) in Québec in 1671.*

Lara, see **Laurent.**

Laraba, Larabee, see **Larrivée.**

Larabelle, from *L'Arabelle*, apparently an alteration of the given name *Annabelle*. — Amer. **Larabell.**

— *Louis Bluteau dit **L'Arabelle**, son of Jacques from Le Gué-de-Velluire in Vendée (Pays de la Loire), m. Geneviève Charland (Claude and Jeanne Pelletier) in Sainte-Famille, Île d'Orléans, QC in 1702.*

Laraby, see **Larrivée.**

Laramée, from *La Ramée*, a placename in France. — Amer. **Laramie, Larmay, Larmie.**

— *Jacques Fissiau dit **Laramée** (Antoine and Jeanne Millet) from Blois in Loir-et-Cher (Centre) m. Anne Monet (Antoine and Françoise Hurtault) in Pointe-aux-Trembles, QC in 1708.*

Laraux, see **L'Heureux.**

Laraway, see **Leroy.**

Lareau, origin undetermined. — Amer. **Lareaux, Laro, Laroe, Larow, Larowe, Larreau, Larro, Larrow.**

— *Jacques (de) **Lareau**/Laraue from Dieppe in Seine-Maritime (Haute-Normandie) m. Anne Fossé in France c. 1650.*

Larivière, either from *Larivière* or *La Rivière*, placenames in France. — Amer. **Lavere, Revier, Reviere, Rivers.**

— *Jacques Bernard, sieur de **Larivière** from France m. Marie-Madeleine Voyer (Pierre and Catherine Crampon) in Québec, QC in 1694.*

— *André Chapdelaine dit **Larivière** (Julien and Jeanne Le Masson) from Plomb in Manche (Basse-Normandie) m. Anne Chèvrefils (François and Marie Lamy) in Québec in 1691.*

— *Jacques Rivière dit **Larivière** (Gaspard and Catherine de Launay) from Rouen in*

Seine-Maritime (Haute-Normandie) m. Catherine Ménard (Jacques and Catherine Forestier) in Boucherville, QC in 1699.

Larmay, Larmie, see **Laramée.**

Laro, see **Lareau.**

Laroche, either from *Laroche* or *La Roche*, placenames in France. — Amer. **Larush, Stone.**

— *Innocent **Laroche** (Innocent and Marguerite Quoy) from Montmorency in Val-d'Oise (Île-de-France) m. Marie Harbour (Michel and Marie Constantineau) in Neuville, QC in 1689.*

— *Jean **Laroche** (Jean and Antoinette Larose) from Chef-Boutonne in Deux-Sèvres (Poitou-Charentes) m. Marie-Suzanne Turpin (Alexandre and Marie Gauthier) in Montréal, QC in 1723.*

Larocque, alteration of either *Rocquebrune* or *Roquebrune*, placenames in France. — Amer. **Larock, Lerock, Lerocque, Rock.**

— *Philibert Couillaud dit **Rocquebrune** from Nevers in Nièvre (Bourgogne) m. Catherine Laporte (Jacques and Nicole Duchesne) in Québec c. 1675.*

Laroe, see **Lareau.**

Laroux, see **Roux.**

Larow, Larowe, Larreau, see **Lareau.**

Larrivée, alteration of *Arrivé*, from *arrivé* 'arrived', probably the nickname of a newcomer in a particular place. — Amer. **Laraba, Larabee, Laraby, Larrabee, Larvey.**

— *Jean **Arrivé** from Luçon in Vendée (Pays de la Loire) m. Jeanne Barbereau in Québec c. 1666.*

Larro, Larrow, see **Lareau** and **Laurent.**

Larue, see **Leroux.**

Larush, see **Laroche.**

Larvey, see **Larrivée.**

Lasage, Lasarge, see **Lesage.**

Lasarte, see **Lacerte.**

Lashaway, see **Lajoie.**

Lashomb, Lashombe, see **Lajambe.**

Lashon, see **Lachance.**

Lashua, Lashuay, see **Lajoie.**

Lashum, see **Lajambe.**

Lashus, see **Lachance.**

Lashway, see **Lajoie.**

Lassard, Lasser, Lassor, see **Lessard.**

Latarte, see **Letarte.**

Latender, Latendre, see **Letendre.**

Latendresse, from Old French *la tendresse* '(the) youth', a soldier's nickname. — Amer. **Latendress, Latondras.**

— *Jean-Baptiste Chebrou dit **Latendresse** (Jean and Marie Petit) from Gençay in Vienne (Poitou-Charentes) m. Madeleine Jarret (Joseph and Marie-Charlotte Lemaire) in Verchères, QC in 1765.*

Latlip, Latlippe, see **Latulippe.**

Latno, see **Létourneau.**

Latondras, see **Latendresse.**

Latourelle, apparently from *La Tourelle*, a placename in France. — Amer. **Latrell, Latterell, Lattrell.**

— *Jean-Baptiste Dubord dit **Latourelle**, son of Julien from Thiviers in Dordogne (Aquitaine), m. Marie Houray (René and Denise Damané) in Champlain, QC in 1709.*

Latourneau, see **Létourneau.**

Latreille, either from *Latreille* or *La Treille*, placenames in France, or from *la treille* 'the vine arbor', a soldier's nickname. — Amer. **Latray.**

— *Léonard Lalande dit **Latreille** (Jean and Marie Larivière) from Magnac-Laval in Haute-Vienne (Poitou-Charentes) m. Gabrielle Beaune (Jean and Marie-Madeleine Bourgery) in Lachine, QC in 1698.*

Latrell, Latterell, Lattrell, see **Latourelle.**

Latulippe, alteration of *la tulipe* 'the tulip', a soldier's nickname. — Amer. **Latlip, Latlippe, Tulip.**

— *Michel Quéret dit **Latulippe** (Michel and ...) from Aix-en-Provence in Bouches-du-Rhône (Provence-Alpes-Côte-d'Azur) m. Françoise Davenne (Charles and Marie Denoyon) in Québec c. 1697.*

Laturno, see **Létourneau.**

Launderville, see **Landreville.**

Laundra, Laundre, Laundrie, Laundry, see **Landry.**

Laurent, from the Latin name *Laurentius*, derived from Laurentum, an ancient Italian city. — Amer. **Lara, Larro, Larrow, Lawrence.**

— *Antoine de Gerlaise dit Saint-Amand and **Laurent**, descendant of Jean-Jacques from Liège in Belgium, m. Marguerite Laviolette (Jacques and Marguerite Duverger) in Trois-Rivières, QC in 1770.*

Laushway, see **Lajoie.**

Lauzon, probable alteration of *(Le) Lozon*, a placename in Manche (Basse-Normandie).
— Amer. **Lauson, Losaw, Loso, Lozen, Lozo, Lozon.**

— *Gilles **Lauzon** (Pierre and Anne Boivin) from Caen in Calvados (Basse-Normandie) m. Marie Archambault (Jacques and Françoise Tourault) in Montréal, QC in 1656.*

Lavac, Lavack, Lavacque, see **Levac.**

Lavake, see **Lévesque.**

Lavalette, see **Laviolette.**

Lavallée, from *La Vallée* or an alteration of *Vallée*, placenames in France. — Amer. **Lavalla, Lavalley, Lavallie, Lavally, Lavelle, Lavellee, Levallee, Lovely.**

— *Jean **Lavallée** dit Petit-Jean from France m. Marguerite Dusson in Québec c. 1671.*

— *Isaac/Étienne Paquet/Pasquier dit **Lavallée** (Mathurin and Marie Fremillon) from Montaigu in Vendée (Pays de la Loire) m. Élisabeth Meunier (Mathurin and Françoise Fafard) in Château-Richer, QC in 1670.*

— *Pierre Vallée dit **Lavallée** (Pierre and Madeleine Dumesnil) from Saint-Saëns in Seine-Maritime (Haute-Normandie) m. Thérèse Leblanc (Léonard and Marie Riton) in Québec, QC in 1665.*

Lavallette, see **Laviolette.**

Lavalley, Lavallie, see **Lavallée** and **Léveillé.**

Lavally, see **Lavallée.**

Lavandier, from Old French *lavandier* 'launderer'. — Amer. **Lavangie, Levangie.**

— Antoine **Lavandier** *from Avranches in Manche (Basse-Normandie) m. Françoise La-vergne (Pierre and Anne Bernon) in Port Toulouse (St. Peter's), NS c. 1732.*

Lavanway, see **Livernois.**

Lavaque, see **Lévesque.**

Lavarn, see **Lavergne.**

Lavarnway, see **Livernois.**

Lavassaur, Lavasser, Lavasseur, see **Levasseur.**

Laveck, see **Lévesque.**

Laveille, see **Léveillé.**

Lavelle, Lavellee, see **Lavallée.**

Lavene, see **Lavigne.**

Laverdure, from *la verdure* 'the greenery', a soldier's nickname. — Amer. **Lavenger.**

— *François Riquet/Riquier dit* **Laverdure** *(Jacques and Michelle Frérard) from Saint-Léger-Dubosq in Calvados (Basse-Normandie) m. Marie-Anne Renaud (Pierre and Françoise Desportes) in Montréal, QC in 1699.*

Lavere, see **Larivière.**

Lavergne, either from *Lavergne* or *La Vergne*, placenames in France. — Amer. **Lavarn, Laverne.**

— *Laurent Buy dit* **Lavergne** *(Pierre and Marie-Françoise ...) from Saint-Jean-de-Côle in Dordogne (Aquitaine) m. Denise Anthoine (François and Guillemette Piro) in Québec in 1670.*

Lavernway, see **Livernois.**

Lavigne, either from *Lavigne* or *La Vigne*, placenames in France, or from *la vigne* 'the vine', a soldier's nickname. — Amer. **Lavene, Lavine, Levigne, Levine.**

— *Jean Brodeur dit* **Lavigne** *(Jean and Françoise Frogeret) from Nieul-le-Dolent in Vendée (Pays de la Loire) m. Marie-Anne Messier (Michel and Anne Lemoine) in Boucherville, QC in 1679.*

— *André Poutré dit* **Lavigne** *(Pierre and Philipotte Racquet) from Valenciennes in Nord (Nord-Pas-de-Calais) m. Jeanne Burel (Daniel and Anne Le Suisse) in Québec, QC in 1667.*

Laviolette, from *la violette* 'the violet', a soldier's nickname. — Amer. **Lavalette, Lavallette, Lovelette, Lovellette.**

— *Guillaume Tougas/Tougard dit* **Laviolette** *(Guillaume and Marie Labbé) from Fatouville in Eure (Haute-Normandie) m. Marie Brazeau (Nicolas and Perrette Billard) in Montréal, QC in 1698.*

Lavoie, from *La Voie*, a placename in France. — Amer. **Lavoy, Laware, Leavitt, Leavoy, Levoy.**

— *Pierre (de)* **Lavoie**/*Lavoye (Pierre and Élisabeth *Vadois) from Aytré in Charente-Maritime (Poitou-Charentes) m. Jacquette Grignon (Pierre and Simone Grisot) in France c. 1650.*

Lawrence, see **Laurent.**

Lawya, Lawyea, see **Loyer.**

Layaou, see **Lagüe.**

Layaw, Layo, see **Langelier.**

Layou, see **Lagüe.**

Lazette, see **Lizotte.**

Leaf, see **Bellefeuille.**

Leanna, see **Lyonnais.**

Leasia, see **Lizé.**

Leavery, see **Lefebvre.**

Leavitt, Leavoy, see **Lavoie.**

Lebarge, see **Laberge.**

Lebean, see **Labine.**

Lebeau, alteration of *Bau,* from the Germanic name *Bavo.* — Amer. **Labeau, Labo, La-boe, Labow, Lebo, Leboe.**

— *Jean Bau/Lebeau dit Lalouette (Mathurin and Louise Garatte) from Saint-Jean-de-Monts in Vendée (Pays de la Loire) m. Étiennette Loret (Jean and Françoise Lefroy) in Boucherville, QC in 1672.*

Lebel, either from *Le Bel,* a placename in France, or from Old French *le bel* 'the handsome one'. — Amer. **Bell, Lebell.**

— *Nicolas Lebel (Clément and Françoise Lagnel) from Illeville-sur-Montfort in Eure (Haute-Normandie) m. Thérèse Mignault (Jean and Louise Cloutier) in Château-Richer, QC in 1665.*

Lebelle, see **Labelle.**

Leboeuf, see **Leboeuf.**

Leberge, see **Laberge.**

Lebine, see **Labine.**

Lebire, probable alteration of *Debuire,* from *de Buire* 'from Buire', a placename in France. — Amer. **Labier.**

— *Narcisse Bulteau dit Lebire, descendant of Noël and Marie-Marguerite Debuire from Rouville in Oise (Picardie), m. Josette Diel (André and Josette-Louise Lussier) in Saint-Constant, QC in 1835.*

Leblanc, from *le blanc* 'the white one', the nickname of an individual with very blond hair. — Amer. **Lablanc, White.**

— *Antoine Leblanc dit Jolicoeur (Martin and Marie *Flaniau)) from Noyon in Oise (Picardie) m. Élisabeth Roy (Antoine and Simone Gaultier) in Sainte-Famille, Île d'Orléans, QC in 1670.*

— *Daniel Leblanc from France m. Françoise Gaudet (Jean and ...) in Acadia c. 1650.*

Lebleu, probable alteration of the German name *Blau,* from *blau* 'blue', the nickname of an individual who usually wore blue clothing. — Amer. **Lablue, Leblue.**

— *Jérémie Lebleu from Germany m. Victoire Maillot (Henri-Vincent and Louise Pépin) in Gentilly, QC in 1812.*

Lebo, Leboe, see **Lebeau.**

Leboeuf, from *le boeuf* 'the bull', the nickname of a strong or hefty individual. — Amer. **Labaff, Labeaf, Labeef, Labeff, Labeouf, Laboeuf, Labouff, Labuff, Lebeouf, Lebouef, Lebuff.**

— *Jacques Leboeuf (Thomas and Nicole Gazeau) from Ciré-d'Aunis in Charente-Maritime (Poitou-Charentes) m. (1) Anne Javelot (André and Séphora Lescure) in Québec, QC in 1667; (2) Antoinette Lenoir (Jean and Antoinette Pirois) in Québec, QC in 1669.*

Lebonte, see **Labonté.**

Lebouef, see **Leboeuf.**

Lebreck, see **Labrecque.**

Lebreux, alteration of *Breux,* a placename in France. — Amer. **Labrue.**

— *François **Breux**/L'Hébreux (Claude and Madeleine Lecompte) from Les Biards in Manche (Basse-Normandie) m. Ursule Caouet (Claude and Marie-Catherine Grondin) in Cap-Saint-Ignace, QC in 1760.*

Lebrun, from *le brun,* same origin as **Bruneau.** — Amer. **Brine, Brown, Labrun, O'Brien.**

— *Vincent **Brun**/**Lebrun** from La Chaussée in Vienne (Poitou-Charentes) m. Renée Breau in Acadia c. 1644.*

Lebuff, see **Leboeuf.**

Lechance, see **Lachance.**

Leclerc, from *le clerc* 'the clerk', the nickname of a scribe. — Amer. **Laclair, Laclaire, Laclare, Laclear, Leclare.**

— *Guillaume **Leclerc** (Antoine and Marie Hérambourg) from Rouen in Seine-Maritime (Haute-Normandie) m. Marie-Thérèse Hunault (Toussaint and Marie Lorgueil) in Montréal, QC in 1676.*

— *Jean **Leclerc** dit Francoeur (Jean and Perrine Merceron) from Nantes in Loire-Atlantique (Pays de la Loire) m. Marie-Madeleine Langlois (Jean and Charlotte-Françoise Bélanger) in Saint-Pierre, Île d'Orléans, QC in 1691.*

Lecompte, variant of *Lecomte,* from *le comte* 'the count', an ironic nickname. — Amer. **Lacount, Lecount.**

— *Pierre Rouillard dit **Lecompte,** descendant of Antoine from Saint-Cosme-en-Vairais in Sarthe (Pays de la Loire), m. Thérèse Lemire (Jean-François and Françoise Niquet) in Baie-du-Febvre, QC in 1764.*

Lecoq, either from *Le Coq,* a placename in France, or from *le coq* 'the rooster', the nickname of a conceited individual or a womanizer. — Amer. **Lacoe.**

— *Jean-Baptiste **Lecoq** dit Ladouceur (Jean and Marguerite Dumesnil) from Rouen in Seine-Maritime (Haute-Normandie) m. Jeanne Houatté (Pierre and Catherine-Angélique Geoffroy) in Fort-Saint-Frédéric (Crown Point), NY in 1757.*

Lecount, see **Lecompte.**

Lecroix, see **Lacroix.**

Lécuyer, from *l'écuyer* 'the squire'. — Amer. **Lagoy, Laquee, Lequier, Spooner.**

— *Antoine **Lécuyer**/Lescuyer from France m. Anne Rabady in Québec c. 1671.*

— *Pierre **Lécuyer**/Lescuyer (René and Marguerite *Reingeaude) from Fontenay-le-Comte in Vendée (Pays de la Loire) m. Marie Juillet (Blaise and Anne-Antoinette de Liercourt) in Montréal, QC in 1670.*

Ledeau, see **Ledoux.**

Ledger, see **Léger.**

Ledoux, either from *Le Doux,* a placename in France, or from *le doux* 'the mild-natured one', the nickname of a pleasant, kindly individual. — Amer. **Ladeau, Ladieu, Ladoux, Ladue, Ledeau, Ledou, Ledue.**

— *Louis **Ledoux** (Louis and Marie Provost) from Le Mans in Sarthe (Pays de la Loire) m. Marie Valiquet (Jean and Renée Loppé) in Montréal, QC in 1679.*

Leduc, from *le duc* 'the duke', an ironic nickname. — Amer. **Laduc, Laduke, Leduke.**

— *Jean **Leduc** (Jean and Cécile Le Chaperon) from Igé in Orne (Basse-Normandie) m. Marie Souligny (Élie and Marie Foulet) in Montréal, QC in 1652.*

— *René **Leduc** (Vincent and Urbaine Renoult) from Brézé in Maine-et-Loire (Pays de* *la Loire) m. Anne Gendreau (Nicolas and Perrine Buet) in Québec, QC in 1664.*

Ledue, see **Ledoux.**

Leduke, see **Leduc.**

Lefebvre, from Old French *le febvre* 'the blacksmith'. — Amer. **Bean, Beane, Lafaive, Lafave, Lafavor, Lafavre, Leavery, Lefave, Lefeber.**

— *Jean-Baptiste **Lefebvre** dit Saint-Jean (Geoffroy and Jeanne Mille) from Amiens in Somme (Picardie) m. Cunégonde Gervaise (Jean and Anne Archambault) in Montréal, QC in 1676.*

— *Louis **Lefebvre** dit Lacroix (Mathieu and Anne Lefrançois) from Paris (Île-de-France) m. Catherine Ferré (Pierre and Marguerite Ferrier) in Québec in 1667.*

— *Pierre **Lefebvre** (Pierre and Jeanne *Cutiloup) from Sceaux in Hauts-de-Seine (Île-de-France) m. Jeanne Auneau in Québec c. 1646.*

— *Pierre **Lefebvre** (Nicolas and Marie *Vauvorin) from Villers-sur-Mer in Calvados (Basse-Normandie) m. Marie Châtaigné (Nicolas and Catherine *Sionnel) in Québec, QC in 1656.*

— *Pierre **Lefebvre** (Robert and Jeanne Autin) from Bois-Guillaume in Seine-Maritime (Haute-Normandie) m. Marguerite Gagné (Pierre and Marguerite Rosée) in Laprairie, QC in 1673.*

— *Pierre **Lefebvre** dit Ladouceur (Guillaume and Marie *Grandeval) from Grez-en-Bouère in Mayenne (Pays de la Loire) m. Marie Marcot (Nicolas and Martine *Tavrey) in Neuville, QC in 1688.*

— *Jean-Baptiste-Étienne Bouffard dit **Lefebvre**, descendant of Jacques from Rouen in Seine-Maritime (Haute-Normandie), m. Marie-Adélaïde Poissant (Pascal and Catherine Bincette) in Laprairie, QC in 1836.*

Lefleur, Leflour, see **Lafleur.**

Lefort, either from *Le Fort*, a placename in France, or from *le fort* 'the strong one', the nickname of a powerful individual. — Amer. **Laford, Lafore, Lafort.**

— *Jean **Lefort** dit Laprairie (Isaac and Anne Tibaud) from Saint-Jean-d'Angély in Charente-Maritime (Poitou-Charentes) m. Marguerite-Françoise Moreau (François and Françoise Gardien) in Laprairie, QC in 1696.*

Lefrançois, from Old French *le François*, the nickname of an individual from the Île-de-France region. — Amer. **Fransway, Lafrancis, Lafrancois.**

— *Charles **Lefrançois** (Charles and Suzanne Montigny) from Muchedent in Seine-Maritime (Haute-Normandie) m. Marie-Madeleine Triot (Jacques and Catherine Guichart) in Québec, QC in 1658.*

Legacy, see **Lagacé.**

Légaré, from Old French *l'esgaré* 'the troubled, abandoned, lost one'. — Amer. **Lagarry, Lagarry.**

— *Nicolas **Légaré** (Gilles and Marguerite Fontaine) from Paris (Île-de-France) m. Anne Dupré (Antoine and Marie-Jeanne Guérin) in Québec, QC in 1690.*

Legassey, see **Lagacé.**

Legault, from *Le Gault*, a placename in France. — Amer. **Lago, Lagoe, Lego.**

— *Noël **Legault** dit Deslauriers (Roch and Marie Le Scour) from Kérinot in Finistère (Bretagne) m. Marie Bénard (Mathurin and Marguerite Viard) in Montréal, QC in 1698.*

Léger, from the Germanic name *Leudgari* composed of *leud* 'people' and *gari* 'spear'. —

Amer. **Ledger**.

— *Pierre Léger dit Parisien (Pierre and Marguerite *Dendase) from Paris (Île-de-France) m. Jeanne Boilard (Jean and Jeanne Maranda) in Québec, QC in 1706.*

Legnard, see **Lagrenade**.

Lego, see **Legault**.

Legraw, see **Legros**.

Legris, either from *Le Gris*, a placename in France, or from *le gris* 'the gray-haired one'. — Amer. **Lagray, Lagree, Legray, Legree**.

— *Adrien Legris dit Lépine (Guillaume and Marie Leclerc) from Paris (Île-de-France) m. Marie-Françoise Branche (René and Marie Varin) in Québec, QC in 1686.*

Legros, from *le gros* 'the big one', the nickname of a stout individual. — Amer. **Lagro, Lagrow, Legraw, Legrow**.

— *Antoine Gros/Legros dit Laviolette (Jean and Marguerite Aupy) from Bourbonne-les-Bains in Haute-Marne (Champagne-Ardenne) m. Jacqueline Aubry (Marin and Anne Leroux) in Québec, QC in 1670.*

— *Pierre Legros dit Saint-Pierre (Jean-Claude and Jeanne Coulardeau) from Roulans in Doubs (Franche-Comté) m. Marie-Françoise Foisy (François and Marie-Élisabeth Végeard) in Verchères, QC in 1761.*

Legue, see **Laiguille**.

Lehay, see **Lahaye**.

Lehman, see **Lemelin**.

Lejeune, from *le jeune* 'the youngster', a nickname serving to differentiate a son from his father or the youngest son from his brothers. — Amer. **Young**.

— *Pierre Lejeune dit Briard from France m. ... Doucet (Germain and ...) in Port-Royal, NS c. 1650.*

Lemay, from *Le May*, a placename in France. — Amer. **Lamay**.

— *Michel Lemay (François and Marie Gaschet) from Chênehutte-Trèves-Cunault in Maine-et-Loire (Pays de la Loire) m. Marie Duteau (Pierre and Jeanne Perrin) in Trois-Rivières, QC in 1659.*

Lemelin, from *le Melin* or *l'Emelin*, from the Germanic name *Amalin*, derived from *amal* 'labor'. — Amer. **Abner, Lehman, Lemlin, Lemna, Lemnah, Lemner**.

— *Jean Lemelin dit (Le) Tourangeau (Noël and Françoise Mélaine) from Chartres in Eure-et-Loir (Centre) m. Marguerite Brassard (Antoine and Françoise Méry) in Québec, QC in 1658.*

Lemerand, see **Lamirande**.

Lemere, see **Lemire**.

Lemerond, see **Lamirande**.

Lemier, see **Lemire**.

Lemieux, from *le mieux*, probably from Old French *miels* 'the best one'. — Amer. **Betters**.

— *Gabriel Lemieux (Thomas and Anne Le Cornu) from Rouen in Seine-Maritime (Haute-Normandie) m. (1) Marguerite Leboeuf (Guillaume and Marguerite Millau) in Québec, QC in 1658; (2) Marthe Beauregard (Jean and Marie Desmarais) in Québec, QC in 1671.*

Lemirande, see **Lamirande**.

Lemire, from Old French *le mire* 'the physician'. — Amer. **Lamear, Lamere, Lamier,**

Lamire, Lemere, Lemier.
— *Jean* **Lemire** *(Mathurin and Jeanne Vanier) from Rouen in Seine-Maritime (Haute-Normandie) m. Louise Marsolet (Nicolas and Marie Barbier) in Québec, QC in 1653.*

Lemlin, Lemna, Lemnah, Lemner, see Lemelin.

Lemoi, see Lemoy.

Lemoine, from *le moine* 'the monk', an ironic nickname. — Amer. **Lamoine, Lamoyne.**
— *Louis Hus dit* **Lemoine,** *descendant of Paul from Montigny in Seine-Maritime (Haute-Normandie), m. Marie-Josèphe Desrosiers (Antoine and Marie-Anne Saint-Yves) in Sorel, QC in 1758.*

Lemorie, see Lamoureux.

Lemoy, from *Le Moy*, a placename in France. — Amer. **Lamoy, Lemoi.**
— *Pierre Lemois/***Lemoy** *(Pierre and Jeanne Pierson) from Ancemont in Meuse (Lorraine) m. Marie-Josèphe Rougeau (Jacques and Marie-Josèphe Coulon) in Québec, QC in 1752.*

Lenaway, see Lanoix.

Leneau, see Luneau.

Leneway, see Lanoix.

Leno, see Gélineau.

Lenoue, see Lanoue.

Lenway, see Lanoix.

Leo, see Charpentier.

Léonard, from the Germanic name *Leonhard* composed of *leon* 'lion' and *hard* 'hard, strong'. — Amer. **Yennard, Yenor.**
— *Joseph Simon dit* **Léonard,** *grandson of Jean from Saint-Sorlin-de-Conac in Charente-Maritime (Poitou-Charentes), m. Marie-Renée Petit (Nicolas and Marie Reguindeau) in Varennes, QC in 1714.*

Lepage, from *le page* 'the pageboy'. — Amer. **Lapage, Page, Paige.**
— *Antoine Pagé/***Lepage** *dit Saint-Antoine from France m. Madeleine Colin in Québec c. 1698.*
— *Louis* **Lepage** *(Étienne and Nicole Berthelot) from Ouanne in Yonne (Bourgogne) m. Sébastienne Loignon (Pierre and Françoise Roussin) in Île d'Orléans, QC in 1667.*

Lepellé, alteration of *le pelé* 'the bald one'. — Amer. **Lapell, Lapelle.**
— *Pierre Lepellé/***Lepelé** *dit ou sieur de Lahaye (Pierre and Jeanne Girardeau) from Hiers-Brouage in Charente-Maritime (Poitou-Charentes) m. Catherine Dodier (Sébastien and Marie Belhomme) in Trois-Rivières, QC c. 1653.*

Lépine, either from *Lépine* or *L'Épine*, placenames in France, or from *l'épine* 'the thorn', a soldier's nickname. — Amer. **Lapean, Lapine.**
— *Gabriel Bérard dit* **Lépine** *(Pierre and Isabelle Guillermain) from Château-du-Loir in Sarthe (Pays de la Loire) m. Geneviève Hayot (Jean and Louise Pelletier) in Québec in 1673.*
— *Nicolas Jolive dit* **Lépine** *(Guillaume and Julienne Monger) from Saint-Maugan in Ille-et-Vilaine (Bretagne) m. Catherine Morin (Jacques and Louise Garnier) in Montréal, QC in 1693.*

Lepitre, alteration of **Pitre.** — Amer. **Lapete.**
— *François Pitre/***Lepitre,** *descendant of Jean from France, m. Antoinette Lupien (Jean-Baptiste and Marie-Antoinette Pinard) in Nicolet, QC in 1750.*

Lepoint, Lepointe, see **Lapointe.**

Lequier, see **Lécuyer.**

Lerette, see **Lirette.**

Lerock, Lerocque, see **Larocque.**

Leroux, from *le roux* 'the redhead'. — Amer. **Larue, Leroue, Wheeler.**

— *François Leroux dit Cardinal (Jean and Jeanne Leblanc) from Senillé in Vienne (Poitou-Charente) m. Marie Renaud (Jean and Catherine Gauthier) in Québec, QC in 1668.*

Leroy, either from *Le Roy*, a placename in France, or a variant of *le roi* 'the king', an ironic nickname. — Amer. **Laraway.**

— *Siméon Roy/Leroy dit Ody/Audy (Richard and Gillette Jacquet) from Créances in Manche (Basse-Normandie) m. Claude Deschalets (François and Jacquette Chevallereau) in Québec, QC in 1668.*

Lesage, from *le sage* 'the wise man'. — Amer. **Lasage, Lasarge.**

— *Jean-Baptiste Lesage (Jean and Marguerite Roussel) from Beaumont-le-Roger in Eure (Haute-Normandie) m. Marie-Josèphe (de) Gerlaise (Jean and Jeanne Trudel) in Trois-Rivières, QC in 1709.*

Lescarbeau, alteration of *Lescarbot*, from *l'escarbot* 'the beetle', a nickname related to some characteristic of this insect. — Amer. **Scarbeau, Scarbo.**

— *Jean Lescarbot dit Beauceron (Jean and Marie *Pilluasdier) from Châteaudun in Eure-et-Loir (Centre) m. Anne Beaudoin (Jean and Marie-Charlotte Chauvin) in Pointe-aux-Trembles, QC in 1683.*

Lespérance, from *l'espérance* '(the) hope', a soldier's nickname. — Amer. **Hope.**

— *Jean-Baptiste Rochereau dit Lespérance (Bernard and Marguerite Durand) from Bordeaux in Gironde (Aquitaine) m. Jeanne-Élisabeth Déry (Maurice and Madeleine Philippeau) in Charlesbourg, QC in 1712.*

— *Jean-Baptiste Talon dit Lespérance (Paul and Marie Bonneau) from Gensac in Gironde (Aquitaine) m. Dorothée Bacon (Joseph and Dorothée Cloutier) in Château-Richer, QC in 1755.*

Lessard, from *Lessard, Lessart, L'Essard* or *L'Essart*, placenames in France. — Amer. **Lassard, Lasser, Lassor, Lessor, Lessert.**

— *Étienne (de) Lessard/Lessart (Jacques and Marie Herson) from Chambois in Orne (Basse-Normandie) m. Marguerite Sevestre (Charles and Marie Pichon) in Québec, QC in 1652.*

Lestage, from *Lestage*, a placename in France. — Amer. **Lestarge.**

— *Jean (de) Lestage (Jean and Saubade Nolibos) from Bayonne in Pyrénées-Atlantiques (Aquitaine) m. Marie-Anne Vermet (Antoine and Barbe Ménard) in Québec, QC in 1691.*

Letarte, alteration *Le Tartre*, a placename in France. — Amer. **Latarte.**

— *René Letartre from La Poterie-au-Perche in Orne (Basse-Normandie) m. Louise Goulet (Thomas and Marie Chalumel) in La Poterie-au-Perche c. 1654.*

Letendre, from Old French *le tendre* 'the young one'. — Amer. **Latender, Latendre, Letender, Letondre.**

— *Pierre Letendre dit Laliberté from France m. Charlotte Morin/Maurice in Québec c. 1668.*

Létourneau, from *l'étourneau* 'the starling', the nickname of a featherbrained individual.

— Amer. **Blackbird, Latno, Latourneau, Laturno, Leturno, Turner.**

— *David **Létourneau** (David and Jeanne Dupen) from Muron in Charente-Maritime (Poitou-Charentes) m. (1) Sébastienne Guéry/Guerry in Muron in 1640; (2) Jeanne Baril (François and Catherine Ligneron) in Saint-Germain-de-Marencennes in Charente-Maritime c. 1653.*

Levac, either an alteration of *La Vaque,* a placename in Somme (Picardie), or of *le vaque,* a regional variant of *la vache* 'the cow', the nickname of a cowherd. — Amer. **Lavac, Lavack, Lavacque, Levacque.**

— *Martin (de) **Levac** dit Bapaume (Pierre and Antoinette Béal) from Bapaume in Pas-de-Calais (Nord-Pas-de-Calais) m. Marie-Josèphe Réaume (Simon and Charlotte Turpin) in Sainte-Anne-de-Bellevue, QC in 1749.*

Levake, see **Lévesque.**

Levallee, see **Lavallée.**

Levangie, see **Lavandier.**

Levasseur, from Old French *le vasseur* 'the vassal'.— Amer. **Lavassaur, Lavasser, Lavasseur, Sister, Sisters.**

— *Laurent **Levasseur** (Jean and Marguerite Maheu) from Bois-Guillaume in Seine-Maritime (Haute-Normandie) m. Marie Marchand (Louis and Françoise Morineau) in Québec, QC in 1670.*

Leveck, see **Lévesque.**

Léveillé, from *l'éveillé* 'the lively one'. — Amer. **Lavalley, Lavallie, Laveille, Smart, Wideawake.**

— *Étienne **Léveillé** (François and Alizon Vivier) from Rouen in Seine-Maritime (Haute-Normandie) m. Élisabeth Lequin (Pierre and Catherine Boldieu) in Québec, QC in 1671.*

— *Jean Serre dit **Léveillé** (François and Marguerite Métayer) from Berson in Gironde (Aquitaine) m. Marguerite Sergent (Thomas and Marie Praisse) in Montréal, QC in 1722.*

— *Louis Truchon dit **Léveillé** (Pierre and Perrine Sirouet) from Abbaretz in Loire-Atlantique (Pays de la Loire) m. Marie-Françoise Beauchamp (Jean and Jeanne Loisel) in Pointe-aux-Trembles, QC in 1687.*

Levert, from Old French *le vert* 'the young, vigorous, lively one'. — Amer. **Neverett, Neverette.**

— *Jean **Levert** from Rouen in Seine-Maritime (Haute-Normandie) m. Françoise Latier in Sainte-Famille, Île d'Orléans, QC in 1669.*

Lévesque, from Old French *l'évesque* 'the bishop', an ironic nickname. — Amer. **Bishop, Lavake, Lavaque, Laveck, Levake, Leveck.**

— *Robert **Lévesque** (Pierre and Marie Caumont) from Hautot-Saint-Sulpice in Seine-Maritime (Haute-Normandie) m. Jeanne Chevalier (Jacques-Alexandre and Marguerite Scoman) in L'Ange-Gardien, QC in 1679.*

Levigne, Levine, see **Lavigne.**

Levoy, see **Lavoie.**

Lewia, see **Louis.**

Lezotte, see **Lizotte.**

L'Heureux, alteration of *Lereau,* from *Le Reau,* a placename in France. — Amer. **Happy, Laraux, Louria, Lurix.**

— Simon **Lereau**/Leureau (René and Marguerite Guillin) from Saint-Cosme-en-Vairais in Sarthe (Pays de la Loire) m. Suzanne Jarousseau (Pierre and Jacquette Tourault) in Québec, QC in 1655.

Libby, see **Labbé.**

Liberty, see **Laliberté.**

Liboiron, derived from *Liboire,* from the Latin name *Liborius.* — Amer. **Bero.**

— Louis **Liboiron** dit Bellefleur (Pierre and Françoise Chaux) from Aigrefeuille-d'Aunis in Charente-Maritime (Poitou-Charentes) m. Marie-Louise Desrochers (François and Marie-Geneviève Renaud) in Sainte-Anne-de-Bellevue, QC in 1759.

Limoges, from *Limoges,* a placename in France. — Amer. **Lamudge.**

— Pierre Amand dit Jolicoeur and **Limoges** (Adrien and Jeanne Videau) from Bordeaux in Gironde (Aquitaine) m. Catherine Grenier (Jean and Françoise Feuilleton) in Montréal, QC in 1698.

Lincourt, apparently from *Lincourt,* a placename in France. — Amer. **Lancor, Lancour, Lancourt.**

— Jean-Baptiste Desorcy dit **Lincourt,** grandson of Michel from Sceaux in Hauts-de-Seine (Île-de-France), m. Marie-Antoinette Desmarais (Paul and Marie Tétreau) in Saint-Sulpice, QC in 1723.

Lirette, alteration of *Hileret* via *Liret,* derived from *Hilaire,* from the Latin name *Hilarius,* derived from *hilaris* 'cheerful, happy'. — Amer. **Lerette, Lorette.**

— François Hileret/**Liret** (Jean and Jacquette Bourdeau) from Fontenay-le-Comte in Vendée (Pays de la Loire) m. Marie-Anne Tessier (Marc and Jacquette Ledoux) in Charlesbourg, QC in 1695.

Lisherness, see **Lajeunesse.**

Little, see **Petit.**

Lively, see **Joyal.**

Livernois, alteration of *Nivernois,* the nickname of a native of Nivernais, a former province in France. — Amer. **Lavanway, Lavarnway, Lavernway.**

— Paul Benoît dit Nivernois/**Livernois** (François and Dimanche Chapelain) from Châtillon-en-Bazois in Nièvre (Bourgogne) m. Élisabeth Gobinet (Nicolas and Marguerite *Lorgeleux/*Loigeleux) in Montréal, QC in 1658.

Lizé, probably derived from *Élisée,* from the Hebrew name *Elisha* composed of *El* 'God' and *yesha* 'salvation', hence 'God is salvation'. — Amer. **Leasia.**

— Jacques **Lizé** dit Saint-Martin (Maurille and Renée Roy) from Angers in Maine-et-Loire (Pays de la Loire) m. Marie-Madeleine André (Antoine and Élisabeth Guilbert) in Montréal, QC in 1733.

Lizotte, alteration of *Lizot,* probably derived from **Lizé.** — Amer. **Lazette, Lezotte.**

— Guillaume **Lizot** (Robert and Catherine Joanne) from La Gravelle in Calvados (Basse-Normandie) m. Anne Pelletier (Jean and Anne Langlois) in Québec, QC in 1670.

Loiseau, either from *L'Oiseau,* a placename in France, or from *l'oiseau* 'the bird', the nickname of a flighty individual. — Amer. **Bird.**

— Pierre **Loiseau** dit Francoeur (François and Françoise Leclerc) from Angers in Maine-et-Loire (Pays de la Loire) m. Jeanne-Léonarde Genest (François and Jeanne Camuset) in Trois-Rivières, QC in 1671.

Loisel(le), from Old French *l'oisel* 'the bird', the nickname of a flighty or lightfooted individual. — Amer. **Loyselle, Loyzelle, Wisell, Wissell.**

— Louis **Loisel** *(Louis and Jeanne Le Terrier) from Courseulles-sur-Mer in Calvados (Basse-Normandie) m. Marguerite Charlot (François and Barbe Girardeau) in Montréal, QC in 1648.*

Lompre, Lomprey, see **Longpré.**

Loncto, see **Lanctôt.**

Londeree, see **Landry.**

Londo, see **Langdeau.**

Londrie, Londry, see **Landry.**

Longdo, see **Langdeau.**

Longe, see **Lange.**

Longevin, Longever, Longeway, see **Langevin.**

Longey, see **Lanier.**

Longlade, see **Langlade.**

Longley, see **Langlois.**

Longpré, from *long pré* 'long lea', a translation of the English name *Longley,* a place-name in England. — Amer. **Lompre, Lomprey.**

— *William Longley/Guillaume* **Longpré** *(William and Jane *Alart) from Deerfield, MA m. Catherine Bleau (François and Catherine Campeau) in Montréal, QC in 1720.*

Longtin, alteration of *Lanquetin* via *Lonquetin,* from *l'Anquetin,* derived from *Anquetil,* from the Germanic name *Ansketill* composed of *Ans,* the name of a god, and *ketill* '(sacrificial) cauldron'. — Amer. **Longtain, Longtine, Longton.**

— *Jérôme* **Longtin**/*Lonquetin (André and Jeanne-Angélique Brière) from Paris (Île-de-France) m. (1) Marie-Catherine Marie (Louis and Mathurine Goard) in Montréal, QC in 1684; (2) Marie-Louise Dumas (René and Marie Lelong) in Laprairie, QC in 1704.*

Longto, Longtoe, see **Lanctôt.**

Longton, see **Longtin.**

Longua, see **Langlois.**

Longver, see **Langevin.**

Longway, see **Langevin** and **Langlois.**

Lonkey, see **Lanthier.**

Lonsway, see **Langevin.**

Lonto, see **Lanctôt.**

Loon, see **Huard.**

Lorette, see **Lirette.**

Loriot, from *loriot* 'oriole', a nickname related to some characteristic of this bird. — Amer. **Lorio.**

— *Jean* **Loriot**/*Lauriot (François and Françoise Mesnard) from Cognac-la-Forêt in Haute-Vienne (Limousin) m. Agathe Merlin (Adrien and Françoise Lebrun) in Québec in 1670.*

Lorrain, from *Lorrain,* the nickname of an individual from Lorraine, a region situated in the northeastern part of France. — Amer. **Lorraine.**

— *Pierre* **Lorrain** *dit Lachapelle from Angliers in Vienne (Poitou-Charentes) m. Françoise Hulin in France c. 1656.*

Losaw, Loso, see **Lauzon.**

Louis, from the Germanic name *Hlodwig* composed of *hlod* 'glory' and *wig* 'combat'. — Amer. **Lewia.**

— **Louis** *Bizier, grandson of Joseph from Languedoc, m. Geneviève Bisson (Étienne and Hélène Vachon) in Lévis, QC in 1837.*

Louria, see **L'Heureux.**

Lovelette, Lovellette, see **Laviolette.**

Lovely, see **Lavallée.**

Loyer, either from the Germanic name *Hlodhari* composed of *hlod* 'glory' and *hari* 'army', or from Old French *l'oyer* 'the gooseherd'. — Amer. **Lawya, Lawyea, Loya, Loyie.**

— *Gabriel **Loyer** dit Desnoyers (Roger and ...) from Rouen in Seine-Maritime (Haute-Normandie) m. (1) Geneviève Gendreau (Pierre and Jeanne Garnier) in L'Ange-Gardien, QC in 1694; (2) Marie-Louise Couvret (Victor and Thérèse Charlot) in Saint-Laurent, Île de Montréal, QC in 1728.*

Loyselle, Loyzelle, see **Loisel(le).**

Lozen, Lozo, Lozon, see **Lauzon.**

Lucia, Lucian, see **Lussier.**

Luck, see **Lachance.**

Luicha, see **Lussier.**

Lumbra, see **Lambert.**

Lunderville, see **Landreville.**

Luneau, alteration of *Louineau* via *Luineau,* derived from *Louin,* from the Germanic name *Hlodwin* composed of *hlod* 'glory' and *win* 'friend'. — Amer. **Leneau.**

— *Pierre **Louineau**/Luineau (Nicolas and Louise *Borseguine) from Saint-Cyr-du-Doret in Charente-Maritime (Poitou-Charentes) m. Marie Bertin (Barthélemi and Anne Richard) in Sainte-Famille, Île d'Orléans, QC in 1678.*

Lupien, from the Latin name *Lupianus,* derived from *lupus* 'wolf'. — Amer. **Lupient, Lupin, Lupine.**

— *Nicolas Baron dit **Lupien** (Lupien and Jeanne Thiesson) from Villenauxe-la-Grande in Aube (Champagne-Ardenne) m. Marie Chauvin (Pierre and Marie-Marthe Hautreux) in Montréal, QC in 1676.*

Lurix, see **L'Heureux.**

Luro, see **Sirois.**

Lusha, Lusian, see **Lussier.**

Lusignan, from *Lusignan,* a placename in Vienne (Poitou-Charentes). — Amer. **Zeno.**

— *Jean Miel/Amiel dit **Lusignan** (Jean and Louise Émonet) from Lusignan in Vienne (Poitou-Charentes) m. Marie-Thérèse Latouche (Roger and Marie Gareau) in Boucherville, QC in 1699.*

Lussier, from Old French *l'ussier* 'the usher'. — Amer. **Dussia, Lucia, Lucian, Luicha, Lusha, Lusian.**

— *Jacques **Lussier**/Lhuissier (Jacques and Marguerite *Darmine) from Paris (Île-de-France) m. Catherine Clérice (Pierre and Marie Lefebvre) in Québec, QC in 1671.*

Lyonnais, from *Lyonnais,* the nickname of an individual from Lyon in Rhône (Rhône-Alpes). — Amer. **Leanna, Lyneis.**

— *Jean-François Bossu dit **Lyonnais** (Claude and Jeanne Suret) from Lyon in Rhône (Rhône-Alpes) m. Élisabeth-Ursule Prou (Jean and Catherine Pinel) in Québec, QC in 1705.*

M

Machia, Macie, see **Messier.**

Macue, see **Mathieu.**

Macy, see **Mercier.**

Magee, Maguy, see **Mailly.**

Maheu, same origin as **Mathieu.** — Amer. **Maher, Mahew, Mayhew, Mayhue, Mayo.**

— *Pierre Maheu/Maheux/Maheust, sieur des Hazards (Jean and Michelle Chauvin) from Mortagne-au-Perche in Orne (Basse-Normandie) m. Jeanne Drouin (Robert and Anne Cloutier) in Québec, QC in 1659.*

Mailhot, alteration of *Maillot,* either from *(Le) Maillot,* a placename in France, or from Old French *maillot* 'mallet', the nickname of someone who worked with this type of implement. — Amer. **Mailhotte, Mayott, Myatt, Myott, Myotte.**

— *René Maillot dit Laviolette (René and Jeanne-Catherine Berger) from Castet-Arrouy in Gers (Midi-Pyrénées) m. Marie Chapacou (Simon and Marie Pacaud) in Québec in 1671.*

Maillé, alteration of *Maguet,* probably from Breton *maget* 'nourished', the nickname of a child found and raised by a nurse. — Amer. **McGee.**

— *Pierre Maguet (Augustin and Françoise Goubillot) from Paris (Île-de-France) m. Catherine Perthuis (Pierre and Claude *Damisé) in Pointe-aux-Trembles, QC in 1686.*

Maillet, either from *(Le) Maillet,* a placename in France, or from *maillet* 'mallet', the nickname of an individual who worked with such an implement. — Amer. **Myers.**

— *Jacques Maillet (Antoine and Françoise Choppart) from Paris (Île-de-France) m. Madeleine Hébert (Antoine and Jeanne Corporon) in Port-Royal, NS in 1720.*

Mailloux, either an alteration of *(Le) Maillou,* a placename in France, or derived from Old French *mail* 'mallet', the nickname of someone who worked with this kind of implement. — Amer. **Mayhew, Mayo, Mayou.**

— *Pierre Mailloux dit Desmoulins (Jacques and Jeanne/Suzanne Arnaud) from Brie-sous-Matha in Charente-Maritime (Poitou-Charentes) m. Anne Delaunay (Louis and Marguerite Cazalede) in Québec, QC in 1661.*

Mailly, from *(Le) Mailly,* a placename in France. — Amer. **Magee, Maguy.**

— *François Mailly (François and Dominique Toussaint) from Nérac in Lot-et-Garonne (Aquitaine) m. Madeleine Dufresne (Pierre and Marie-Madeleine Crépeau) in Saint-Laurent, Île d'Orléans, QC in 1727.*

Mainville, alteration of *Miéville* via *Miville,* a placename in Switzerland. — Amer. **Manville, Mayville.**

— *Pierre Miville dit Le Suisse from Fribourg in Switzerland m. Charlotte Maugis in France c. 1631.*

Malépart, probable alteration of Old French *mal espart* 'bad division, separation'. — Amer. **Maleport.**

— *Jean Malépart dit Tourangeau (Sébastien and Madeleine Crosnier) from Tours in*

Indre-et-Loire (Centre) m. Marie-Thérèse Dubé (Pierre and Marie-Thérèse Boucher) in Montréal, QC in 1733.

Malo, alteration of *Saint-Malo*, a placename in Ille-et-Vilaine (Bretagne). — Amer. **Milo.**

— *Jean Hayet dit Saint-Malo/**Malo** (Gilles and Jeanne Héreau) from Saint-Malo in Ille-et-Vilaine (Bretagne) m. Catherine Galbrun (Simon and Françoise Duverger) in Pointe-aux-Trembles, QC in 1680.*

Maloche, see **Meloche.**

Malonso, Malonson, see **Melançon.**

Malosh, see **Meloche.**

Mandeville, from *Mandeville*, a placename in France. — Amer. **Montville, Monville.**

— *Jean **Mandeville** from Rouen in Seine-Maritime (Haute-Normandie) m. Françoise Mousseau (Jacques and Marguerite Sauviot) in Québec c. 1680.*

Manny, see **Many.**

Manor, Manore, see **Ménard.**

Manosh, see **Meloche.**

Manville, see **Mainville.**

Many, alteration of *Magny*, from *(Le) Magny*, a placename in France. — Amer. **Manny.**

— *Nicolas **Magny** dit Ladouceur (Nicolas and Marie-Barbe Dumesnil) from Paris (Île-de-France) m. Marie Cloutier (Charles and Anne Thibault) in Château-Richer, QC in 1743.*

Marceau, from the Latin name *Marcellus*, derived from *Marcus*. — Amer. **Marsaw.**

— *François **Marceau** (André and Marie Grant) from Thiré in Vendée (Pays de la Loire) m. Marie-Louise Beaupère (Gilles and Nicole Lechef) in Sainte-Famille, Île d'Orléans, QC in 1671.*

Marcelain, see **Marsolais.**

Marcell, see **Marcil.**

Marcellais, see **Marsolais.**

Marcelle, see **Marcil.**

Marchand, either from *(Le) Marchand*, a placename in France, or from *marchand* 'merchant'. — Amer. **Merchant.**

— *Jacques **Marchand**/Lemarchand from Caen in Calvados (Basse-Normandie) m. Françoise Capel (Julien and Laurence Lecomte) in Québec in 1660.*

Marcher, see **Mercure.**

Marcheterre, alteration of *marche à terre* 'walks on the ground', the nickname of a foot soldier. — Amer. **Mashtare, Mushtare, Walker.**

— *Antoine Dandurand dit **Marchàterre** (Jean and Marguerite La Beauce) from Paris (Île-de-France) m. Marie Vérieu (Nicolas and Marguerite Hiardin/Hyardin) in Sainte-Famille, Île d'Orléans, QC in 1696.*

Marcia, Marcier, see **Mercier.**

Marcil, from the Latin name *Marcilius*, derived from *Marcus*. — Amer. **Marcell, Marcelle.**

— *André **Marcil**/Marsil dit L'Espagnol (Guilbert and Perronne Clairbout) from Saint-Omer in Pas-de-Calais (Nord-Pas-de-Calais) m. Marie Lefebvre (Antoine and Hélène Cavet) in Trois-Rivières, QC in 1671.*

Marco, Marcoe, see **Marcoux.**

Marcotte, alteration of *Marcot,* derived from *Marc,* from the Latin name *Marcus.* — Amer. **Marcott.**

— *Jacques **Marcot** (Charles and Jacqueline Baucher) from Fécamp in Seine-Maritime (Haute-Normandie) m. Élisabeth Salé (Pierre and Françoise Lupia) in Québec in 1670.*

Marcoux, either from *Marcou* or *Marcoux,* placenames in France, or from the Germanic name *Marcwulf* composed of *marca* 'border' and *wulf* 'wolf'. — Amer. **Marco, Marcoe, Stewart.**

— *Pierre **Marcoux**/Marcou (Claude and Marie Junot) from Cry in Yonne (Bourgogne) m. Marthe (de) Rainville (Paul and Rolline Poète) in Québec, QC in 1662.*

Marcure, see **Mercure.**

Marier, alteration of *Marié,* from *marié* 'married', probably the nickname of a married man used to distinguish him from an unmarried namesake. — Amer. **Maryea, Murray.**

— *Jacques **Marié**/Lemarié from Angoulême in Charente (Poitou-Charentes) m. Marie Morin in France c. 1652.*

Markee, Markey, see **Marquis.**

Marleau, alteration of *Merlot,* derived from *merle* 'blackbird', the nickname of someone who liked to sing or whistle. — Amer. **Marlow, Marlowe.**

— *André **Merlot** dit Laramée from France m. Marie Roy (Jean and Françoise Bouet) in Lachine, QC in 1678.*

Marnay, from *Marnay,* a placename in France. — Amer. **Marney.**

— *Louis **Marnay** dit Richelieu (Jacques and Renée-Jeanne Morineau) from Faye-la-Vineuze in Indre-et-Loire (Centre) m. Marie-Josèphe Couturier (Jean-Baptiste and Marie-Marguerite Beauchamp) in Montréal, QC in 1758.*

Marois, from *Le/La/Les Marois,* placenames in France. — Amer. **Morois, Morway.**

— *Guillaume **Marois** (Charles and Catherine Livrade) from Paris (Île-de-France) m. Catherine Laberge (Robert and Françoise Gausse) in L'Ange-Gardien, QC in 1687.*

Marquis, either from *(Le) Marquis,* a placename in France, or from *marquis* 'marquess', an ironic nickname. — Amer. **Markee, Markey.**

— *Charles **Marquis** (Charles and Jeanne Bignon) from Mortagne-sur-Sèvre in Vendée (Pays de la Loire) m. Agnès Giguère (Robert and Aimée Miville) in Beaupré, QC in 1698.*

Marsaw, see **Marceau.**

Marseille, from *Marseille,* a placename in Bouches-du-Rhône (Provence-Alpes-Côte-d'Azur). — Amer. **Marseilles.**

— *Jean-Sébastien Natte dit **Marseille** (Jean-Noël and Françoise Gassin) from Marseille in Bouches-du-Rhône (Provence-Alpes-Côte-d'Azur) m. Marguerite Duchesneau (Pierre and Marie-Catherine Barbeau) in Québec, QC in 1758.*

Marsha, Marshall, see **Mercier.**

Marsolais, alteration of *Marsolet,* apparently derived from *Mars* via *Marsol,* from the Latin name *Medardus,* derived from the Germanic name *Madhard* composed of *mad* 'respect, reverence' and *hard* 'hard, strong'. — Amer. **Marcelain, Marcellais.**

— *Jean Lemire dit **Marsolet,** son of Jean from Rouen in Seine-Maritime (Haute-Normandie), m. Élisabeth Bareau (Jean and Jeanne Cusson) in Montréal, QC in 1703.*

Martel, either from *(Le) Martel,* a placename in France, or from Old French *martel* '(sledge) hammer', probably the nickname of a blacksmith. — Amer. **Martell.**

— *Honoré **Martel** dit Lamontagne (Jean and Marie Duchesne) from Paris (Île-de-*

France) m. Marguerite Lamirault (François and Jeanne Clos) in Québec, QC in 1668.

Maryea, see **Marier.**

Mashtare, see **Marcheterre.**

Mashue, see **Masseau.**

Mason, see **Masson.**

Masse, from *(La) Masse,* a placename in France. — Amer. **Morse, Moss.**

*— Pierre **Masse** from France m. Marie Pinet in Québec, QC in 1644.*

Massé, either from *Massé* or an alteration of *Macé,* placenames in France. — Amer. **Massey, Mossey.**

*— Jean **Massé** dit Sancerre (Jacques and Jeanne Bernard) from La Mothe-Saint-Héray in Deux-Sèvres (Poitou-Charentes) m. Marie Beaudet (Laurent and Marguerite-Louise Crevier) in Laprairie, QC in 1704.*

Masseau, alteration of *Manseau,* a variant of *Manceau,* the nickname of an individual from *Mans,* a region in Sarthe (Pays de la Loire), or one from *Maine,* a former province in France. — Amer. **Mashue.**

*— Jacques **Manseau**/Manceau (Étienne and Marie Métayer) from Fontenay-le-Comte in Vendée (Pays de la Loire) m. Marguerite Latouche (Jean and Marie Touellon) in Québec, QC in 1673.*

Massey, see **Massé.**

Massicot, derived from *Thomas,* from the Greek name *Thomas,* from Syriac *toma* 'twin'. — Amer. **Mexico.**

*— Jacques **Massicot** (Jacques and Jeanne Landri) from Le Gicq in Charente-Maritime (Poitou-Charentes) m. Marie-Catherine Baril (Jean and Marie Guillet) in Batiscan, QC in 1696.*

Masson, alteration of *Thomasson,* derived from the Greek name *Thomas,* from Syriac *toma* 'twin'. — Amer. **Mason.**

*— Jean **Masson** (François and Thérèse Hébert) from Saint-Georges-de-Montaigu in Vendée (Pays de la Loire) m. Anne Greslon (Jacques and Jeanne Vignault) in Neuville, QC in 1699.*

Masta, variant of *Masteau,* derived from *Masset,* an alteration of *Thomasset,* same origin as **Masson.** — Amer. **Mastaw.**

*— Mathurin **Masta** (Jacques and Marie Coulaude) from Saint-Denis-la-Chevasse in Vendée (Pays de la Loire) m. Antoinette Éloy (Jean and Antoinette Poité) in Montréal, QC in 1665.*

Matevia, see **Métivier.**

Mathieu, from the Hebrew name *Mattiyah* via Latin *Matthæus,* from *mattath* 'gift' and *yah* 'Lord', hence 'gift of the Lord'. — Amer. **Macue, Mathews, Matthews, Micue.**

*— Jean **Mathieu** (Jean and Isabelle *Monnachau) from Montignac-Charente in Charente-Maritime (Poitou-Charentes) m. Anne Letartre (René and Louise Goulet) in Château-Richer, QC in 1669.*

Matott, see **Méthot.**

Matthews, see **Mathieu.**

Mauger, from the Germanic name *Madalgari* composed of *madal* (> *mal*) 'council, reunion' and *gari* 'spear'. — Amer. **Moge.**

*— Jacques Gadois dit **Mauger,** grandson of Pierre from Igé in Orne (Basse-Normandie), m. Marie-Madeleine-Jacquette Chorel (François and Marie-Anne Aubuchon) in*

Montréal, QC in 1714.

Maurice, from the Latin name *Mauritius/Mauricius,* derived from *Maurus* 'Mauritanian', the nickname of a swarthy individual. — Amer. **Morris.**

— *Simon Arrivé dit* **Maurice,** *son of Maurice from Saint-Denis-la-Chevasse in Vendée (Pays de la Loire), m. Marie-Catherine Garand (Pierre and Renée Chanfrain) in Saint-François, Île d'Orléans, QC in 1709.*

Mayhew, see **Maheu** and **Mailloux.**

Mayhue, see **Maheu.**

Mayo, see **Maheu** and **Mailloux.**

Mayott, see **Mailhot.**

Mayou, see **Mailloux.**

Mayville, see **Mainville.**

McCure, see **Mercure.**

McGee, see **Maillé.**

McQueen, see **Moquin.**

Meilleur, probable alteration of *Mayeur,* from Old French *maire,* either 'town councillor' or 'greater, major, principal', the nickname of the eldest in a family. — Amer. **Miller.**

— *Jacques* **Meilleur/Lemeilleur** *(Jacques and Catherine Le Boulanger) from Rouen in Seine-Maritime (Haute-Normandie) m. Marie Valade (André and Sarah Cousseau) in Québec, QC in 1677.*

Melançon, variant of *Malançon/Malençon,* derived from Old French *malence* 'illness', the nickname of a sickly individual. — Amer. **Malonso, Malonson.**

— *Pierre* **Melançon/Melanson** *dit Laverdure from France m. Priscilla ... in England c. 1631.*

Meloche, probable alteration of *Meloches,* a placename in Gironde (Aquitaine). — Amer. **Maloche, Malosh, Manosh, Melosh, Menoche, Molash.**

— *François* **Meloche** *(François and Thérèse Renu) from Frontenay-Rohan-Rohan in Deux-Sèvres (Poitou-Charentes) m. Marie Mouflet (Jean and Anne Dodin) in Montréal, QC in 1700.*

Melot, Melott, Melotte, see **Milot(te).**

Ménard, from the Germanic name *Maginhard* composed of *magin* 'strength' and *hard* 'hard, strong'. — Amer. **Manor, Manore, Menone, Miner, Minnon, Minor.**

— *Jacques* **Ménard** *dit Lafontaine (Jean and Anne Savinelle) from Mervent in Vendée (Pays de la Loire) m. Catherine Forestier (Jean and Julienne Coiffé) in Trois-Rivières, QC in 1657.*

— *Joseph* **Ménard** *of undetermined origin m. Marie-Louise Brisset (Jean-Baptiste and Marie Forcier) in Saint-Cuthbert, QC in 1789.*

— *Pierre* **Ménard** *dit Saint-Onge from France m. Marguerite Deshayes in Québec c. 1670.*

Ménéclier, alteration of *Ménéglier,* probably from Old French *marreglier* 'churchwarden, beadle'. — Amer. **Miniclier.**

— *Nicolas* **Ménéclier** *de Monrochaud (Louis and Anne Jacopé) from Broyes in Marne (Champagne-Ardenne) m. Marie-Charlotte Trudel (René and Marie-Anne Liénard) in Québec, QC in 1757.*

Menoche, see **Meloche.**

Menone, see **Ménard.**

Mény, alteration of *Mesnil* via *Mesny,* a placename in France. — Amer. **Minnie.**
— *Claude Mesny/Mesnil (André and Antoinette Valentin) from Saint-Jean-d'Aubrigoux in Haute-Loire (Auvergne) m. Marie Deniger (Bernard and Marguerite Raisin) in Laprairie, QC in 1694.*

Meraw, see **Amirault.**

Merchant, see **Marchand.**

Mercier, from Old French *mercier* 'merchant'. — Amer. **Macy, Marcia, Marcier, Marsha, Marshall, Mercia, Mercy, Mersha.**
— *Julien Mercier (François and Roberte Cornilleau) from Tourouvre in Orne (Basse-Normandie) m. Marie Poulin (Claude and Jeanne Mercier) in Québec, QC in 1654.*

Mercille, alteration of *Marcil,* from the Latin name *Marcilius,* derived from *Marcus.* — Amer. **Merseal.**
— *André Marcil/Marsil dit L'Espagnol (Guilbert and Perronne Clairbout) from Saint-Omer in Pas-de-Calais (Nord-Pas-de-Calais) m. Marie Lefebvre (Antoine and Hélène Cavet) in Trois-Rivières, QC in 1671.*

Mercure, from the Latin name *Mercurius.* — Amer. **Marcher, Marcure, McCure.**
— *François Mercure from Villenouvelle in Haute-Garonne (Midi-Pyrénées) m. Marie Perrault (Joseph and Marie Gagné) in Sainte-Famille, Île d'Orléans, QC in 1707.*

Mercy, see **Mercier.**

Mere, see **Myre.**

Mero, see **Amirault** and **Miron.**

Meron, see **Miron.**

Merrow, see **Amirault** and **Miron.**

Merseal, see **Mercille.**

Mersha, see **Mercier.**

Messier, from Old French *messier* 'rural policeman'. — Amer. **Machia, Macie.**
— *Jacques Messier (David and Marguerite Bar/Barc) from Saint-Denis-le-Thiboult in Seine-Maritime (Haute-Normandie) m. Marie-Renée Couillard (François and Esther Dannessé) in Québec c. 1685.*

Metevia, Metevier, see **Métivier.**

Méthot, alteration of *Métot,* apparently derived from Old French *meiteier* 'tenant farmer, sharecropper'. — Amer. **Matott, Metott.**
— *Abraham Méthot/Métot (Jacques and Françoise Auzou/Ozou) from Pont-Audemer in Eure (Haute-Normandie) m. Marie-Madeleine Mézeray (René and Nicole Gareman) in Québec in 1673.*

Métivier, from Old French *mestivier* 'harvester, reaper'. — Amer. **Matevia, Metevia, Metevier, Metiva.**
— *Barthélemi Groinier dit Métivier, son of Nicolas from La Roche-Guyon in Val-d'Oise (Île-de-France), m. Marguerite Descaries (Michel and Marie Cuillerier) in Montréal, QC in 1730.*

Metott, see **Méthot.**

Meunier, either from *meunier* 'miller' or an alteration of *Migner,* a variant of *Mignier,* from *minier* 'miner'. — Amer. **Miller.**
— *Pierre Meunier dit Bellerose (Nicolas and Catherine Geny) from Vaxy in Moselle (Lorraine) m. Marie-Josèphe Côté (Pierre and Marie-Josèphe Charland) in Saint-Antoine-de-Tilly, QC in 1762.*

— Pierre **Meunier** dit Lapierre (Bertrand and Madeleine Guibourg) from Rennes in Ille-et-Vilaine (Bretagne) m. Barbe Richaume (Pierre and Marthe Arnu) in Québec in 1675.

— André **Mignier** dit Lagacé (Michel and Catherine Masson) from Le Bois-Plage-en-Ré in Charente-Maritime (Poitou-Charentes) m. Jacquette Michel (Jacques and Jeanne Dupont) in Québec, QC in 1668.

Meuse, see **Mius.**

Mexico, see **Massicot.**

Meyett, Meyette, see **Millet(te).**

Meyre, see **Myre.**

Micha, see **Moquin.**

Michaud, derived from *Michel*, from the Hebrew name *Mikha'el* 'who is like God?'. — Amer. **Mishoe, Mishou, Mitchell.**

— Pierre **Michaud**/*Micheau* (Antoine and Marie Train) from Fontenay-le-Comte in Vendée (Pays de la Loire) m. Marie Ancelin (René and Claire Rousselot) in Château-Richer, QC in 1667.

Micue, see **Mathieu.**

Miller, see **Dumoulin, Meilleur, Meunier** and **Millier.**

Millet(te), either from *(Le) Millet*, a placename in France, or from *millet* 'millet', the nickname of a producer or seller. — Amer. **Meyett, Meyette, Millett.**

— Nicolas **Millet** dit Le Beauceron (Jacques and Jeanne Vincent) from Neuville-aux-Bois in Loiret (Centre) m. Catherine Lorion (Mathurin and Françoise Morinet) in Montréal, QC in 1657.

Millier, alteration of **Millet.** — Amer. **Miller.**

— Pierre **Millier**/*Millet* (Vincent and Claude Penin) from Mirebeau in Vienne (Poitou-Charentes) m. Marie Salois (Claude and Anne Mabile/Mabille) in Saint-Laurent, Île d'Orléans, QC in 1702.

Milo, see **Malo.**

Milot(te), derived from the Germanic name *Milo*, from *mil* 'good, generous'. — Amer. **Melot, Melott, Melotte.**

— Jean **Milot** dit Le Bourguignon (Philibert and Chrétienne/Christine Saunois) from Vermenton in Yonne (Bourgogne) m. Mathurine Thibault (Étienne and Jeanne de La Mothe) in Montréal, QC in 1663.

Miner, see **Ménard.**

Miniclier, see **Ménéclier.**

Minnie, see **Mény.**

Minnon, Minor, see **Ménard.**

Mireau, see **Amirault.**

Miron, alteration of *Migneron*, derived from *Mignier*, an alteration of *minier* 'miner'. — Amer. **Mero, Meron, Merrow.**

— Laurent **Migneron** (Pierre and Françoise Plessis) from Chizé in Deux-Sèvres (Poitou-Charentes) m. Anne Saint-Denis (Pierre and Vivienne Bunel) in Québec in 1666.

Mishoe, Mishou, see **Michaud.**

Mitchell, see **Michaud** and **St-Michel.**

Mius, probably from Old French *mius* 'the best'. — Amer. **Meuse, Muse.**

— Philippe **Mius,** sieur d'Entremont probably from Seine-Maritime (Haute-Norman-

die) m. Madeleine Hélie in Acadia c. 1649.

Moblo, see **Mombleau**.

Moen, see **Faucher**.

Moge, see **Mauger**.

Moineau, from *moineau* 'sparrow', the nickname of a light-footed or flighty individual. — Amer. **Moino**.

— *Michel **Moineau** dit Jamoneau (Louis and Marthe Gauthier) from Augé in Deux-Sèvres (Poitou-Charentes) m. Marie Jodoin (Claude and Anne Thomas) in Boucherville, QC in 1688.*

Moisan, same origin as **Moïse**. — Amer. **Moison**.

— *Pierre **Moisan** (Jacques and Françoise Fontaine) from Dieppe in Seine-Maritime (Haute-Normandie) m. Barbe Rotot (Geoffroy and Catherine Carrieux) in Québec, QC in 1673.*

Moïse, from the Hebrew name *Mosheh* 'liberator, savior' via Latin *Moyses*. — Amer. **Moses**.

— *Rigobert Dupuis dit **Moïse**, descendant of François from Saint-Laurent-sur-Gorre in Haute-Vienne (Limousin), m. Judith Roger (Jean-Baptiste and Agathe Beaudoin) in Laprairie, QC in 1782.*

Moison, see **Moisan**.

Molash, see **Meloche**.

Molleur, alteration of the German name *Moller*, from Low German *moller* 'miller'. — Amer. **Mollere, Muller**.

— *Pierre **Molleur** dit L'Allemand (Joseph and Catherine Joseph) from Ulm in Germany m. Jeanne Quenneville (Mathurin and Jeanne Latouche) in Québec, QC in 1671.*

Momany, see **Montminy**.

Mombleau, alteration of *Maublot*, from *Le Maublot*, a placename in Vosges (Lorraine). — Amer. **Moblo, Mumblo, Mumblow**.

— *Pierre **Maublot** dit Latulippe (Nicolas and Marie Deschamps) from Nancy in Meurthe-et-Moselle (Lorraine) m. Marie-Clémence Laroche (Jean and Marie-Suzanne Turpin) in Montréal, QC in 1739.*

Momenee, Momeny, Mominee, see **Montminy**.

Monet(te), alteration of *Moinet*, derived from *moine* 'monk', an ironic nickname. — Amer. **Monett**.

— *Antoine **Monet**/Moinet (Laurent and Louise Petit) from Saintes in Charente-Maritime (Poitou-Charentes) m. Françoise Hurtault (Jean and Françoise de La Haye) in Pointe-aux-Trembles, QC in 1684.*

Mongeau, derived from *Demonge*, a regional variant of *Dominique*, from the Latin name *Dominicus*, derived from *dominus* 'master'. — Amer. **Monjeau, Mosher**.

— *Pierre **Mongeau** (Jacques and Jeanne Clémenceau) from Chagnolet in Charente-Maritime (Poitou-Charentes) m. Louise Dubois in France c. 1645.*

Mongeon, same origin as **Mongeau**. — Amer. **Mosher**.

— *Nicolas **Mongeon** (Nicolas and Andrée Brillart) from Montargis in Loiret (Centre) m. Marguerite-Geneviève Chevalier (Jean and Marie-Geneviève Avice) in Beauport, QC in 1723.*

Mongrain, probable alteration of *Maugrain*, from Old French *mau grain* 'bad grain', probably the nickname of a miller. — Amer. **Mongraw**.

— *Pierre Lafond dit **Mongrain**, son of Étienne from Saint-Laurent-de-la-Barrière in Charente-Maritime (Poitou-Charentes), m. Marie-Madeleine Rivard (Nicolas and Catherine de Saint-Père) in Québec in 1677.*

Monjeau, see **Mongeau**.

Monmaney, see **Montminy**.

Monpas, see **Montpas**.

Montambault, alteration of *Montembault*, a placename in Mayenne (Pays de la Loire).
— Amer. **Montambo**.

— *Michel **Montambault** dit Léveillé (Étienne and Marguerite Belliers) from Choisy-en-Brie in Seine-et-Marne (Île-de-France) m. Marie Mesuré (Étienne and Cécile Girard) in Québec in 1665.*

Montee, Montey, Montie, see **Monty**.

Montminy, origin undetermined. — Amer. **Momany, Momenee, Momeny, Mominee, Monmaney, Mumley**.

— *Guillaume **Montminy**/Montmesnil (René and Marguerite Verdon) from La Rochelle in Charente-Maritime (Poitou-Charentes) m. Marguerite Gobeil (Jean and Jeanne Guyet/Guillet) in Saint-Jean, Île d'Orléans, QC in 1688.*

Montpas, alteration of *Maupas*, a placename in France. — Amer. **Monpas**.

— *Nicolas **Maupas** dit Saint-Hilaire (Pierre and Chardine Fez/Fay) from Vaudry in Calvados (Basse-Normandie) m. Agnès Guillemet (Nicolas and Marie Sel) in Saint-Jean, Île d'Orléans, QC in 1698.*

Montreuil, apparently from *Montreuil*, a placename in France. — Amer. **Montrey, Montrie, Montroy**.

— *Jean Sédilot dit **Montreuil**, son of Louis from Gif-sur-Yvette in Essonne (Île-de-France), m. (1) Marie-Claire (de) Lahogue (Gilles and Marie Le Brun) in Québec, QC in 1669; (2) Charlotte-Françoise Poitras (Jean and Marie-Sainte Vié) in Québec, QC in 1689.*

Montville, see **Mandeville**.

Monty, from *Le Monty*, a placename in Aveyron (Midi-Pyrénées)— Amer. **Montee, Montey, Montie**.

— *Jean **Monty** (Dominique and Jeanne Benoist) from Saint-Bertrand-de-Comminges in Haute-Garonne (Midi-Pyrénées) m. Marie-Marthe Poyer (Jacques and Marguerite Dubois) in Chambly, QC in 1729.*

Monville, see **Mandeville**.

Moore, see **Populus**.

Mooso, see **Mousseau**.

Moquin, derived from *moqueur* 'mocker'. — Amer. **McQueen, Micha**.

— *Mathurin **Moquin** (Mathurin and Élisabeth Lefebvre) from Saumur in Maine-et-Loire (Pays de la Loire) m. Suzanne Beaujean (Élie and Suzanne Cougnon) in Montréal, QC in 1672.*

Moran, Morang, see **Morin**.

Moras, from *Moras*, a placename in France. — Amer. **Moross**.

— *Claude **Moras** (Godefroy and Anne Desroches) from Paris (Île-de-France) m. Thérèse Samson (Antoine and Catherine Larue) in Sainte-Foy, QC in 1741.*

Moreau, either from *(Le) Moreau*, a placename in France, or from the Latin name *Maurellus*, derived from *Maurus* 'Mauritanian', the nickname of a swarthy individual. —

Amer. **Morrow**.

— Jean **Moreau** (Jean and Catherine Leroux) from Parthenay in Deux-Sèvres (Poitou-Charentes) m. Marie-Anne Rodrigue (Jean and Anne Roy) in Québec, QC in 1692.

— Louis Cantin dit **Moreau**, descendant of Nicolas from Gonneville-sur-Honfleur in Calvados (Basse-Normandie), m. Françoise Parisien (Joseph and Marguerite Martin) in Qu'Appelle, SK in 1882.

— Pierre-François (de) Jordy/Desjordy/Desourdy dit **Moreau**, son of François from Carcassonne in Aude (Languedoc-Roussillon), m. Charlotte Foisy (Jacques and Marie-Charlotte Végeard) in Saint-Sulpice, QC in 1746.

Morel, either from (Le) Morel, a placename in France, or the same origin as **Moreau**. — Amer. **Morell, Morrell, Morrill**.

— Guillaume **Morel** (Guillaume and Jeanne Mathieu) from Paris (Île-de-France) m. Marie Baret (Jean and Jeanne Bitouset) in Beaupré, QC in 1690.

— Olivier **Morel**, sieur de La Durantaye (Thomas and Alliette du Houssay) from Le Gâvre in Loire-Atlantique (Pays de la Loire) m. Françoise Duquet (Denis and Catherine Gauthier) in Québec, QC in 1670.

Morin, either from (Le) Morin, a placename in France, or from the Latin name Maurinus, derived from Maurus 'Mauritanian', the nickname of a swarthy individual. — Amer. **Moran, Morang, Morong, Morrin, Morrow, Murray**.

— Pierre **Morin** dit Boucher from Normandie m. Marie-Madeleine Martin (Pierre and Catherine Vigneau) in Acadia c. 1661.

— Pierre **Morin** (Jacques and Hilaire Guéry) from Saint-Étienne-de-Brillouet in Vendée (Pays de la Loire) m. Catherine Lemesle (Jean and Marguerite Renard) in Québec, QC in 1672.

— Pierre **Morin** (Pierre and Marguerite Laurent) from Plaine-Haute in Côtes-d'Armor (Bretagne) m. Marie-Madeleine Lépinay/Lespinay (Jean and Catherine Granger) in Beauport, QC in 1694.

Morisset(te), derived from Morisse, a variant of **Maurice**. — Amer. **Morisett, Morissett, Morrisett, Morrissett, Morsett, Morsette, Mousette**.

— Jean **Morisset**/Moricet (Paul and Mathurine Guillois) from Surgères in Charente-Maritime (Poitou-Charentes) m. Jeanne Choret (Mathieu and Sébastienne Veillon) in Québec, QC in 1669.

Morois, see **Marois**.

Morong, see **Morin**.

Moross, see **Moras**.

Morrell, Morrill, see **Morel**.

Morrin, see **Morin**.

Morris, see **Maurice**.

Morrisett, Morrissett, see **Morisset(te)**.

Morrow, see **Moreau** and **Morin**.

Morse, see **Masse**.

Morsett, Morsette, see **Morisset(te)**.

Morway, see **Marois**.

Moses, see **Moïse**.

Mosher, see **Mongeau** and **Mongeon**.

Moss, see **Masse**.

Mossey, see **Massé.**

Mossow, see **Mousseau.**

Mothé, alteration of *Timothée,* from the Greek name *Timotheos* composed of *time* 'honor, respect' and *theos* 'God', hence 'honoring God'. — Amer. **Mutty.**

— *Timothée Thibodeau dit **Mothé**, descendant of Pierre from France, m. (1) Marguerite Aucoin (Martin and Élisabeth Boudrot) in Acadia c. 1761; (2) Élisabeth Bélanger (Jean-Baptiste and Marie-Angélique Vézina) in Beauport, QC in 1771.*

Mousaw, see **Mousseau.**

Mousette, see **Morisset(te).**

Mousseau, from *(Le) Mousseau,* a placename in France. — Amer. **Mooso, Mossow, Mousaw, Mousso, Mussaw, Musseau.**

— *Jacques **Mousseau** dit Laviolette (Nicolas and Jacquine Janot) from Azay-le-Rideau in Indre-et-Loire (Centre) m. Marguerite Sauviot (Jean and Louise Brodeur) in Montréal, QC in 1658.*

Muller, see **Molleur.**

Mumblo, Mumblow, see **Mombleau.**

Mumley, see **Montminy.**

Murray, see **Marier** and **Morin.**

Muse, see **Mius.**

Mushtare, see **Marcheterre.**

Mussaw, Musseau, see **Mousseau.**

Mutty, see **Mothé.**

Myatt, see **Mailhot.**

Myers, see **Maillet.**

Myott, Myotte, see **Mailhot.**

Myre, alteration of **Lemire.** — Amer. **Mere, Meyre.**

— *Jean **Lemire** (Mathurin and Jeanne Vanier) from Rouen in Seine-Maritime (Haute-Normandie) m. Louise Marsolet (Nicolas and Marie Barbier) in Québec, QC in 1653.*

N

Nadeau, either a variant of Occitan *Nadal,* same origin as **Noël,** or derived from *Bernad,* same origin as **Bernard.** — Amer. **Neadeau, Neadow, Neddeau, Neddo, Neddow, Nedeau, Nedo, Nido.**
— *Jean **Nadeau** (Jean and Marie Raffel) from Le Gué-de-Velluire in Vendée (Pays de la Loire) m. Marie-Anne Dumont (Julien and Catherine Topsan) in Saint-Jean, Île d'Orléans, QC in 1696.*
— *Ozanie-Joseph **Nadeau** dit Lavigne (Macia and Jeanne Despins) from Genouillac in Charente (Poitou-Charentes) m. Marguerite Abraham (Godegrand and Denise Fleury) in Québec in 1665.*

Nailor, see **Cloutier.**

Naneville, see **Laneuville.**

Naro, Narreau, Narrow, see **Noreau.**

Naylor, see **Cloutier.**

Neadeau, see **Nadeau.**

Neadle, see **Laiguille.**

Neadow, Neddeau, Neddo, Neddow, Nedeau, Nedo, see **Nadeau.**

Needle, see **Laiguille.**

Nephew, Neveau, see **Neveu.**

Neverett, Neverette, see **Levert.**

Neveu, from Old French *neveu* 'grandson, nephew'. — Amer. **Nephew, Neveau, Nevue.**
— *Jean **Neveu**/Nepveu (Gilles and Claude Gaudron) from Poitiers in Vienne (Poitou-Charentes) m. Catherine Godin (Pierre and Jeanne Rousselière) in Lachine, QC in 1688.*
— *Jean-Baptiste-Louis **Neveu**/Nepveu (Jean-Baptiste and Marie-Françoise Pachot) from Blois in Loir-et-Cher (Centre) m. Marie-Josèphe Janson (Jean-Baptiste and Marie-Josèphe Lord) in L'Assomption, QC in 1770.*

Newall, see **Noël.**

Newcity, see **Villeneuve.**

Newell, see **Noël.**

Newton, Newtown, Newvine, see **Villeneuve.**

Nice, see **Joly.**

Nichols, see **Nicole.**

Nicolas, from the Greek name *Nikolaos* via Latin *Nicolaus,* from *nike* 'victory' and *laos* 'people', hence 'prevailing among the people'. — Amer. **Nicklaw.**
— *Pierre Bourcier dit **Nicolas,** descendant of Jean from Chenac-Saint-Seurin-d'Uzet in Charente-Maritime (Poitou-Charentes), m. Jovide Brault (Germain and Amable Poitras) in Saint-Joachim, QC in 1826.*

Nicole, from the Greek name *Nikolaos* composed of *nike* 'victory' and *laos* 'people', hence 'prevailing among the people'. — Amer. **Nichols.**

— *Olivier **Nicole** (Luc and Gillette Basset) from Kairon in Manche (Basse-Normandie) m. Louise Brochu (Jean-Baptiste and Suzanne Garand) in Saint-Vallier, QC in 1765.*
Nido, see Nadeau.
Noël, from *Noël* 'Christmas', a name given to an individual born on that day or around that time of year. — Amer. **Newall, Newell.**
— *François **Noël** (Pierre and Élisabeth Augustin) from Chiré-en-Montreuil in Vienne (Poitou-Charentes) m. Nicole Legrand (Nicolas and Anne Duplessis) in Québec, QC in 1669.*
Nolet, derived from names such as *Bernolet, Renolet, Arnolet*. — Amer. **Nollette.**
— *Sébastien **Nolet** dit Larivière (Vincent and Jeanne Martel) from Sainte-Pexine in Vendée (Pays de la Loire) m. Jeanne Auger (Savinien and Marie Ruelle) in Québec, QC in 1671.*
Noreau, variant of *Noireau*, derived from *noir* 'black (haired)'. — Amer. **Naro, Narreau, Narrow, Noreault, Noro.**
— *Mathurin **Noreau** (Jean and Marie Patureau) from Saint-Georges-des-Coteaux in Charente-Maritime (Poitou-Charentes) m. Marie-Josèphe Marchet (Jean and Marie-Jeanne Gély) in Québec, QC in 1722.*
Normand, from *Normand*, the nickname of a native of Normandie, a former province in France. — Amer. **Norman.**
— *Gervais **Normand**/Lenormand (François and Radegonde Gadois) from Igé in Orne (Basse-Normandie) m. Léonarde Jouault in Igé c. 1635.*
Normandin, derived from **Normand.** — Amer. **Lamonda, Lamonday, Lamondia, Lamondie.**
— *Daniel **Normandin** (Jacob and Marie Viaud) from Rochefort in Charente-Maritime (Poitou-Charentes) m. Louise Hayot (Jean and Louise Pelletier) in Sorel, QC in 1687.*
Noro, see Noreau.
Nourry, from the Germanic name *Nodric* composed of *nod* 'need' and *ric* 'powerful'. — Amer. **Nourie.**
— *François Parmentier dit **Nourry**, grandson of Louis from Lyon in Rhône (Rhône-Alpes), m. Louise Camirand (André and Marie Lord) in Pointe-du-Lac, QC in 1805.*

O

Oben, see **Aubin.**
Obershaw, Obeshaw, see **Aubuchon.**
Obey, see **Aubé** and **Aubin.**
Obin, see **Aubin.**
Obrey, see **Aubry.**
O'Brien, see **Lebrun.**
Obuchon, see **Aubuchon.**
Oby, see **Aubé.**
Oclair, O'Clair, see **Auclair.**
Ocoin, O'Coin, see **Aucoin.**
Odett, Odette, O'Dett, O'Dette, see **Audet(te).**
Oge, Ogea, Ogee, see **Auger.**
O'Quinn, see **Aucoin.**
Oshia, see **Auger.**
Ostiguy, probable alteration of *Aosteguia*, a placename in Pyrénées-Atlantiques (Aquitaine). — Amer. **Austin.**
  *— Dominique **Ostiguy** dit Domingue (Jean and Catherine Chevery) from Arcangues in Pyrénées-Atlantiques (Aquitaine) m. Marie-Marguerite Parent (Pierre and Marie-Catherine James) in Chambly, QC in 1754.*
Ouellet(te), probable alteration of *Houellet*, derived from Old French *ho(u)el* 'mattock', the nickname of a maker or a worker who used such an implement. — Amer. **Ouelett, Ouellett, Ouilette, Wallett, Wallette, Wellet, Wellette, Wilette, Willet, Willete, Willett, Willette.**
  *— René **Ouellet** (François and Isabelle Barré) from Paris (Île-de-France) m. (1) Anne Rivet in Québec, QC in 1666; (2) Thérèse Mignault (Jean and Louise Cloutier) in Québec, QC in 1679.*
Ouimet(te), probable alteration of *Wi(l)met*, derived from *Willaume*, a regional variant of *Guillaume*, from the Germanic name *Wilhelm* composed of *wil* 'will' and *helm* 'helmet'. — Amer. **Wemett, Wemette, Wimett, Wimette.**
  *— Jean **Ouimet** (Nicolas and Perrette Nicaise) from Vrigny in Marne (Champagne-Ardenne) m. Renée Gagnon (Jean and Marguerite Cauchon) in Québec in 1660.*
Oven, see **Dufour.**
Overshon, see **Aubuchon.**

P

Pacquette, see **Paquet(te).**

Page, Paige, see **Lepage.**

Paillé, from *Paillé,* a placename in France. — Amer. **Pay, Paye, Payea, Payie.**

— *Léonard Paillé (André and Catherine Geoffroy) from Pressac in Vienne (Poitou-Charentes) m. Louise Vachon (Paul and Marguerite Langlois) in Québec in 1678.*

Papillon, either from *(Le) Papillon,* a placename in France, or from *papillon* 'butterfly', the nickname of a flighty individual. — Amer. **Butterfly, Flagg.**

— *Étienne Papillon (François and Michelle Fabre) from La Rochelle in Charente-Maritime (Poitou-Charentes) m. Geneviève Garnier (François and Jacqueline Freslon) in Neuville, QC in 1691.*

Papin, same origin as **Pépin.** — Amer. **Pappan.**

— *Pierre Papin (François and Michelle Laigneau) from Sablé-sur-Sarthe in Sarthe (Pays de la Loire) m. Anne Pelletier (Mathurin and Catherine Lagneau) in Montréal, QC in 1665.*

Papineau, derived from **Papin.** — Amer. **Papinaw, Pappa.**

— *Samuel Papineau dit Montigny (Samuel and Marie Delain/Delaine) from Montigny in Deux-Sèvres (Pays de la Loire) m. Catherine Quévillon (Adrien and Jeanne Hunault) in Rivière-des-Prairies, QC in 1704.*

Pappan, see **Papin.**

Paquet(te), either the same origin as **Paquin** or an alteration of *Pasquier,* from *(Le) Pasquier,* a placename in France. — Amer. **Pacquette, Parker, Parquette, Pauquette, Perket, Perkett, Perkins, Pocket, Pockett, Pockette, Poquet, Poquette, Pouquette.**

— *Isaac/Étienne Paquet/Pasquier dit Lavallée (Mathurin and Marie Fremillon) from Montaigu in Vendée (Pays de la Loire) m. Élisabeth Meunier (Mathurin and Françoise Fafard) in Château-Richer, QC in 1670.*

— *Méry Paquet/Pasquier (Annet and Marguerite Genet) from Poitiers in Vienne (Poitou-Charentes) m. Vincente Beaumont in France c. 1638.*

— *Noël Paquet dit Larivière (Thomas and Anne Liaudin) from Verdun in Meuse (Lorraine) m. Marguerite Beaudet (Laurent and Marguerite-Louise Crevier) in Chambly, QC in 1709.*

Paquin, derived from *Paque,* from the Latin name *Pascha,* from Hebrew *pasah* 'Passover'. — Amer. **Perkins, Pikey.**

— *Nicolas Paquin (Jean and Renée Frémont) from La Poterie-Cap-d'Antifer in Seine-Maritime (Haute-Normandie) m. Marie-Françoise Plante (Jean and Françoise Boucher) in Château-Richer, QC in 1676.*

Paradis, from *(Le) Paradis,* a placename in France. — Amer. **Paradee, Paradise, Parady, Pardis, Paridee, Parody.**

— *Pierre Paradis (Jacques and Michelle Pelle) from Mortagne-au-Perche in Orne (Basse-Normandie) m. Barbe Guyon (Jean and Mathurine Robin) in France in 1632.*

Paranteau, Paranto, see **Parenteau.**

Pardis, see **Paradis.**

Paré, from Old French *paré* 'dressed, finished', the nickname of a worker who carded and smoothed woolen cloth. — Amer. **Perry.**

— *Robert **Paré** (Mathieu and Marie Joannet) from Saint-Laurent-Rochefort in Loire (Rhône-Alpes) m. Françoise Lehoux (Jacques and Marie Meilleur) in Québec, QC in 1653.*

Parent, from Old French *parent* 'father', a nickname used to distinguish a father and son with the same given name. — Amer. **Parrent, Parron.**

— *Pierre **Parent**/Parant (André and Marie Coudré) from Mortagne-sur-Gironde in Charente-Maritime (Poitou-Charentes) m. Jeanne Badeau (Jacques and Anne Ardouin) in Québec, QC in 1654.*

Parenteau, derived from **Parent.** — Amer. **Paranteau, Paranto, Paronto, Parranto, Pronto.**

— *Pierre **Parenteau** dit Lafontaine (Jean and Marguerite *Fouestre) from Bazauges in Charente-Maritime (Poitou-Charentes) m. Madeleine Tisserand (Louis and Louise Destré) in Québec, QC in 1673.*

Paridee, see **Paradis.**

Pariseau, derived from *Paris*, from the Latin name *Patricius*, from *patricius* 'patrician'. — Amer. **Pariso, Parizo, Periso, Perrizo.**

— *Jean Delpé dit **Pariseau** (Jean and Marguerite Delmas) from Rodez in Aveyron (Midi-Pyrénées) m. Renée Lorion (Mathurin and Jeanne Bizet) in Montréal, QC in 1674.*

Parisien, from *Parisien* 'Parisian', the nickname of a native of Paris. — Amer. **Parisian.**

— *Pierre Léger dit **Parisien** (Pierre and Marguerite *Dendase) from Paris (Île-de-France) m. Jeanne Boilard (Jean and Jeanne Maranda) in Québec, QC in 1706.*

Pariso, Parizo, see **Pariseau.**

Parker, see **Paquet(te).**

Paro, see **Perrault** and **Perron.**

Parody, see **Paradis.**

Paronto, see **Parenteau.**

Parot, see **Perrot(te).**

Parquette, see **Paquet(te).**

Parranto, see **Parenteau.**

Parrent, see **Parent.**

Parro, see **Perrault.**

Parron, see **Parent.**

Parrot, see **Perrot(te).**

Parrow, see **Perras** and **Perrault.**

Passeno, Passinault, Passineau, Passino, see **Pinsonnault.**

Patenaude, alteration of Old French *pate(r)nostre* 'rosary', the nickname of a maker. — Amer. **Patenode, Patnaud, Patnaude, Patneau, Patneaude, Patno, Patnod, Patnode, Patnoe, Patnude, Pattenaude.**

— *Nicolas **Patenaude**/Patenostre (Nicolas and Adrienne Simon) from Berville in Seine-Maritime (Haute-Normandie) m. Marguerite Breton (Antoine and Sainte Paulin) in Québec, QC in 1651.*

Patraw, see **Pétrin.**

Patrick, see **Patry.**

Patro, Patrow, see **Poitras.**

Patry, from the Latin name *Patricius*, from *patricius* 'patrician'. — Amer. **Patrick.**
— André **Patry** *(René and Renée Cousinet) from Airvault in Deux-Sèvres (Poitou-Charentes) m. Henriette Cartois (Lambert and Marie Lambert) in Québec, QC in 1675.*

Pattenaude, see **Patenaude.**

Pauquette, see **Paquet(te).**

Pauzé, probable alteration of *Pauzet*, a placename in Gironde (Aquitaine). — Amer. **Posey.**
— Jacques **Pauzé**/*Posé (Jean and Isabelle Hébert) from La Rochelle in Charente-Maritime (Poitou-Charentes) m. Marie Jobidon (Louis and Marie de Ligny) in Québec, QC in 1678.*

Pay, Paye, Payea, Payie, see **Paillé.**

Payrot, see **Perrot(te).**

Payseno, see **Pinsonnault.**

Peach, see **Poirier.**

Peacor, see **Picard.**

Pealo, see **Pilon.**

Pearo, see **Perrault** and **Perron.**

Peartree, see **Poirier.**

Pease, see **Therrien.**

Peashey, see **Piché.**

Peat, see **Pitre.**

Peatee, see **Petit.**

Peats, see **Pitre.**

Pechette, see **Pichette.**

Pecor, Pecore, see **Picard.**

Pecott, Pecotte, see **Picotte.**

Pednault, probable alteration of *Pédenaut* or *Pédenau*, placenames in France. — Amer. **Pelno, Peno.**
— Pierre-Étienne **Pednault** *(Michel and Catherine Mélaine/Mestay) from Saint-Martin-de-Ré in Charente-Maritime (Poitou-Charentes) m. Marie-Gertrude Bouchard (François and Marguerite Simard) in Baie-Saint-Paul, QC in 1732.*

Peet, Peete, Peets, see **Pitre.**

Peidlow, see **Piédalue.**

Pelcher, Pelchy, see **Pelletier.**

Pelican, see **Péloquin.**

Pelin, see **Pilon.**

Pelkey, Pelkie, Pelky, see **Pelletier.**

Pelland, alteration of *Pellan*, a placename in Bretagne. — Amer. **Pellant.**
— Yves Martin dit **Pelland** *(Julien and Marie Binard) from Péaule in Morbihan (Bretagne) m. Marie Piet (Jean and Marguerite Chemereau) in Québec in 1699.*

Pellerin, alteration of *pèlerin* 'pilgrim'. — Amer. **Pellerine, Pelrine, Pelroy.**
— Étienne **Pellerin** *from France m. Jeanne Savoie (François and Catherine Lejeune) in Acadia c. 1675.*

Pelletier, from *pelletier* 'furrier'. — Amer. **Pelcher, Pelchy, Pelkey, Pelkie, Pelky, Pel-**

litier, **Pilkey**.

— *Guillaume* **Pelletier**/*Peltier dit Gobloteur (Éloi and Françoise Matte) from Bresolettes in Orne (Basse-Normandie) m. Michelle Mabille (Guillaume and Étiennette *Monhé) in France in 1619.*

Pelno, see **Pednault**.

Pelo, Pelon, see **Pilon**.

Péloquin, either from the medieval name *Peloquinus* or derived from Occitan *pelhoc* 'rag', the nickname of a ragman or of someone dressed in tatters. — Amer. **Pelican**.

— *François* **Péloquin** *dit Crédit (Mathurin and Ambroise Syllard) from Niort in Deux-Sèvres (Poitou-Charentes) m. Marie Niquet (Pierre and Françoise Lemoine) in Trois-Rivières, QC in 1699.*

Pelott, Pelotte, see **Pilote**.

Pelow, see **Pilon**.

Pelrine, Pelroy, see **Pellerin**.

Penell, see **Pinel**.

Peno, see **Pednault**.

Penor, see **Pinard**.

Pensoneau, see **Pinsonnault**.

Pépin, from the Germanic name *Pipin*. — Amer. **Peppan, Peppin, Pippen**.

— *Antoine* **Pépin** *dit Lachance (André and Jeanne Chevalier) from Le Havre in Seine-Maritime (Haute-Normandie) m. Marie Teste (Jean and Louise Talonneau) in Québec, QC in 1659.*

— *Robert* **Pépin** *(Jean and Jeanne Dumont) from Grisy in Calvados (Basse-Normandie) m. Marie Crête (Jean and Marguerite Gaulin) in Québec, QC in 1670.*

Périard, alteration of *Périllard*, probably from *Le Périllard*, a placename in Loir-et-Cher (Centre). — Amer. **Perior, Periord**.

— *Nicolas* **Périllard** *dit Bourguignon (Nicolas and Nicole Baraton) from Auxerre in Yonne (Bourgogne) m. Jeanne Sabourin (Jean and Mathurine Renaud) in Montréal, QC in 1695.*

Perica, see **Perruquier**.

Périgord, from *Périgord*, a former province in France. — Amer. **Perigard**.

— *François Marquet dit* **Périgord** *(François and Marie Barison) from Chapelle-Gonaguet in Dordogne (Aquitaine) m. Marie-Louise Galarneau (Charles and Geneviève Greslon) in Québec, QC in 1706.*

Perior, Periord, see **Périard**.

Periso, see **Pariseau**.

Perket, Perkett, see **Paquet(te)**.

Perkins, see **Paquet(te)** and **Paquin**.

Pero, see **Perrault** and **Perron**.

Perras, from *Perras*, a placename in France. — Amer. **Parrow, Perro**.

— *Pierre* **Perras** *dit Lafontaine (Pierre and Jeanne Lasnier) from La Rochelle in Charente-Maritime (Poitou-Charentes) m. Denise Lemaître (Denis and Catherine Deharme) in Montréal, QC in 1660.*

Perrault, derived from *Pierre*, from the Latin name *Petrus*, derived from *petra* 'rock, stone'. — Amer. **Paro, Parro, Parrow, Pearo, Pero, Perro**.

— *Nicolas* **Perrault**/*Perrot (François and Marie Sirot) from Darcey in Côte-d'Or*

(Bourgogne) m. Madeleine Raclos (Idebon and Marie Viennot) in Québec in 1671.
— *Louis Leparon dit **Perrault**, son of Pierre from Derval in Loire-Atlantique (Pays de la Loire), m. Marie-Josèphe Normandeau (Pierre and Marguerite Rancourt) in Québec, QC in 1751.*

Perrica, see **Perruquier**.

Perrizo, see **Pariseau**.

Perro, see **Perras** and **Perrault**.

Perron, either from *(Le) Perron*, a placename in France, or the same origin as **Perrault**.
— Amer. **Dupperon, Paro, Pearo, Pero, Poro**.
— *Daniel **Perron** dit Suire (François and Jeanne Suire) from Dompierre-sur-Mer in Charente-Maritime (Poitou-Charentes) m. Louise Gargottin (Jacques and Françoise Bernard) in Château-Richer, QC in 1664.*

Perrot(te), same origin as **Perrault**. — Amer. **Parot, Parrot, Payrot, Perrott**.
— *Albert **Perrot** (... and Marie Monal) from Aulas in Gard (Languedoc-Roussillon) m. Marie-Louise Létourneau (Louis and Marie-Angélique Desnoyers) in Saint-Charles-sur-Richelieu, QC in 1761.*

Perruquier, from *perruquier* 'wigmaker'. — Amer. **Perica, Perrica**.
— *Édouard Amelot dit **Perruquier**, descendant of Jacques from Dieppe in Seine-Maritime (Haute-Normandie), m. Émilie Sauvage (Jean-Olivier and Marie-Louise Leroux) in Sain-Anicet, QC in 1845.*

Perry, see **Paré** and **Poirier**.

Peryea, see **Poirier**.

Peshette, see **Pichette**.

Pete, see **Pitre**.

Petee, see **Petit**.

Peters, see **Pitre**.

Petit, from *petit* 'little, small', either the nickname of a short individual or the youngest in the family. — Amer. **Little, Peatee, Petee, Petite**.
— *Nicolas **Petit** dit Lapré/Laprée (Nicolas and Catherine Ancelin) from Le Gué-d'Alleré in Charente-Maritime (Poitou-Charentes) m. Marie Pouponnel (Jean and Michelle Boulet) in Trois-Rivières, QC in 1656.*
— *Pierre **Petit** dit Gobin (François and Jeanne Gobin) from Lyon in Rhône (Rhône-Alpes) m. Marguerite Véron (Étienne and Marie Moral) in Trois-Rivières, QC in 1692.*
— *Pierre **Petit** dit Saint-Pierre (Jean and Marie Blot) from Évreux in Eure (Haute-Normandie) m. Judith Miville (Pierre and Marie-Anne Roy) in Québec in 1758.*

Petitpas, probably from *Le Petit Pas*, a placename in France. — Amer. **Pitts**.
— *Claude **Petitpas**, sieur de Lafleur from France m. Catherine Bugaret (Bernard and ...) in Acadia c. 1658.*

Petre, Petri, Petrie, see **Pitre**.

Pétrin, alteration of *Patrin*, probably derived from *pâtre* 'shepherd'. — Amer. **Patraw**.
— *François **Pétrin**/Patrin (François and Marie Bachelier) from Grez-Neuville in Maine-et-Loire (Pays de la Loire) m. Marguerite-Antoinette Parenteau (Pierre-Louis and Marguerite Laurent) in Yamaska, QC in 1743.*

Petry, see **Pitre**.

Phaneuf, alteration of *Farnworth* via *Farnsworth*, a placename in England. — Amer. **Faneuf, Faneuff, Fenoff**.

— *Mathias Farnsworth/**Phaneuf** (Mathias and Sarah Nutting) from Groton in Massachusetts m. Catherine Charpentier (Jean and Françoise Hunault) in Rivière-des-Prairies, QC in 1713.*

Pharmer, see **Therrien**.

Phelix, see **Félix**.

Philie, alteration of Breton *Fily*, from the Latin name *Filius*, from *filius* 'son'. — Amer. **Filie**.

— *Michel **Fily**, sieur de Kerrigou (Jean and Jeanne Provost) from Spézet in Finistère (Bretagne) m. Marie-Madeleine Plumereau (Julien and Jeanne Barbier) in Montréal, QC in 1705.*

Picard, from *Picard*, the nickname of a native of Picardie, a former province in France. — Amer. **Peacor, Pecor, Pecore**.

— *Philippe Destroismaisons dit **Picard** (Adrien and Antoinette Leroux) from Montreuil in Pas-de-Calais (Nord-Pas-de-Calais) m. Martine Crosnier (Pierre and Jeanne Rotreau) in Château-Richer, QC in 1669.*

— *Alexandre Noiret dit **Picard** (Louis and Marie-Louise Braillon) from Thenailles in Aisne (Picardie) m. Jeanne Quenneville (Jean-Baptiste and Marie-Madeleine Guilbert) in Montréal, QC in 1756.*

Piché, probable variant of *Pichet*, same origin as **Pichette**. — Amer. **Peashey**.

— *Pierre **Piché**/Picher/Pichet dit Lamusette (Pierre and Anne Piaut/Piot) from Faye-la-Vineuze in Indre-et-Loire (Centre) m. Catherine Durand (Pierre and Jacquette Courtois) in Québec, QC in 1665.*

Pichette, alteration of Old French *pichet* '(measuring) pot', either the nickname of a potter or a measurer. — Amer. **Pechette, Peshette**.

— *Jean **Pichet** from Poitiers in Vienne (Poitou-Charentes) m. Madeleine Leblanc (Jean and Madeleine Nicolet) in Québec c. 1665.*

Picotte, alteration of *Picot*, either from *(Le) Picot*, a placename in France, or from Old French *picot* 'pickaxe', the nickname of an individual who used such an implement. — Amer. **Pecott, Pecotte**.

— *Pierre **Picot**/Picault (Pierre and Andrée Leblanc) from Neuville-en-Beaumont in Manche (Basse-Normandie) m. Marie-Madeleine Brosseau (Nicolas and Madeleine Huppé) in Charlesbourg, QC in 1720.*

Pidgeon, see **Pigeon**.

Piédalue, alteration of *Pied d'Aloue*, a placename in Yonne (Bourgogne). — Amer. **Peidlow, Piedlow**.

— *Julien **Piédalue** dit Laprairie/Prairie (Pierre and Marie Dolbeau) from Courtalain in Eure-et-Loir (Centre) m. Françoise Aupry (Louis-Bertrand and Anne Dumas) in Laprairie, QC in 1722.*

Pigeon, from Old French *pigeon* 'fledgling, squab', the nickname of a breeder or seller. — Amer. **Pidgeon**.

— *Pierre **Pigeon** (Claude and Françoise Philippe) from Paris (Île-de-France) m. Jeanne Godard (Robert and Antoinette Grandpierre) in Montréal, QC in 1662.*

Pikey, see **Paquin**.

Pilkey, see **Pelletier**.

Pilon, from *(Le) Pilon*, a placename in France. — Amer. **Pealo, Pelin, Pelo, Pelon, Pelow**.

— *Antoine* **Pilon** *(Thomas and Madeleine Ruault) from Bayeux in Calvados (Basse-Normandie) m. Marie-Anne Brunet (Mathieu and Marie Blanchard) in Montréal, QC in 1689.*

Pilote, either from *Pilote*, a placename in France, or from *pilote* 'pilot', the nickname of an individual who steered a ship. — Amer. **Pelott, Pelotte.**

— *Léonard* **Pilote** *from La Rochelle in Charente-Maritime (Poitou-Charentes) m. Denise Gauthier in France in 1644.*

Pinard, from *Pinard*, a placename in France. — Amer. **Penor.**

— *Louis* **Pinard** *(Jean and Marguerite Gaigneur) from La Rochelle in Charente-Maritime (Poitou-Charentes) m. (1) Marie-Madeleine Hertel (Jacques and Marie Marguerie) in Trois-Rivières, QC in 1658; (2) Marie-Ursule Pépin (Guillaume and Jeanne Méchin) in Champlain, QC in 1680.*

Pinel, from *(Le) Pinel*, a placename in France. — Amer. **Penell, Pinelle.**

— *Nicolas* **Pinel** *(Jean and Thomasse de la Haye) from Campagnolles in Calvados (Basse-Normandie) m. Madeleine Maraud/Marraud (Mathieu and Jeanne Gay/Guay) in France in 1630.*

Pinet(te), from *(Le) Pinet*, a placename in France. — Amer. **Pinnette, Spruce.**

— *Pierre* **Pinet** *(Julien and Antoinette Beauval/Coquerelle) from Chalandrey in Manche (Basse-Normandie) m. Marguerite Michaud (Louis and Marie-Geneviève Albert) in Kamouraska, QC in 1765.*

Pinsonnault, derived from *pinson* 'chaffinch', the nickname of an individual who liked to sing or whistle. — Amer. **Passeno, Passinault, Passineau, Passino, Payseno, Pensoneau.**

— *François* **Pinsonnault** *dit Lafleur from Saintes in Charente-Maritime (Poitou-Charentes) m. Anne Leper in Québec c. 1673.*

Pippen, see **Pépin.**

Pitre, from Old French *pistre* 'baker'. — Amer. **Peat, Peats, Peet, Peete, Peets, Pete, Peters, Petre, Petri, Petrie, Petry, Pitt.**

— *Jean* **Pitre** *from France m. Marie Pesseley (Isaac and Barbe Bajolet) in Acadia c. 1665.*

Pitts, see **Petitpas.**

Plamondon, derived from *Plamont*, a placename in France. — Amer. **Plumadore.**

— *Philippe* **Plamondon** *dit Lafleur from Lapeyrouse in Puy-de-Dôme (Auvergne) m. Marguerite Clément (Jean and Madeleine Surget) in Laprairie, QC in 1680.*

Plankey, see **Plantier.**

Plante, from *Plante*, a placename in France. — Amer. **Plant, Plaunt.**

— *Jean* **Plante** *(Nicolas and Isabelle Chauvin) from Laleu in Charente-Maritime (Poitou-Charentes) m. Françoise Boucher (Marin and Perrine Mallet) in Québec, QC in 1650.*

Plantier, from *(Le) Plantier*, a placename in France. — Amer. **Plankey, Plonkey.**

— *Jean-Baptiste* **Plantier** *dit Lagrenade (François and Jeanne Rivel) from Rivel in Aude (Languedoc-Roussillon) m. Marie-Josèphe Choquet (Nicolas and Marie-Anne Casavant) in Varennes, QC in 1760.*

Planty, see **Laplante.**

Plaunt, see **Plante.**

Playful, see **Joyal.**

Plonkey, see **Plantier.**

Plonty, see **Laplante.**

Plouffe, alteration of *Blouf* via *Plouf*, probably from the Germanic name *Biliwulf* composed of *bili* 'kind, nice' and *wulf* 'wolf'. — Amer. **Ploof, Plouf, Plouff, Pluff.**

— Jean **Plouf/Blouf** *(Antoine and Geneviève Demest) from Paris (Île-de-France) m. Marie-Madeleine Guilleboeuf (Nicolas and Madeleine *Vavilin) in Montréal, QC in 1669.*

Plourde, either an alteration of *Pelourde*, a placename in Gironde (Aquitaine), or derived from *Mouterre-sur-Blourde*, a placename in Vienne (Poitou-Charentes). — Amer. **Plourd, Plude, Splude.**

— René **Plourde** *(François and Jeanne Gremillon) from Vouneuil-sur-Vienne in Vienne (Poitou-Charentes) m. Jeanne-Marguerite Bérubé (Damien and Jeanne Savonnet) in Rivière-Ouelle, QC in 1697.*

Pluff, see **Plouffe.**

Plumadore, see **Plamondon.**

Pocket, Pockett, Pockette, see **Paquet(te).**

Podvin, see **Potvin.**

Poirier, from *(Le) Poirier*, a placename in France. — Amer. **Peach, Peartree, Perry, Peryea, Poirer, Poirior, Porrier, Pouria, Puariea, Purrier.**

— Jean **Poirier** *from France m. Jeanne Chebrat (Antoine and Françoise Chaumoret) in France or Acadia c. 1647.*

— Jean **Poirier** *dit Lajeunesse (Jean and Jeanne Ribairo) from Molières in Lot (Midi-Pyrénées) m. Marie Langlois (Thomas and Marie de Neufville) in Montréal, QC in 1668.*

— Joseph **Poirier** *dit Desloges (Jacques and Françoise Brunet) from Lathus-Saint-Rémy in Vienne (Poitou-Charentes) m. Marie Gauthier (Pierre and Charlotte Roussel) in Montréal, QC in 1709.*

— Nicolas **Poirier** *(Pierre and Suzanne Fonteneau) from Les Brouzils in Vendée (Pays de la Loire) m. Anne Rabouin (Jean and Marguerite Ardiot) in Montréal, QC in 1689.*

Poissant, variant of *puissant* 'strong, powerful'. — Amer. **Fish, Fisher.**

— Jacques **Poissant** *dit La Saline (Jacques and Isabelle Magor) from Marennes in Charente-Maritime (Poitou-Charentes) m. Marguerite Bessette (Jean and Anne Seigneur) in Québec c. 1699.*

Poisson, from *poisson* 'fish', probably the nickname of a fishmonger. — Amer. **Fish, Fisher.**

— Jean **Poisson** *(Jean and Barbe Broust) from Mortagne-au-Perche in Orne (Basse-Normandie) m. Jacqueline Chamboy (Jacques and Marguerite Fauvel) in France in 1644.*

Poitras, alteration of *Po(i)dras*, probably derived from Breton *poder* 'potter'. — Amer. **Patro, Patrow, Putraw.**

— Jean **Poitras/Poidras** *(Laurent and Renée Bertin/Breton) from Cugand in Vendée (Pays de la Loire) m. (1) Marie-Sainte Vié (Robert and Sainte Paulin) in Québec, QC in 1664; (2) Marie-Anne Lavoie (Pierre and Isabelle Aupé) in Québec, QC in 1695.*

Poland, see **Poulin.**

Politte, alteration of *Hypolite*, a variant of *Hippolyte*, from the Greek name *Hippolytos* composed of *hippos* 'horse' and the stem of *luein* 'to let loose', hence 'letting horses loose'. — Amer. **Polite**.

— *Hypolite Paul Robert Roussin dit* **Politte**, *descendant of Jean from Tourouvre in Orne (Basse-Normandie), m. Marie-Anne Boyer (Nicolas and Dorothée Olivier) in Ste. Genevieve, MO in 1797.*

Polyot, see **Pouliot**.

Pomainville, alteration of *Pommainville*, a placename in Orne (Basse-Normandie). — Amer. **Pomerville, Pommenville, Pommerville**.

— *Henri Brault dit* **Pomainville**/*Pominville (Jean and Suzanne Jousseaume) from Ballon in Charente-Maritime (Poitou-Charentes) m. Claude (de) Chevrainville (Jacques and Marguerite-Léonarde Baudon) in Québec, QC in 1665.*

Pombrio, see **Pontbriand**.

Pomerleau, alteration of *Pamerleau*, origin undetermined. — Amer. **Pomelow, Pumarlo**.

— *Noël Vachon dit* **Pamerleau**, *son of Paul from La Copechagnière in Vendée (Pays de la Loire), m. Monique Giroux (Toussaint and Marie Godard) in Beauport, QC in 1695.*

Pomerville, Pommenville, Pommerville, see **Pomainville**.

Pontbriand, alteration of *Briand*, a variant of *Brien*, from Breton *brient* 'preeminence, privilege', probably the nickname of a pretentious individual. — Amer. **Pombrio**.

— *Jean-Baptiste Briand dit* **Pontbriand**, *grandson of Jean-Baptiste from Nanteuil-en-Vallée in Charente (Poitou-Charentes), m. Thérèse Perron (Eustache and Thérèse Arpin) in Sorel, QC in 1794.*

Ponton, from *(Le) Ponton*, a placename in France. — Amer. **Ponto**.

— *Pierre-André* **Ponton** *dit Saint-Germain (Pierre-André and Geneviève Troisvallets) from Saint-Germain-en-Laye in Yvelines (Île-de-France) m. Marie-Jeanne Thomas (Paul and Marie-Josèphe Barbeau) in Montréal, QC in 1756.*

Pooler, see **Poulin**.

Popour, see **Poupart**.

Populus, from Latin *populus* 'people', the nickname of a cantor. —Amer. **Moore**.

— *Joseph Douge dit* **Populus** *(Laurent and Catherine Chudau) from Saint-Rémy in Haute-Saône (Franche-Comté), m. Geneviève Duval (Guillaume and Marie-Françoise Jérémie) in Pointe-aux-Trembles, QC in 1766.*

Poquet, Poquette, see **Paquet(te)**.

Poro, see **Perron**.

Porrier, see **Poirier**.

Portwine, see **Potvin**.

Posey, see **Pauzé**.

Potvin, alteration of *Poitevin*, the nickname of a native of Poitou, a former province in France. — Amer. **Podvin, Portwine, Potvine, Potwin, Pudvah, Pudvan**.

— *Louis* **Poitevin** *dit Saint-Louis (Pierre and Marie Magulot) from Mouzon in Ardennes (Champagne-Ardenne) m. Madeleine Blosse (Jean and Marie-Catherine Cauchon) in Berthier-en-Haut, QC in 1767.*

— *Émery Arpin/Herpin dit* **Poitevin** *(Pierre and Catherine *Osbéré) from Poitiers in Vienne (Poitou-Charentes) m. Marie-Jacqueline Coulon (Auffray and Françoise Tierce) in Québec in 1689.*

Poulin, alteration of Old French *poulain* 'young animal', a nickname apparently related to an individual's youth or liveliness. — Amer. **Colt, Coltey, Colty, Poland, Pooler**.

— Claude **Poulin**/Poulain (Pascal and Marie Levert) from Rouen in Seine-Maritime (Haute-Normandie) m. Jeanne Mercier in Québec, QC in 1639.

— Jean **Poulin** (Jacques and Marie Violette) from Méru in Oise (Picardie) m. Louise Paré (Robert and Françoise Lehoux) in Beaupré, QC in 1667.

Pouliot, probable variant of *Pouillot*, derived from Old French *po(u)ille* 'louse', the nickname of a lice-ridden individual. —Amer. **Polyot, Pullyard.**

— Charles **Pouliot**/Poulliot (Jean and Jeanne Josse) from Saint-Cosme-en-Varais in Sarthe (Pays de la Loire) m. Françoise Meunier (Mathurin and Françoise Fafard) in Québec in 1667.

Poupart, from Old French *poupart/poupard* 'young child', the nickname of a babyfaced individual. — Amer. **Popour, Poupore.**

— Pierre Poupard/**Poupart** (Jean and Marguerite Frichet) from Saint-Denis in Seine-Saint-Denis (Île-de-France) m. Marguerite Perras (Pierre and Denise Lemaître) in Laprairie, QC in 1682.

Pouquette, see **Paquet(te).**

Pouria, see **Poirier.**

Prairie, from *(La) Prairie*, a placename in France. — Amer. **Prarie.**

— Julien Piédalue dit Laprairie/**Prairie** (Pierre and Marie Dolbeau) from Courtalain in Eure-et-Loir (Centre) m. Françoise Aupry (Louis-Bertrand and Anne Dumas) in Laprairie, QC in 1722.

Predom, Predum, Preedom, see **Prud'homme.**

Préfontaine, from *Préfontaine*, a placename in France. — Amer. **Prefountain.**

— Antoine Fournier dit **Préfontaine** (Denis and Catherine *Desabeux) from Beaumont-sur-Oise in Val-d'Oise (Île-de-France) m. Marie Ronceray (Jean and Jeanne Servignan) in Boucherville, QC in 1688.

Prégent, variant of *Prigent*, from Breton *prit* '(nice) appearance' and *gent* 'lineage, family'. — Amer. **Prashaw, Prejean.**

— Louis Prigent/**Prégent** dit L'Oeillet (François and Jeanne Kervennan) from Le Tréhou in Finistère (Bretagne) m. Anne Mallet (Pierre and Anne Hardy) in Montréal, QC in 1698.

Premo, see **Primeau.**

Preo, see **Briard.**

Prévost, from Old French *prevost* 'magistrate, registrar'. — Amer. **Prevo.**

— Martin **Prévost** (Pierre and Charlotte Viet) from Montreuil in Seine-Saint-Denis (Île-de-France) m. Marie Manitabéouich (Roch and ...) in Québec, QC in 1644.

Prew, see **Proulx.**

Primeau, derived from Old French *prim(e)* 'first', the nickname of the eldest in a family. — Amer. **Premo, Primeaux.**

— François **Primeau**/Primot from Normandie m. Marie Deniau (Martin and Louise-Thérèse Le Breuil) in Laprairie, QC in 1687.

Progin, alteration of *Progens*, a placename in Switzerland. — Amer. **Progen.**

— François **Progin** (François and Marie Masson) from Switzerland m. Catherine Blais (Guillaume and Madeleine Gagnon) in Lacadie, QC in 1820.

Pronto, see **Parenteau.**

Prosper, from the Latin name *Prosper*, from *prosper* 'happy, prosperous'. — Amer. **Prespare.**

— *Joseph Desgroseilliers dit* **Prosper**, *descendant of Claude from Montigny-Lengrain in Aisne (Picardie), m. Catherine Bisaillon (Amable and Marie-Catherine Dupuis) in Laprairie, QC in 1817.*

Proulx, alteration of *Prou*, from *prou*, a regional variant of Old French *preu* 'brave, wise, expert'. — Amer. **Prew, Proue, Prue**.

— *Jean* **Prou** *(Jean and Louise Vallée) from Saumur in Maine-et-Loire (Pays de la Loire) m. Jacquette Fournier (Guillaume and Françoise Hébert) in Québec, QC in 1673.*

Provancha, see **Provencher**.

Proveau, see **Provost**.

Provençal, from *Provençal*, the nickname of a native of Provence, a former province in France. — Amer. **Provencial**.

— *Antoine Isoir dit* **Provençal** *(Blaise and Françoise* *Sarbacan*) from Aix-en-Provence in Bouches-du-Rhône (Provence-Alpes-Côte-d'Azur) m. Marie-Thérèse (de) Rainville (Jean and Élisabeth* *de La Guéripière*) in Beauport, QC in 1699.*

Provencher, alteration of *(La) Provenchère*, a placename in France. — Amer. **Provancha, Provoncha**.

— *Sébastien* **Provencher**/*Provenchère from France m. Marguerite Manchon in Québec in 1663.*

Provencial, see **Provençal**.

Provoncha, see **Provencher**.

Provost, alteration of **Prévost**. — Amer. **Proveau, Provo, Provoe**.

— *Martin* **Prévost** *(Pierre and Charlotte Vien) from Montreuil in Seine-Saint-Denis (Île-de-France) m. Marie-Olivier Sylvestre (Roch Manitouabéouich and ...) in Québec, QC in 1644.*

Prud'homme, alteration of Old French *preu d'homme* 'honest man'. — Amer. **Predom, Predum, Preedom**.

— *Louis* **Prud'homme**/*Prudhomme (Claude and Isabelle* *Aliomet*) from Pomponne in Seine-et-Marne (Île-de-France) m. Roberte Gadois (Pierre and Louise Mauger) in Montréal, QC in 1650.*

Prue, see **Proulx**.

Puariea, see **Poirier**.

Pudvah, Pudvan, see **Potvin**.

Pullyard, see **Pouliot**.

Pumarlo, see **Pamerleau**.

Purrier, see **Poirier**.

Putraw, see **Poitras**.

Q

Quarter, see **Cartier.**

Quenell, see **Quesnel.**

Quenneville, alteration of *Le Quenneville,* a placename in Seine-Maritime (Haute-Normandie). — Amer. **Kenville, Kinville, Quennville, Quenville.**

— *Jean **Quenneville** (Pierre and Jeanne Sacquespée) from Rouen in Seine-Maritime (Haute-Normandie) m. Denise Marié (Pierre and Jeanne Loret) in Montréal, QC in 1674.*

Queor, see **Couillard.**

Quéret, from *(Le) Quéret,* a placename in France. — Amer. **Carie, Carrie.**

— *Michel Quéret dit **Latulippe** (Michel and ...) from Aix-en-Provence in Bouches-du-Rhône (Provence-Alpes-Côte-d'Azur) m. Françoise Davenne (Charles and Marie Denoyon) in Québec c. 1697.*

Quesnel, from *(Le) Quesnel,* a placename in France. — Amer. **Canell, Cannell, Quenell, Quesnell, Quesnelle.**

— *Olivier **Quesnel** (Pierre and Marie Poulard) from Bayeux in Calvados (Basse-Normandie) m. Catherine Prudhomme (Louis and Roberte Gadois) in Montréal, QC in 1680.*

Quévillon, alteration of *Quevillon,* a placename in Seine-Maritime (Haute-Normandie). — Amer. **Couvillion, Covyeau, Covyeow.**

— *Adrien **Quévillon** (Nicolas and Marie Vauquelin) from Saint-Ouen-le-Mauger in Seine-Maritime (Haute-Normandie) m. Jeanne Hunault (Toussaint and Marie Lorgueil) in Montréal, QC in 1672.*

Quillia, see **Coallier.**

Quintal, from Old French *quintal* 'hundred pound weight', probably the nickname of a heavyset individual. — Amer. **Chantell, Kentile.**

— *François **Quintal** (Nicolas and Marie Genin) from La Rochelle in Charente-Maritime (Poitou-Charentes) m. Marie Gauthier (Charles and Catherine Camus) in Québec, QC in 1678.*

Quinville, see **Quenneville.**

Qulia, see **Coallier.**

R

Rabatoy, see **Robitaille.**

Rabedeau, see **Robidoux.**

Rabida, see **Robidas.**

Rabideau, Rabideaux, Rabidou, Rabidoux, see **Robidoux.**

Rabior, see **Robillard.**

Rabitoy, Rabtoy, see **Robitaille.**

Racette, alteration of *Rasset* via *Racet,* derived from *Rasse,* from the Germanic name *Radizo,* derived from *rad* 'counsel'. — Amer. **Russet, Russett, Russette.**

— *Jean Rasset/**Racet** (Pierre and Jeanne du Thil) from Sainte-Geneviève in Seine-Maritime (Haute-Normandie) m. Jeanne Chapeau (Pierre and Madeleine Duval) in Québec, QC in 1678.*

Racicot, alteration of *Rassicot,* same origin as **Racette.** — Amer. **Rasco, Rascoe, Rasicot, Roscoe.**

— *Jacques **Racicot** dit Léveillé (Michel and Geneviève Allard) from Château-Gontier in Mayenne (Pays de la Loire) m. Marie-Jeanne Labbé (Jean and Marie-Anne Faye) in Québec, QC in 1715.*

Racine, either from *(La) Racine,* a placename in France, or from *racine* 'root', the nickname of a producer or seller of root vegetables. — Amer. **Root, Russell.**

— *Étienne **Racine** (René and Marie Loysel) from Fumichon in Calvados (Basse-Normandie) m. Marguerite Martin (Abraham and Marguerite Langlois) in Québec, QC in 1638.*

Raiche, alteration of the German name *Resch,* from Middle High German *resch* 'lively, cheerful, active'. — Amer. **Rash, Rashe.**

— *Jean-Baptiste Resch/**Raiche** (Mathias and Agathe *Bourgrine) from Elzach in Germany m. Madeleine Voyer (Pierre and Ursule Moisan) in L'Ancienne-Lorette, QC in 1788.*

Rainault, see **Raynaud.**

Rainville, from *Rainville,* a placename in Orne (Basse-Normandie). — Amer. **Ranville, Raville, Renville.**

— *Paul (de) **Rainville** (Jean and Jeanne Brechet) from Touques in Calvados (Basse-Normandie) m. Roline Poète/Poite in Touques c. 1638.*

Ramo, see **Raymond.**

Rancourt, from *Rancourt,* a placename in France. — Amer. **Ranco, Ronco.**

— *Joseph **Rancourt**/Rancour (Pierre and Jeanne-Claude de Boisandré) from Caen in Calvados (Basse-Normandie) m. (1) Marie Parent (Pierre and Jeanne Badeau) in Beauport, QC in 1685; (2) Françoise Daveau (Charles and Marguerite d'Aubigny) in Château-Richer, QC in 1701.*

Ranger, from the Germanic name *Ranghari* composed of *rang* 'curved' and *hari* 'army'. — Amer. **Roshia.**

— Hubert **Ranger** dit Laviolette *(Pierre and Jeanne Boutin) from La Rochelle in Charente-Maritime (Poitou-Charentes) m. Anne Girardin (Léonard and Charlotte Jolivet) in Lachine, QC in 1686.*

Ranville, see **Rainville.**

Rasberry, see **Laframboise.**

Rasco, Rascoe, see **Racicot.**

Rash, see **Raiche.**

Rashaw, see **Rochon.**

Rashe, see **Raiche.**

Rasicot, see **Racicot.**

Raspberry, see **Laframboise.**

Ratay, see **Ratté.**

Ratelle, alteration of *Ratel,* from *ratel,* a regional variant of *râteau* 'rake', the nickname of an individual who used this implement. — Amer. **Ratell, Rattell.**

— *Pierre **Ratel** (Michel and Marguerite Gosset) from Rouen in Seine-Maritime (Haute-Normandie) m. Marie Lemaire (Joseph and Élisabeth Dupré) in Montréal, QC in 1669.*

Ratté, alteration of *Raté,* a probable variant of *Ratet,* derived from *rat* 'rat', the nickname of a wily individual. — Amer. **Ratay, Ratta, Rattay, Rattie, Rayta.**

— *Jacques **Raté** (François and Jacquette Huguet) from Laleu in Charente-Maritime (Poitou-Charentes) m. Anne Martin (Abraham and Marguerite Langlois) in Québec, QC in 1658.*

Rattell, see **Ratelle.**

Rattie, see **Ratté.**

Rault, alteration of *Raoul,* from the Germanic name *Radwulf* composed of *rad* 'counsel' and *wulf* 'wolf'. — Amer. **Rau, Reau.**

— *Alexandre Raoul/**Rault**/Rheault (Louis and Jacquette Robin) from Deyrançon in Deux-Sèvres (Poitou-Charentes) m. Marie Desrosiers (Antoine and Anne Leneuf) in Trois-Rivières, QC in 1664.*

Raville, see **Rainville.**

Raymond, from the Germanic name *Raginmund* composed of *ragin* 'counsel' and *mund* 'protection'. — Amer. **Ramo, Raymo, Remo.**

— *Toussaint **Raymond** dit Passe-Campagne (Berthomé and Marguerite Chaudier) from Roullet in Charente (Poitou-Charentes) m. Barbe Pilet (François and Françoise Loisel) in Montréal, QC in 1696.*

— *Jean Bertrand dit Toulouse and **Raymond** (Raymond and Jeanne Aubry) from Saint-Lizier-du-Planté in Gers (Midi-Pyrénées) m. Louise Drousson (Robert and Jeanne Tardé) in Laprairie, QC in 1699.*

— *Romain Phocas dit **Raymond** (Renaud and Catherine de Gaspart) from Langon in Gironde (Aquitaine) m. Thérèse Saint-Pierre (Pierre and Marie Gerbert) in Québec c. 1715.*

Raynaud, same origin as **Renaud.** — Amer. **Rainault.**

— *Jean **Raynaud**/Reynaud dit Blanchard (Antoine and Jacqueline Le Noble) from La Serre-Bussière-Vieille in Creuse (Limousin) m. Catherine Millet (Nicolas and Catherine Lorion) in Montréal, QC in 1671.*

Rayno, see **Renaud.**

Rayta, see **Ratté.**

Reandeau, Reando, see **Riendeau.**

Reau, see **Rault.**

Reaulo, see **Rouleau.**

Réaume, apparently from the Germanic name *Raginhelm* composed of *ragin* 'counsel' and *helm* 'helmet'. — Amer. **Reome, Reyome, Rheome.**

— *René Réaume (Jean and Marie Chevalier) from Aytré in Charente-Maritime (Poitou-Charentes) m. Marie Chevreau (Cathien and Étiennette Jallée) in Québec, QC in 1665.*

Rebidoux, Rebidue, see **Robidoux.**

Recor, Record, Recore, see **Ricard.**

Reevis, see **Rivet.**

Reil, see **Riel.**

Reindeau, see **Riendeau.**

Rell, Relle, see **Harel.**

Remo, see **Raymond.**

Renadette, see **Renaudette.**

Renaud, from the Germanic name *Raginwald* composed of *ragin* 'counsel' and *wald* 'power, authority'. — Amer. **Arno, Erno, Rayno, Reneau, Renno, Reno, Rhino.**

— *Guillaume Renaud/Regnault (Guillaume and Suzanne de la Haye) from Saint-Jouin-Bruneval in Seine-Maritime (Haute-Normandie) m. Marie de Lamarre (David and Anne *Busevestre) in Québec, QC in 1668.*

— *Jean-Baptiste Renaud/Arnaud dit Deslauriers (Jean and Marie Forget) from Astaillac in Corrèze (Limousin) m. Marie-Anne Provost (René and Anne Daudelin) in Varennes, QC in 1705.*

— *Mathurin Renaud (Mathurin and Gabrielle Routy) from Ars-en-Ré in Charente-Maritime (Poitou-Charentes) m. Marie Pelletier (François and Michelle Le Challe) in Québec, QC in 1669.*

— *René Arnaud/Renaud (Julien and Françoise Fonteneau) from Cugand in Vendée (Pays de la Loire) m. Marie Vignier (Samuel and Anne Renaud) in Québec, QC in 1668.*

Renaudette, alteration of *Renaudet*, derived from **Renaud.** — Amer. **Renadette.**

— *Joseph-Jean-Baptiste Renaudet (David and Marguerite Moreau) from Bordeaux in Gironde (Aquitaine) m. Marie-Madeleine Ménard (Maurice and Madeleine Couc) in Chambly, QC in 1717.*

Reneau, Renno, Reno, see **Renaud.**

Renville, see **Rainville.**

Reome, see **Réaume.**

Reopel, Reopelle, see **Riopel.**

Revard, see **Rivard.**

Revier, Reviere, see **Larivière.**

Revoir, Revor, Revord, Revoy, see **Rivard.**

Reyome, Rheome, see **Réaume.**

Rhino, see **Renaud.**

Ricard, same origin as **Richard.** — Amer. **Recor, Record, Recore, Ricord.**

— *Jean Ricard from France m. Madeleine Pineau (Pierre and Anne Boyer) in Québec c. 1675.*

Richard, from the Germanic name *Richard* composed of *ric* 'powerful' and *hard* 'hard, strong'. — Amer. **Rich, Richards.**

— *Antoine-François Richard (Charles and Marguerite Alain) from Saint-Pair in Manche (Basse-Normandie) m. Cécile Doucet (Magloire and Hélène Amirault) in Wedgeport, NS in 1797.*

— *François Richard (Jean and Anne Christin) from Auray in Morbihan (Bretagne) m. Anne Comeau (Jean and Françoise Hébert) in Port-Royal, NS in 1710.*

— *Guillaume Richard dit Lafleur (Jean and Anne Meusnier) from Saint-Léger in Charente-Maritime (Poitou-Charentes) m. Agnès Tessier (Urbain and Marie Archambault) in Montréal, QC in 1675.*

— *Pierre Richard (Antoine and Olive Noël/Nouel) from Saint-Georges-des-Coteaux in Charente-Maritime (Poitou-Charentes) m. Françoise Miville (François and Marie Langlois) in Cap-Saint-Ignace, QC in 1680.*

Richer, alteration of *Ériché*, a variant of *Hériché/Héricher*, from the Germanic name *Harigari* composed of *hari* 'army' and *gari* 'spear'. — Amer. **Richey, Ritchie.**

— *Jacques Ériché/Richer dit Louveteau (Jacques and Catherine Pain) from Louvetot in Seine-Maritime (Haute-Normandie), m. Marie Geoffrion (Pierre and Marie Priault) in Montréal, QC in 1698.*

Rickey, see **Riquier.**

Ricord, see **Ricard.**

Riel, from *(Le) Riel,* a placename in France. — Amer. **Reil, Rielle.**

— *Jean-Baptiste Riel dit Lirlande (Jean-Baptiste and Louise Lafontaine) from Limerick in Ireland m. Louise Coutu (François and Jeanne Verdon) in Sorel, QC in 1704.*

Riendeau, alteration of *Reguindeau*, probable variant of *Raguideau*, derived from regional French *raguider* 'to watch, spy on', the nickname of a nosy individual. — Amer. **Reandeau, Reando, Reindeau, Yandeau, Yando, Yondo.**

— *Joachim Reguindeau dit Joachim (Pierre and Andrée Martineau) from La Rochelle in Charente-Maritime (Poitou-Charentes) m. Madeleine Aleton/Alton (Nicolas and Marie Fant) in Québec in 1669.*

Riggie, see **Royer.**

Riopel, origin undetermined. — Amer. **Dupell, Dupelle, Reopel, Reopelle, Upell, Yeupell.**

— *Pierre Riopel (Pierre and Marguerite Dubois) from Saint-Georges-d'Oléron in Charente-Maritime (Poitou-Charentes) m. Marie Julien (Jean and Madeleine Guérin) in L'Ange-Gardien, QC in 1687.*

Riquier, from the Germanic name *Richari* composed of *ric* 'powerful' and *hari* 'army'. — Amer. **Rickey.**

— *François Riquet/Riquier dit Laverdure (Jacques and Michelle Frérard) from Saint-Léger-Dubosq in Calvados (Basse-Normandie) m. Marie-Anne Renaud (Pierre and Françoise Desportes) in Montréal, QC in 1699.*

Ritchie, see **Richer.**

Rivait, see **Rivet.**

Rivard, apparently derived from Old French *river* 'to prowl about, to indulge in debauchery', the nickname of a carouser or womanizer. — Amer. **Revard, Revoir, Revor, Revord, Revoy, Rivers, Rivord.**

— *Nicolas Rivard dit Lavigne (Pierre and Jeanne Mullard) from Tourouvre in Orne*

(Basse-Normandie) m. Catherine Saint-Père (Étienne and Marie-Madeleine Couteau) in Québec c. 1653.

Rivers, see **Larivière.**

Rivet, from *(Le) Rivet,* a placename in France. — Amer. **Reevis, Rivait, Rivett, Rivette.**
— *Étienne Rivet/Rivest from La Rochelle in Charente-Maritime (Poitou-Charentes) m. Marie Comeau (Pierre and Rose Bayon) in Acadia c. 1676.*
— *Maurice Rivet/Rivest (Jacques and Marie Guery) from La Rochelle in Charente-Maritime (Poitou-Charentes) m. Marie Cusson (Jean and Marie Foubert) in Québec in 1671.*

Rivord, see **Rivard.**

Robair, Robar, Robare, see **Robert.**

Robarge, see **Roberge.**

Robear, see **Robert.**

Robedeau, Robedeaux, see **Robidoux.**

Robellard, see **Robillard.**

Rober, Robere, see **Robert.**

Roberge, from the Germanic name *Hrodberga* composed of *hrod* 'glory' and *berga,* derived from *bergan* 'hide, preserve'. — Amer. **Robarge.**
— *Pierre Roberge dit Lapierre (Jacques and Claudine Buret) from Saint-Germain-le-Vasson in Calvados (Basse-Normandie) m. Françoise Loignon (Pierre and Françoise Roussin) in Sainte-Famille, Île d'Orléans, QC in 1679.*
— *Pierre Roberge dit Lacroix (Jacques and Claudine Buret) from Saint-Germain-le-Vasson in Calvados (Basse-Normandie) m. Marie Lefrançois (Charles and Marie-Madeleine Triot) in Château-Richer, QC in 1684.*

Robert, from the Germanic name *Hrodbehrt* composed of *hrod* 'glory' and *berht* 'bright'. — Amer. **Robair, Robar, Robare, Robear, Rober, Robere, Roberts.**
— *Louis Robert dit Lafontaine (André and Catherine Bonin) from La Rochelle in Charente-Maritime (Poitou-Charentes) m. Marie Bourgery (Jean-Baptiste and Marie Gendre) in Trois-Rivières, QC in 1666.*

Robetoy, see **Robitaille.**

Robichaud, derived from **Robert** via *Robiche.* — Amer. **Robichau, Robichaux, Robicheaux.**
— *Étienne Robichaud from France m. Françoise Boudrot (Michel and Michelle Aucoin) in Acadia c. 1663.*

Robidas, probably derived from **Robert.** — Amer. **Rabida.**
— *Jacques Robidas dit Manseau (Gabriel and Anne Crespin) from Le Mans in Sarthe (Pays de la Loire) m. Louise (de) Guitre (Louis and Renée de Seine) in Montréal, QC in 1692.*

Robidoux, alteration of *Robidou,* probably derived from **Robert.** — Amer. **Rabedeau, Rabideau, Rabideaux, Rabidou, Rabidoux, Rebidoux, Rebidue, Robedeau, Robedeaux, Robideau, Robideaux, Roubideaux, Rubadeau, Rubado, Rubidoux.**
— *André Robidou dit L'Espagnol (Emmanuel and Catherine Alve) from Santa María in Spain m. Jeanne Denot (Antoine and Catherine Leduc) in Québec, QC in 1667.*

Robillard, derived from **Robert** via *Robil.* — Amer. **Rabior, Robellard, Robilard, Rubeor.**
— *Claude Robillard from France m. Marie Grandin in Québec c. 1672.*

Robitaille, origin undetermined. — Amer. **Rabatoy, Rabitoy, Rabtoy, Robetoy, Robtoy.**
— *Pierre* **Robitaille** *(Jean and Martine Cormont) from Saint-Georges in Pas-de-Calais (Nord-Pas-de-Calais) m. Marie Maufay (Pierre and Marie Duval) in Québec in 1675.*
Rochefort, from *Rochefort,* a placename in France. — Amer. **Rushford.**
— *Jean Huret dit* **Rochefort** *from France m. Madeleine Judic in Acadia c. 1660.*
Rocheleau, alteration of *(Le) Rochereau,* a placename in France. — Amer. **Rochleau, Rushlaw, Rushlo, Rushlow.**
— *Jean-Baptiste* **Rochereau** *dit Lespérance (Bernard and Marguerite Durand) from Bordeaux in Gironde (Aquitaine) m. Jeanne-Élisabeth Déry (Maurice and Madeleine Philippeau) in Charlesbourg, QC in 1712.*
— *Michel* **Rochereau** *from Lagord in Charente-Maritime (Poitou-Charentes) m. Marie Bigot (François and Marguerite Drapeau) in Québec c. 1664.*
Rochon, either from *(Le) Rochon* or *(Le) Rocheron,* placenames in France. — Amer. **Rashaw.**
— *Gervais* **Rocheron/Rochon** *(Julien and Martine Lemoyne) from Saint-Cosme-en-Vairais in Sarthe (Pays de la Loire) m. Marie-Madeleine Guyon (Claude and Catherine Colin) in Sainte-Famille, Île d'Orléans, QC in 1671.*
Rock, see **Larocque.**
Rocker, see **Bercier.**
Rodrigue, alteration of Portuguese *Rodrigues,* from the Germanic name *Hrodric* composed of *hrod* 'glory' and *ric* 'powerful'. — Amer. **Roderick, Roderigue, Roderique, Rodrick.**
— *João Rodrigues/Jean* **Rodrigue** *(João and Susana da Cruz) from Lisbon (Lisboa) in Portugal m. Anne Leroy (François and Anne Bourdois) in Québec, QC in 1671.*
— *Sebastião Rodrigues/Sébastien* **Rodrigue** *dit L'Espagnol (João and Maria ...) from Évora in Portugal m. Marie-Anne Parent (Joseph and Marguerite Vinet) in Les Cèdres, QC in 1757.*
Roett, see **Rouet(te).**
Rogers, see **Royer.**
Rolo, see **Rouleau.**
Rompré, apparently from *Rompré* or an alteration of *Romprey,* placenames in France. — Amer. **Romprey.**
— *Mathurin Lévesque dit* **Rompré,** *son of Pierre from Doue-la-Fontaine in Maine-et-Loire (Pays de la Loire), m. Marie-Madeleine Morand (Pierre and Marie-Madeleine Grimard) in Batiscan, QC in 1712.*
Ronco, see **Rancourt.**
Rondeau, from *(Le) Rondeau,* a placename in France. — Amer. **Rondo, Rondow.**
— *Pierre* **Rondeau** *(Jean and Jacquette Paillereau) from Marsilly in Charente-Maritime (Poitou-Charentes) m. Marie Ancelin (René and Marie Juin) in Saint-Jean, Île d'Orléans, QC in 1683.*
Rookey, see **Routhier.**
Root, see **Racine.**
Roscoe, see **Racicot.**
Rosebush, see **Desrosiers.**
Roshia, see **Ranger.**

Rosseau, see **Rousseau.**

Roubideaux, see **Robidoux.**

Rouet(te), alteration of *(Le) Rouet*, a placename in France. — Amer. **Roett, Wheel.**
— *Pierre-Joseph Rouet dit Vive-L'Amour (Pierre and Catherine Pelletier) from Cambrai in Nord (Nord-Pas-de-Calais) m. Marie-Josèphe Biron (François and Marie-Jeanne Rognon) in Trois-Rivières, QC in 1759.*

Rouleau, derived from *Roul*, from the Germanic name *Hrodwulf* composed of *hrod* 'glory' and *wulf* 'wolf'. — Amer. **Reaulo, Rolo, Rulo.**
— *Gabriel Rouleau dit Sansoucy from Tourouvre in Orne (Basse-Normandie) m. Mathurine Leroux (Antoine and Jeanne Jouary) in Québec in 1652.*

Roussain, see **Roussin.**

Rousseau, either from *(Le) Rousseau*, a placename in France, or derived from *roux* 'redhead'. — Amer. **Brooks, Rosseau, Rusaw, Russeau.**
— *Antoine Rousseau dit Labonté (Jean and Blaise Moricet) from Bournand in Vienne (Poitou-Charentes) m. Marie Roinay (François and Perrine Meunier) in Québec c. 1675.*
— *Thomas Rousseau (Honoré and Marie Boillerot) from Oroux in Deux-Sèvres (Poitou-Charentes) m. Madeleine Olivier (Jean and Louise Prévost) in Québec, QC in 1667.*

Roussel, either from *(Le) Roussel*, a placename in France, or derived from *roux* 'redhead'. — Amer. **Roussell, Russel, Russell.**
— *Alain Roussel (Mathurin and Françoise Nicolas) from Pleslin-Trigavou in Côtes-d'Armor (Bretagne) m. Geneviève Bonnier (Jacques and Geneviève Migneron) in La Baleine, NS in 1730.*
— *François Roussel (François and Reine Lemarchand) from Dinan in Côtes-d'Armor (Bretagne) m. Marie Roy (Jean-Baptiste and Angélique Cassé) in Saint-Vallier, QC in 1743.*
— *Guillaume Roussel dit Sansoucy (Jean and Marie Lefebvre) from Dieppe in Seine-Maritime (Haute-Normandie) m. Nicole Filiatrault (René and Jeanne Hérault) in Montréal, QC in 1700.*

Roussin, either from *(Le) Roussin*, a placename in France, or derived from *roux* 'redhead'. — Amer. **Roussain, Russin.**
— *Jean Roussin (Pierre and Jeanne *Nyeullé) from Tourouvre in Orne (Basse-Normandie) m. Madeleine Giguère (Jean and Madeleine Viette) in Tourouvre in 1622.*

Routhier, from the Germanic name *Hrodhari* composed of *hrod* 'glory' and *hari* 'army'. — Amer. **Rookey.**
— *Jean Routhier/Routier (Jean and Rogère Houssaye) from Dieppe in Seine-Maritime (Haute-Normandie) m. Catherine Méliot (François and Marie Chanson) in Québec, QC in 1662.*

Roux, either from *(Le) Roux*, a placename in France, or from *roux* 'redhead'. — Amer. **Laroux.**
— *Simon Roux/Leroux dit Sanschagrin (François-Brice and Marguerite Perrin) from Mirecourt in Vosges (Lorraine) m. Marie-Louise Lemay (François and Marie-Louise Perrault) in Saint-Pierre-les-Becquets, QC in 1760.*

Rowe, see **Tétreau.**

Roy, either from *(Le) Roy*, a placename in France, or a variant of *roi* 'king', an ironic

nickname. — Amer. **King.**
— *Antoine* **Roy** *dit Desjardins (Olivier and Catherine Bodard) from Joigny in Yonne (Bourgogne) m. Marie Major (Jean and Marguerite Le Pelé) in Québec, QC in 1668.*
— *Jacques* **Roy** *(Jacques and Jacquette Dugast) from La Châtaigneraie in Vendée (Pays de la Loire) m. Marie Roy (François and Marie Cécire) in Lachine, QC in 1747.*
— *Jean* **Roy**/*Leroy (André and Marie Dubois) from Marans in Charente-Maritime (Poitou-Charentes) m. Françoise Bouet in France c. 1659.*
— *Jean* **Roy** *dit Laliberté from Saint-Malo in Ille-et-Vilaine (Bretagne) m. Marie Aubois in Acadia c. 1686.*
— *Mathurin* **Roy** *from La Rochelle in Charente-Maritime (Poitou-Charentes) m. Marguerite Biré in France c. 1638.*
— *Nicolas* **Roy**/*Leroy (Louis and Anne Lemaître) from Dieppe in Seine-Maritime (Haute-Normandie) m. Jeanne Lelièvre (Guillaume and Judith Riquet/Riquier) in France in 1658.*
— *Pierre* **Roy** *from Poitiers in Vienne (Poitou-Charentes) m. Françoise Dagenais in Île Jésus, QC c. 1688.*
Royer, either from the Germanic name *Hrodhari* composed of *hrod* 'glory' and *hari* 'army', or from Old French *roier* 'wheelwright'. — Amer. **Riggie, Rogers, Royea, Ryea.**
— *Jean* **Royer** *(Jean and Marie *Paise) from Saint-Cosme-en-Vairais in Sarthe (Pays de la Loire) m. Marie Targer (Daniel and Louise Martin) in Château-Richer, QC in 1663.*
Rubadeau, Rubado, see **Robidoux.**
Rubeor, see **Robillard.**
Rubidoux, see **Robidoux.**
Rulo, see **Rouleau.**
Rusaw, see **Rousseau.**
Rushford, see **Rochefort.**
Rushlaw, Rushlo, Rushlow, see **Rocheleau.**
Russeau, see **Rousseau.**
Russel, see **Roussel.**
Russell, see **Racine** and **Roussel.**
Russet, Russett, Russette, see **Racette.**
Russin, see **Roussin.**
Ryea, see **Royer.**

S

Sabourin, derived from Occitan *sabour* 'flavor, taste', the nickname of a pleasant, amiable individual. — Amer. **Sabra, Sabrey, Sauberan.**
— *Jean **Sabourin** (Jean and Antoinette Pinault) from Montalembert in Deux-Sèvres (Poitou-Charentes) m. Mathurine Renaud in La Rochelle in Charente-Maritime (Poitou-Charentes) in 1665.*

Sabre, see **Savaria.**

Sabrey, see **Sabourin.**

Saintdennis, see **St-Denis.**

Saintfrancis, see **St-François.**

Saintgeorge, see **St-Georges.**

Saintgermain, Saintgermaine, see **St-Germain.**

Saintjames, Saintjock, see **St-Jacques.**

Saintjohn, see **St-Jean.**

Saintlawrence, see **St-Laurent.**

Saintmarie, Saintmary, see **Ste-Marie.**

Saintpeter, Saintpeters, see **St-Pierre.**

Salois, origin uncertain. — Amer. **Salter, Saltus, Salway.**
— *Claude **Salois** from Lille in Nord (Nord-Pas-de-Calais) m. Anne Mabille in Québec c. 1666.*

Salt, see **Decelle.**

Salter, Saltus, Salway, see **Salois.**

Sampica, see **Sanspitié.**

Sampier, see **St-Pierre.**

Samson, from the Hebrew name *Shimshon* via Greek *Sampson*, derived from *shemesh* 'sun'. — Amer. **Sampson.**
— *Gabriel **Samson**/Sanson (Toussaint and Catherine Chevalier) from Saint-Gatiendes-Bois in Calvados (Basse-Normandie) m. Françoise Durand (Martin and Françoise Brunet) in Québec, QC in 1669.*

Sancomb, see **St-Côme.**

Sancraint, Sancrainte, Sancrant, see **Sanscrainte.**

Sanctuaire, alteration of *Santoire*, from *La Santoire*, a placename in France. — Amer. **Sanctuary.**
— *Jérôme **Santoire** (Antoine and Antoinette Pradier) from Ardes in Puy-de-Dôme (Auvergne) m. Marie-Amable Trudeau (Étienne and Marie-Françoise Marcil) in Longueuil, QC in 1761.*

Sandville, see **Senneville.**

Sangrey, see **Sansregret.**

Sanscrainte, from *sans crainte* 'without fear, fearless', the nickname of a soldier. — Amer. **Sancraint, Sancrainte, Sancrant, Soncrant.**

— *Jean Romain/Roman dit **Sanscrainte** (Charles and Catherine Coste) from Angoulê-me in Charente (Poitou-Charentes) m. Marie-Josèphe Leblanc (Julien and Anne Vani-er) in Montréal, QC in 1722.*

Sansoucy, from Old French *sans soucy* 'without care, carefree', a soldier's nickname. — Amer. **Sansoucie.**

— *Pierre James/Jamme/Jacques dit **Sansoucy**, son of William from Wimborne in Eng-land, m. Marie-Madeleine Simon (Joseph and Marie-Renée Petit) in Longue-Pointe, QC in 1744.*

Sanspitié, from *sans pitié* 'without pity, pitiless', a soldier's nickname. — Amer. **Sampi-ca.**

— *Raphaël Dessent/Descent dit **Sanspitié** (Dominique and Louise David) from Bor-deaux in Gironde (Aquitaine) m. Anne Boursier (Jean and Marie-Marthe Thibodeau) in Montréal, QC in 1699.*

Sanspree, see **St-Esprit.**

Sansregret, from *sans regret* 'without regret, unregretful', a soldier's nickname. — Amer. **Sangrey.**

— *Jean-Baptiste Briand dit **Sansregret** (Jean-Baptiste and Anne Labrande) from Nan-teuil-en-Vallée in Charente (Poitou-Charentes) m. Marie-Anne Baillargeon (Nicolas and Marie-Thérèse Harel) in Repentigny, QC in 1722.*

Santa, see **St-Onge.**

Santamore, see **St-Amour.**

Santaw, see **St-Onge.**

Santhany, Santhony, see **St-Denis.**

Santimaw, see **St-Amand.**

Santimore, see **St-Amour.**

Santo, Santor, see **St-Onge.**

Santspree, see **St-Esprit.**

Sanville, see **Senneville.**

Sarault, from the Germanic name *Sarwald* composed of *sar* 'armor' and *wald* 'power, authority'. — Amer. **Sarrault.**

— *Jean **Sarault** dit Laviolette (Isaac and Jacquette Archambault) from Saint-Sympho-rien in Deux-Sèvres (Poitou-Charentes) m. Catherine Brossard (Urbain and Urbaine Hodiau) in Montréal, QC in 1689.*

Sarrazin, variant of *Sarrasin* 'Saracen', the name given to Muslims in the Middle Ages, the nickname of a dark-skinned individual. — Amer. **Buckwheat.**

— *Nicolas **Sarrazin**/Sarazin (Nicolas and Nicole Héron) from Paris (Île-de-France) m. Marie-Catherine Blondeau (François and Nicole Rolland) in Charlesbourg, QC in 1680.*

Sasseville, from *Sasseville*, a placename in Seine-Maritime (Haute-Normandie). — Amer. **Sausville, Sosville.**

— *Pierre **Sasseville** (Marin and Catherine Vaillant) from Fauville-en-Caux in Seine-Maritime (Haute-Normandie) m. Marie Leseigneur (Jean and Jeanne Godailler) in Château-Richer, QC in 1670.*

Sauberan, see **Sabourin.**

Saucier, variant of Old French *saussier* 'sauce cook, sauce seller'. — Amer. **Socea, So-chia, Socia, Soucier.**

— Louis **Saucier/Saussier** (Charles and Charlotte Clairet) from Paris (Île-de-France) m. Marguerite Gaillard (Jean-Baptiste and Catherine Lomelle) in Québec, QC in 1671.

Saulnier, from Old French saulnier 'salt merchant'. — Amer. **Sonia, Sonier, Sonnier.**

— Louis **Saulnier** from France m. Louise Bastineau in Acadia c. 1684.

Sault, see **Decelle.**

Saumier, variant of Old French som(m)ier 'baggage, gear', the nickname of a driver of beasts of burden or a carrier. — Amer. **Somers.**

— Nicolas Sommier/**Saumier** dit Lajeunesse (Michel and Marguerite Barbier) from Cugney in Haute-Saône (Franche-Comté) m. Marie Loisel (Michel and Isabelle Monet) in Sainte-Rose, QC in 1763.

Sausville, see **Sasseville.**

Sauvageau, derived from Sauvage, the nickname of a coarse, unsociable individual. — Amer. **Savageau.**

— Claude **Sauvageau** (Jean and Marguerite Auvray) from Marcé-sur-Esves in Indre-et-Loire (Centre) m. Jeanne Legendre (Isaac and Claude *Lentonne) in Québec in 1669.

Sauvé, from the Latin name Salvatus, derived from salvus 'healthy, safe'. — Amer. **Sauvie, Soffa, Sopha, Souva, Sova, Sovay, Sovey, Sovie.**

— Pierre **Sauvé** dit Laplante (François and Marie Malleret) from Libourne in Gironde (Aquitaine) m. Marie Michel (Jean and Marie Marchessault) in Lachine, QC in 1696.

Savageau, see **Sauvageau.**

Savard, apparently from the Germanic name Sabhard composed of sab, origin undetermined, and hard 'hard'. — Amer. **Savor.**

— Simon **Savard** (Simon and Marguerite Vinante) from Montreuil in Seine-Saint-Denis (Île-de-France) m. Marie Hourdouil (Quentin and Marie Souhaité) in France c. 1654.

Savaria, variant of Savari(e)au, derived from Savary, from the Germanic name Sabaric composed of sab of undetermined origin and ric 'powerful'. — Amer. **Sabre.**

— Jacques Savariau/**Savaria** (Simon and Barbe Bouillat) from Ars-en-Ré in Charente-Maritime (Poitou-Charentes) m. Suzanne Lacroix (Jacques and Anne Perrault) in Québec, QC in 1672.

Savor, see **Savard.**

Sawyer, Sayen, see **Séguin.**

Scarbeau, Scarbo, see **Lescarbeau.**

Scherette, see **Charette.**

Scioneaux, see **Sionneau.**

Sear, see **Cyr.**

Sears, see **Cyr** and **St-Cyr.**

Searway, see **Sirois.**

Secore, see **Sicard.**

Sédilot, derived from Old French sedil 'seat', the nickname of a maker or seller. — Amer. **Sedlow, Sedelow.**

— Louis **Sédilot/Sédillot** from Gif-sur-Yvette in Essonne (Île-de-France) m. Marie Grimoult in France c. 1633.

Segouin, see **Sigouin.**

Séguin, from the Germanic name Sigwin composed of sig 'victory' and win 'friend'. — Amer. **Sawyer, Sayen, Sequin, Seyuin.**

— *François* **Séguin** *dit Ladéroute (Laurent and Marie Massieu) from Saint-Aubin-en-Bray in Oise (Picardie) m. Jeanne Petit (Jean and Jeanne Gaudreau) in Boucherville, QC in 1672.*

Sempier, see **St-Pierre**.

Senay, alteration of *Senet*, either from Old French *sené* 'sensible, wise, careful' or derived from the Germanic name *Sinard* composed of *sin* 'old' and *hard* 'hard, strong'. — Amer. **Senna, Snay**.

— *Nicolas* **Senet** *dit Laliberté (Pierre and Suzanne Varnier) from Vitry-le-François in Marne (Champagne-Ardenne) m. Marie-Gertrude Daunay (Antoine and Marie Richard) in Boucherville, QC in 1689.*

Sénécal, regional variant of *sénéchal* 'seneschal', either an ironic nickname or that of an officer of the law. — Amer. **Senical, Snickles**.

— *Adrien* **Sénécal**/*Senécal dit Laframboise (Nicolas and Marie Petit) from Bénouville in Seine-Maritime (Haute-Normandie) m. Jeanne Lecomte in Harfleur in Seine-Maritime in 1666.*

Senna, see **Senay**.

Senneville, apparently from *Senneville*, a placename in France. — Amer. **Sandville, Sanville**.

— *Jean Lefebvre dit* **Senneville**, *grandson of Pierre from Sceaux in Hauts-de-Seine (Île-de-France), m. Madeleine Châtenay (Jean and Marie-Anne Hébert) in Batiscan, QC in 1722.*

Sequin, see **Séguin**.

Seroy, see **Sirois**.

Seymore, see **Simard**.

Seymour, see **Cinq-Mars** and **Simard**.

Seyuin, see **Séguin**.

Shackett, Shackette, see **Choquette**.

Shallow, see **Chalut**.

Shambo, see **Archambault**.

Shampay, see **Champigny**.

Shampine, see **Champagne**.

Shampo, see **Champeau**.

Shanaway, see **Chênevert**.

Shangraw, see **Gingras**.

Shappee, Shappy, see **Chaput**.

Sharai, see **Jarret**.

Sharbino, Sharbono, see **Charbonneau**.

Sharette, see **Charette**.

Sharkey, see **Chartier**.

Sharland, see **Charland**.

Sharleville, see **Charleville**.

Sharlow, see **Chaloux**.

Sharon, see **Charron**.

Sharrai, see **Jarret**.

Sharrett, Sharrette, see **Charette**.

Sharron, Sharrow, see **Charron**.

Shartrand, see **Chartrand.**

Shatney, see **Châteauneuf.**

Shatraw, see **Chartrand.**

Shaurette, see **Charette.**

Sheff, see **Cheff.**

Sheltra, see **Chartré.**

Shennett, Shennette, see **Chenette.**

Shepard, see **Berger, Chabot** and **Chaput.**

Sheperd, see **Chaput.**

Shequin, see **Chicoine.**

Sherbert, see **Chabot.**

Shinavar, Shinevar, Shinevare, Shinevarre, see **Chênevert.**

Sholan, see **Jolin.**

Sholette, see **Cholette.**

Shonio, see **Chagnon.**

Shontell, Shontelle, see **Chantal.**

Shonyo, see **Chagnon.**

Shor, Shore, see **Giard.**

Shorett, Shorette, see **Charette.**

Shorkey, see **Chartier.**

Shortsleeve, Shortsleeves, see **Courtemanche.**

Shorty, see **Châtigny.**

Shosey, see **Chaussé.**

Shoulette, see **Cholette.**

Shovah, Shovan, Shovar, Shoven, Shover, see **Chauvin.**

Shum, see **Lajambe.**

Shumar, Shumard, see **Chamard.**

Shurette, see **Charette.**

Shurn, see **Charron.**

Sicard, from the Germanic name *Sighard* composed of *sig* 'victory' and *hard* 'hard'. — Amer. **Secore.**
— *Jean **Sicard** (Nicolas and Michelle Bobine) from Mornac-sur-Seudre in Charente-Maritime (Poitou-Charentes) m. Catherine Lauzon (Gilles and Marie Archambault) in Montréal, QC in 1681.*

Sicotte, alteration of *Sicot,* a variant of *Sicaud,* from the Germanic name *Sigwald* composed of *sig* 'victory' and *wald* 'power, authority'. — Amer. **Cicotte.**
— *Jean **Sicot**/Sicaud (Guillaume and Jeanne Fafard) from Dolus-d'Oléron in Charente-Maritime (Poitou-Charentes) m. Marguerite Maclin (Nicolas and Suzanne Larose) in Montréal, QC in 1662.*

Sigouin, same origin as **Séguin.** — Amer. **Segouin.**
— *Jean **Sigouin** (Jacques and Jeanne Le Ber) from La Ferté-Macé in Orne (Basse-Normandie) m. Lucrèce Billot (Marin and Marie Laquesse) in Québec, QC in 1669.*

Silver, see **Sylvain.**

Simard, from the Germanic name *Sigmar* composed of *sig* 'victory' and *mar* 'famous'. — Amer. **Seymore, Seymour.**
— *Pierre **Simard** dit Lombrette (Marsault and Ozanne Soullet) from Puymoyen in Cha-*

rente (Poitou-Charentes) m. Suzanne Durand (Louis and Françoise Levrauld) in Angoulême in Charente in 1635.

Simoneau, derived from *Simon*, from the Hebrew name *Shimon* via Greek *Simon*, derived from *shama* 'he heard'. — Amer. **Simonds, Simoneaux.**

— *René Simoneau/Simonneau dit Sanschagrin (René and Marguerite de La Praye) from Bouin in Vendée (Pays de la Loire) m. Jeanne Moreau (Jean and Anne Couture) in Saint-Laurent, Île d'Orléans, QC in 1699.*

Singelais, see **St-Gelais.**

Sionneau, derived from *Sion*, from Hebrew *Tziyyon* 'Zion'. — Amer. **Scioneaux.**

— *Mathurin Sionneau dit Dumoulin/Desmoulins (Luc and Jeanne Briault) from Sainte-Pazanne in Loire-Atlantique (Pays de la Loire) m. Marie Anne Guibault (Louis and Marie Lefebvre) in La Pérade, QC in 1694.*

Sirois, probable alteration of *Sirouet*, derived from *Sirou*, from the Germanic name *Sarwulf* composed of *sar* 'armor' and *wulf* 'wolf'. — Amer. **Cyrway, Luro, Searway, Seroy.**

— *François Sirois dit Duplessis (Jean and Marie-Angélique Dumond/Dumont) from Saint-Germain-en-Laye in Yvelines (Île-de-France) m. (1) Marie-Anne Thiboutot (Jacques and Marie Boucher) in Rivière-Ouelle, QC in 1713; (2) Marie-Françoise Roy (Pierre and Marie-Anne Martin) in Québec in 1721.*

Sister, Sisters, see **Levasseur.**

Smart, see **Léveillé** and **Vaillancourt.**

Snay, see **Senay.**

Snickles, see **Sénécal.**

Snow, see **Arseneau** and **Chenard.**

Socea, Sochia, Socia, see **Saucier.**

Soffa, see **Sauvé.**

Solo, probable variant of *Solu*, from Breton *sol* 'heel', a nickname possibly having to do with an individual's shoes. — Amer. **Soleau.**

— *Pierre-Henri Solo (Pierre and Jeanne-Marie Portais) from Nantes in Loire-Atlantique (Pays de la Loire) m. Anne-Thérèse Gamelin (Pierre and Marie-Jeanne Maugras) in Saint-François-du-Lac, QC in 1727.*

Somers, see **Saumier.**

Soncrant, see **Sanscrainte.**

Sonia, Sonier, Sonnier, see **Saulnier.**

Sopha, see **Sauvé.**

Sorel, alteration of *Chorel*, from Old French *chorel* 'choir member, chorister'. — Amer. **Sorell, Sorelle, Sorrell, Surrell.**

— *Hilaire Chorel/Sorel dit Léveillé (Pierre and Anne ...) from Saint-Sernin in Aude (Languedoc-Roussillon) m. Geneviève Brault (Georges and Marie-Madeleine Marchand) in Québec, QC in 1715.*

Sosville, see **Sasseville.**

Soucier, see **Saucier.**

Soucisse, alteration of **Soucy.** — Amer. **Soucise, Sucese, Susice.**

— *Pierre-Louis Soucy/Soucisse, descendant of Jean from Abbeville in Somme (Picardie), m. Marie-Rose Marois (Jean-Baptiste and Marguerite Bohémier) in Mascouche, QC in 1778.*

Soucy, from *Soucy,* a placename in France. — Amer. **Sucy.**

— *Jean* **Soucy** *dit Lavigne (Claude and Françoise Seraine) from Abbeville in Somme (Picardie) m. Jeanne Savonet (Jacques and Antoinette Babillet) in Québec c. 1670.*

Soulière, alteration of *Sullière,* apparently from *La Sullière,* a placename in Deux-Sèvres (Pays de la Loire). — Amer. **Souilliere, Soulia, Soulier, Soullier, Soulor, Sulier.**

— *Nicolas* **Sullière** *dit Tranchemontagne (Vincent and Marie *Navence) from Quimper in Finistère (Bretagne) m. Marie-Marguerite Leblanc (Antoine and Élisabeth Roy) in Saint-Jean, Île d'Orléans, QC in 1691.*

Souva, Sova, Sovay, Sovey, Sovie, see **Sauvé.**

Splude, see **Plourde.**

Spooner, see **Cuillerier** and **Lécuyer.**

Spruce, see **Pinet(te).**

Stacy, see **Tessier.**

Staie, see **Jetté.**

St-Amand, alteration of *Saint-Amand,* either a placename in France or a soldier's nickname. — Amer. **Santimaw.**

— *Louis André dit* **Saint-Amand** *(Jacques and Jeanne Vinet) from Taillebourg in Charente-Maritime (Poitou-Charentes) m. Marguerite Samson (Pierre and Catherine Gauthier) in Lachine, QC in 1730.*

St-Amour, alteration of *Saint-Amour,* a soldier's nickname. — Amer. **Santamore, Santimore.**

— *Pierre Payet dit* **Saint-Amour** *(Pierre and Marie Martin) from Sainte-Florence in Gironde (Aquitaine) m. Louise Tessier (Urbain and Marie Archambault) in Montréal, QC in 1671.*

St-Antoine, alteration of *Saint-Antoine,* a placename in France. — Amer. **Anthony.**

— *Antoine Vacher dit* **Saint-Antoine** *(François and Marguerite Pascal) from Condatlès-Montboissier in Puy-de-Dôme (Auvergne) m. Marie-Marguerite Pelletier (François and Anne Gignard) in Montréal, QC in 1723.*

St-Aubin, alteration of *Saint-Aubin,* a placename in France. — Amer. **Centerbar.**

— *Louis-Charles Conscient dit de* **Saint-Aubin** *(Henri and Marie-Anne Decreil) from Bolbec in Seine-Maritime (Haute-Normandie) m. Marie-Angélique Alarie (Joseph and Geneviève Desgagnés) in Québec, QC in 1766.*

Stay, see **Jetté.**

St-Côme, apparently from *Saint-Côme,* a placename in France. — Amer. **Sancomb.**

— *Pierre Gagné dit* **Saint-Côme,** *grandson of Pierre from Igé in Orne (Basse-Normandie), m. Marie-Madeleine Baudreau (Urbain and Mathurine Juillet) in Montréal, QC in 1712.*

St-Cyr, alteration of *Saint-Cyr,* either a placename in France or a soldier's nickname. — Amer. **Sears.**

— *Pierre Deshayes dit* **Saint-Cyr** *from France m. Marguerite Guillet (Pierre and Jeanne Saint-Père) in Québec c. 1677.*

St-Denis, alteration of *Saint-Denis,* a soldier's nickname. — Amer. **Dennis, Saintdennis, Santhany, Santhony, Stdennis, Stdenny.**

— *Jacques Denis dit* **Saint-Denis** *(Michel and Catherine Le Tellier) from Caen in Calvados (Basse-Normandie) m. Anne Gauthier (Pierre and Charlotte Roussel) in Lachine, QC in 1689.*

Steady, see **Tranquille.**

Ste-Marie, alteration of *Sainte-Marie*, an ironic nickname derived from the surname *Marie*. — Amer. **Saintmarie, Saintmary, Stmarie, Stmary.**

— *Louis Marie dit **Sainte-Marie** (Louis and Marguerite Peigné) from Tours in Indre-et-Loire m. Mathurine Goard (Gilles and Catherine Léger) in Montréal, QC in 1667.*

St-Esprit, derived from *Pont-Saint-Esprit*, a placename in Gard (Languedoc-Roussillon). — Amer. **Sanspree, Santspree.**

— *François Plantier dit **Saint-Esprit** (François and Anne Horas) from Pont-Saint-Esprit in Gard (Languedoc-Roussillon) m. Marie-Reine Janot (Jean-Baptiste and Anne-Geneviève Renaud) in Saint-Charles-sur-Richelieu, QC in 1764.*

Stewart, see **Marcoux.**

St-François, alteration of *Saint-François*, apparently from a placename in France. — Amer. **Saintfrancis, Stfrancis.**

— *François-Michel Messier, sieur de **Saint-François**, son of Michel from Saint-Denis-le-Thiboult in Seine-Maritime (Haute-Normandie), m. Marie-Anne Amiot (Jean-Baptiste and Geneviève Guyon) in Varennes, QC in 1706.*

St-Gelais, alteration of *Saint-Gelais*, a placename in Deux-Sèvres (Poitou-Charentes). — Amer. **Singelais.**

— *Simon Pradet dit Laforge and **Saint-Gelais** (Gaspard and Élisabeth Chaigneau) from Niort in Deux-Sèvres (Poitou-Charentes) m. Geneviève Charron (Jean and Geneviève Dupil) in Saint-Pierre, Île d'Orléans, QC in 1730.*

St-Georges, alteration of *Saint-Georges*, a placename in France. — Amer. **Saintgeorge, Stgeorge.**

— *Jacques (de) Laporte dit **Saint-Georges** (Jacques and Marie Hamelin) from Nocé in Orne (Basse-Normandie) m. Nicole Duchesne (François and Marie Rolet) in Montréal, QC in 1657.*

St-Germain, alteration of *Saint-Germain*, a placename in France. — Amer. **Germaine, Saintgermain, Saintgermaine, Stgermain, Stgermaine.**

— *Jean Gazaille dit **Saint-Germain** (Jean and Aubine Reynier) from Sarrazac in Dordogne (Aquitaine) m. Jeanne Touzé (Jean and Jeanne Finot) in Québec, QC in 1668.*

St-Jacques, alteration of *Saint-Jacques*, an ironic nickname derived from the first name *Jacques*. — Amer. **Saintjames, Saintjock, Stjames, Stjock.**

— *Jacques-Joseph Cheval dit Chevalier and **Saint-Jacques** (Thomas and Gillette Nevé) from Tournai in Belgium m. Marie Cousineau (Jean and Jeanne Bénard) in Montréal, QC in 1725.*

St-Jean, alteration of *Saint-Jean*, an ironic nickname derived from the first name *Jean*. — Amer. **Saintjohn, Stjohn.**

— *Jean Anctil dit **Saint-Jean** (Louis and Jeanne Fontaine) from Ducey in Manche (Basse-Normandie) m. Marguerite Lévesque (François-Robert and Marie-Charlotte Aubert) in Rivière-Ouelle, QC in 1738.*

— *Jean-Baptiste Laperche dit **Saint-Jean** (Jean-Baptiste and Marguerite Cousineau) from Saint-Martin-de-Goyne in Gers (Midi-Pyrénées) m. Françoise Émery (Antoine and Marie Devault) in Boucherville, QC in 1700.*

Stjock, see **St-Jacques.**

Stjohn, see **St-Jean.**

St-Laurent, alteration of *Saint-Laurent*, an ironic surname derived from the surname

Laurent. — Amer. **Saintlawrence, Stlawrence.**

— *Pierre Laurent dit **Saint-Laurent** (Étienne and Marguerite Viger) from Périgueux in Dordogne (Aquitaine) m. Constance Garinet (François and Catherine Lepage) in Saint-François, Île d'Orléans, QC in 1699.*

Stmars, see **Cinq-Mars.**

Stmarie, Stmary, see **Ste-Marie.**

St-Michel, alteration of *Saint-Michel*, a placename in France. — Amer. **Mitchell.**

— *François Circé dit/sieur de **Saint-Michel** (François and Anne Véron) from Paris (Île-de-France) m. Marie-Madeleine Berthelot (Maurice and Marie Prévost) in Québec, QC in 1680.*

Stone, see **Desroches, Lapierre** and **Laroche.**

St-Onge, alteration of *Saintonge* via *Saint-Onge*, the nickname of a native of Saintonge, a former province in France. — Amer. **Santa, Santaw, Santo, Santor.**

— *Jacques Payan dit Saintonge/**Saint-Onge** (François and Madeleine Cantin) from Sainte-Colombe in Charente-Maritime (Poitou-Charentes) m. Louise Morin (Pierre and Catherine Le Mesle) in Québec, QC in 1699.*

St-Ours, apparently an alteration of *Saint-Ours*, a placename in France. — Amer. **Stores.**

— *Jacques-Amable Payan dit **Saint-Ours**, descendant of Jacques from Sainte-Colombe in Charente-Maritime (Poitou-Charentes), m. Abigail Potter in Stillwater, NY in 1781.*

St-Pierre, alteration of *Saint-Pierre*, a placename in France. — Amer. **Saintpeter, Saintpeters, Sampier, Sempier, Stpeter, Stpeters.**

— *Pierre (de) **Saint-Pierre** (Michel and Françoise Engrand) from Rouen in Seine-Maritime (Haute-Normandie) m. Marie Gerbert (Mathurin and Élisabeth Targer) in Sainte-Famille, Île d'Orléans, QC in 1679.*

St-Roch, alteration of *Saint-Roch*, a placename in France. — Amer. **Strock.**

— *Jacques Lagarde dit **Saint-Roch** (Mathurin and Suzanne Nolin) from Paris (Île-de-France) m. Marie-Catherine Lafargue (François and Catherine Quenneville) in Montréal, QC in 1749.*

Strong, see **Dufort** and **Trahan.**

Sucese, see **Soucisse.**

Sucy, see **Soucy.**

Sulier, see **Soulière.**

Supernault, Supernaw, Superneau, Supernor, Supprise, Supri, Suprise, Supry, see **Surprenant.**

Surette, alteration of *Suret*, a probable variant of *Seuret*, derived from *Sévère*, from the Latin name *Severus*, from *severus* 'strict, solemn, serious'. — Amer. **Surrett, Surrette.**

— *Pierre Suret/**Surette** (Noël and Françoise Colarde) from Marans in Charente-Maritime (Poitou-Charentes) m. Jeanne Pellerin (Étienne and Jeanne Savoie) in Port-Royal, NS in 1709.*

Surprenant, alteration of *Supernant*, origin uncertain. — Amer. **Supernault, Supernaw, Superneau, Supernor, Supprise, Supri, Suprise, Supry, Surprise.**

— *Jacques Supernant/**Surprenant** dit Sansoucy (Jacques and Louise Roquet) from Saint-Martin-du-Vieux-Bellême in Orne (Basse-Normandie) m. Jeanne Denot (Antoine and Catherine Leduc) in Laprairie, QC in 1678.*

Surrell, see **Sorel.**

Surrett, Surrette, see **Surette.**

Susice, see **Soucisse.**

Suzor, origin undetermined. — Amer. **Susor.**

   — *François **Suzor** (François and Étiennette Guillais) from Blois in Loir-et-Cher (Centre) m. Charlotte Couture (Eustache and Marguerite Bégin) in Beaumont, QC in 1733.*

Sweeney, see **Choinière** and **Chouinard.**

Sweenor, Swenor, Swinyer, see **Chouinard.**

Sylvain, from the Latin name *Silvanus*, derived from *silva* 'forest, wood'. — Amer. **Silver.**

   — *Pierre Veau dit **Sylvain**, son of Sylvain from Valençay in Indre (Centre), m. Catherine Racine (François and Marie Baucher) in Beaupré, QC in 1722.*

Sylvestre, from the Latin name *Silvester*, derived from *silva* 'forest, wood'. — Amer. **Sylvester.**

   — *Nicolas **Sylvestre** dit Champagne (Nicolas and Tanche Colson) from Pont-sur-Seine in Aube (Champagne-Ardenne) m. Barbe Neveu (Jean and Anne Ledet) in Québec, QC in 1667.*

Syr, Syre, see **Cyr.**

Syriac, see **Tiriac.**

T

Tacey, Tacia, Tacy, see **Tessier**.

Taillon, probable alteration of *Le Taillon,* a placename in France. — Amer. **Tyo**.
— *Olivier Michel dit Le Tardif and **Taillon** (Gilles and Barbe Émard) from La Rochelle in Charente-Maritime (Poitou-Charentes) m. Marie-Madeleine Cauchon (Jean and Madeleine Miville) in Château-Richer, QC in 1671.*

Talon, from the Germanic name *Talo,* derived from *tal* 'valley'. — Amer. **Heald**.
— *Étienne **Talon** dit Le Bourdelois (Simon and Jeanne Murat) from Bordeaux in Gironde (Aquitaine) m. Jeanne Lavergne (François and Françoise Lefrançois) in Rivière-Ouelle, QC in 1698.*

Tardif, from Old French *tardif* 'slow (of body or mind)'. — Amer. **Tardie, Tardiff**.
— *Olivier **Tardif**/Letardif (Jean and Clémence Houart) from Étables-sur-Mer in Côtes-d'Armor (Bretagne) m. Barbe Émard (Jean and Marie Bineau) in France in 1648.*

Taro, see **Thériault**.

Tarrien, see **Therrien**.

Tatreau, Tatro, Tatroe, Tatrow, see **Tétreau**.

Tavernier, from Old French *tavernier* 'innkeeper'. — Amer. **Tavernia**.
— *Julien **Tavernier** dit Sanspitié (François and Marie Marquant) from Namps-au-Mont in Somme (Picardie) m. Marie-Anne Girouard (Antoine and Marie-Anne Barré) in Montréal, QC in 1749.*

Taylor, see **Couturier** and **Therrien**.

Tayrien, see **Therrien**.

Tebear, see **Thibert**.

Tebeau, see **Thibault**.

Tebedo, Tebidor, see **Thibodeau**.

Tebo, Tebolt, see **Thibault**.

Tefoe, see **Thiffault**.

Terio, see **Thériault**.

Terriah, Terrian, see **Therrien**.

Terrio, see **Thériault**.

Terrion, see **Therrien**.

Teson, see **Tison**.

Tessier, from Old French *tessier* 'weaver'. — Amer. **Stacy, Tacey, Tacia, Tacy, Tracy**.
— *Louis-François **Tessier** dit Laforest (Daniel and Marie Raimbault) from Saint-Martin-de-Saint-Maixent in Deux-Sèvres (Poitou-Charentes) m. Thérèse Dupuis (François and Marguerite Banliac) in Cap-de-la-Madeleine, QC in 1728.*
— *Urbain **Tessier** dit Lavigne (Arthur and Jeanne Même) from Château-la-Vallière in Indre-et-Loire (Centre) m. Marie Archambault (Jacques and Françoise Tourault) in Québec, QC in 1648.*

Tétreau, probably derived from Old French *testre/tistre* 'to weave', the nickname of a weaver. — Amer. **Rowe, Tatreau, Tatro, Tatroe, Tatrow, Tetro.**

— *Louis **Tétreau**/Tétrault (Mathurin and Marie Bernard) from Louin in Deux-Sèvres (Pays de la Loire) m. Noëlle Landeau (Jean and Marie Aubert) in Trois-Rivières, QC in 1663.*

Theabo, Thebeau, Thebeault, see **Thibault.**

Théberge, from the Germanic name *Theodberga* composed of *theod* 'people' and *berga,* derived from *bergan* 'to hide, preserve'. — Amer. **Debarge.**

— *Louis **Théberge** (Louis and Sébastienne Pelchat) from Les Biards in Manche (Basse-Normandie) m. Marie-Geneviève Chouinard (Eustache and Marie-Madeleine Bérubé) in Montmagny, QC in 1747.*

Thebert, see **Thibert.**

Thebo, see **Thibault.**

Theriac, see **Tiriac.**

Thériault, derived from *Thierry,* from the Germanic name *Theodoric* composed of *theod* 'people' and *ric* 'powerful'. — Amer. **Taro, Terio, Terrio, Therio, Therrio.**

— *Jean **Thériot**/Thériault from Martaizé in Vienne (Poitou-Charentes) m. Perrine Reau in France c. 1636.*

Therrien, alteration of Old French *terrien* 'owner of a farmland'. — Amer. **Farmer, Lander, Pease, Pharmer, Tarrien, Taylor, Tayrien, Terriah, Terrian, Terrion, Therrian.**

— *Pierre **Therrien**/Terrien (André and Marie Foucauld) from La Rochelle in Charente-Maritime (Poitou-Charentes) m. Gabrielle Mineau (Jean and Jeanne Caillé) in Sainte-Famille, Île d'Orléans, QC in 1670.*

Therrio, see **Thériault.**

Thibault, from the Germanic name *Theodbald* composed of *theod* 'people' and *bald* 'bold'. — Amer. **Tebeau, Tebo, Tebolt, Theabo, Thebeau, Thebeault, Thebo, Thibeaux, Thiebault, Tibeau.**

— *François **Thibault** (Louis and Renée Gauthier) from La Flotte in Charente-Maritime (Poitou-Charentes) m. Élisabeth-Agnès Lefebvre (Guillaume and Barbe Viot) in Beaupré, QC in 1670.*

Thibert, from the Germanic name *Theodberht* composed of *theod* 'people' and *berht* 'bright'. — Amer. **Tebear, Thebert.**

— *Jean **Thibert** (Émiliand and Claudine Richard) from Saint-Usuge in Saône-et-Loire (Bourgogne) m. Marie-Angélique Mercier (Pierre and Marie-Catherine Chamberland) in Cap-Saint-Ignace, QC in 1736.*

— *Jean-Marie **Thibert** dit Marion (Joachim and Marie Guillemin) from Saint-Denis-de-Vaux or Saint-Jean-de-Vaux in Saône-et-Loire (Bourgogne) m. Marie-Louise Pélissier (Pierre and Marie-Clémence Harel) in Yamaska, QC in 1744.*

Thibodeau, from the Germanic name *Theodbald* composed of *theod* 'people' and *bald* 'bold'. — Amer. **Bodo, Tebedo, Tebidor, Thebodo, Thibadeau, Thibedeau, Thibideau, Thibodaux, Thibodeaux, Thibodo, Tibado, Tibedeau, Tibedo.**

— *Pierre **Thibodeau** from France m. Jeanne Thériot (Jean and Perrine Reau) in Acadia c. 1660.*

Thiebault, see **Thibault.**

Thiffault, alteration of *Tiffaut* or *Tifaut,* placenames in France. — Amer. **Tefoe, Thiefault, Thyfault.**

— *Jacques Tifault/**Thiffault** (Antoine and Marguerite Moreau) from Gironde-sur-Dropt in Gironde (Aquitaine) m. Marie-Anne Lécuyer (Antoine and Anne Rabady) in Batiscan, QC in 1687.*

Thivierge, alteration of *Thibierge*, same origin as **Théberge**. — Amer. **Verge**.

— *Hippolyte **Thibierge** (Étienne and Magdeleine Chaillou) from Blois in Loir-et-Cher (Centre) m. Renée Hervé/Hervet (Gabriel and Marguerite Lorillau) in Blois in 1653.*

Thouin, from the Germanic name *Theodwin* composed of *theod* 'people' and *win* 'friend'. — Amer. **Twine**.

— *Roch **Thouin** (Antoine and Perrette Gagnon) from Saint-Martin-le-Gaillard in Seine-Maritime (Haute-Normandie) m. Denise Colin (Jacques and Nicole Fontaine) in Boucherville, QC in 1673.*

Thout, see **Thuot**.

Threehouse, see **Destroismaisons**.

Thuot, derived from the Germanic name *Theodwald* composed of *theod* 'people' and *wald* 'power, authority'. — Amer. **Thout**.

— *Pierre-Edmé **Thuot** dit Duval (Pierre-Edmé and Marie-Louise Duval) from Tonnerre in Yonne (Bourgogne) m. Marie Fournier (Antoine and Marie Ronceray) in Montréal, QC in 1712.*

Thyfault, see **Thiffault**.

Tibado, see **Thibodeau**.

Tibeau, see **Thibault**.

Tibedeau, Tibedo, see **Thibodeau**.

Tiriac, origin undetermined. — Amer. **Syriac, Theriac**.

— *François **Tiriac** dit Laforest (Jacques and Marie-Agnès Monigon) from Paris (Île-de-France) m. Marie-Madeleine Bénard (Jean and Marie-Madeleine Périllard) in Montréal, QC in 1748.*

Tison, derived from Old French *tieis* 'German'. — Amer. **Teson**.

— *Jean-Baptiste-Joseph **Tison** (François and Jeanne-Françoise-Joseph Collery) from Valenciennes in Nord (Nord-Pas-de-Calais) m. Marie-Anne Picard (François and Marguerite Cusson) in Montréal, QC in 1760.*

Tooper, see **Toupin**.

Torango, see **Tourangeau**.

Tougas, alteration of *Tougard*, from the Germanic name *Thorgard* composed of *Thor*, the god of thunder, and *gard* 'enclosure'. — Amer. **Tougaw, Tugaw**.

— *Guillaume **Tougas**/Tougard dit Laviolette (Guillaume and Marie Labbé) from Fatouville in Eure (Haute-Normandie) m. Marie Brazeau (Nicolas and Perrette Billard) in Montréal, QC in 1698.*

Toupin, apparently from Old Occitan *toupin* 'little earthen pot', the nickname of a maker or seller. — Amer. **Tooper**.

— *Pierre **Toupin** dit Lapierre (Guillaume and Jeanne Arnault/Arnaud) from Rouffiac in Charente (Poitou-Charentes) m. Mathurine Graton (Pierre and Marie Boucher) in Québec, QC in 1670.*

Tourangeau, from *Tourangeau*, the nickname of an individual from Touraine, a former province in France. — Amer. **Torango**.

— *Philippe Guillet dit **Tourangeau** (Jean and Jeanne Dutartre) from Saint-Pierre-des-Corps in Indre-et-Loire (Centre) m. Angélique Martineau (Pierre and Antoinette Du-*

moutier) in Québec, QC in 1725.

Tourville, apparently from *Tourville,* a placename in France. — Amer. **Troville, Turville.**

— *Augustin Hubou dit **Tourville**, grandson of Mathieu from Le Mesnil-Durand in Calvados (Basse-Normandie), m. Élisabeth Forget (Louis and Élisabeth Éthier) in Saint-François, Île Jésus, QC in 1712.*

Toussaint, from *Toussaint* 'All Saints' Day', the name given to a child born on that day or around that time of year. — Amer. **Tousant, Tusa, Tuson.**

— *Jean-Baptiste Cusson dit **Toussaint**, descendant of Jean from Sainte-Marguerite-sur-Duclair in Seine-Maritime (Haute-Normandie), m. Adeline Ratté (David and Dorothée Martin) in Henryville, QC in 1859.*

— ***Toussaint** Leroux dit Cardinal, descendant of François from Senillé in Vienne (Poitou-Charente), m. Catherine Audet (Charles and Catherine Brosseau) in Saint-Luc, QC in 1836.*

Trackey, see **Trottier.**

Tracy, see **Tessier.**

Trahan, probably derived from Old Breton *trech* 'victory'. — Amer. **Strong, Trahant, Trayah.**

— *Guillaume **Trahan** (Nicolas and Renée Desloges) from Montreuil-Bellay in Maine-et-Loire (Pays de la Loire) m. Madeleine Brun (Vincent and Renée Breau) in Port-Royal, NS c. 1666.*

Trank, see **Trinque.**

Tranquille, from *tranquille* 'quiet', the nickname of a calm, placid individual. — Amer. **Steady.**

— *Pierre Jourdanais/Jourdonnais dit **Tranquille** (Pierre and Jeanne Clair) from Bossey in Haute-Savoie (Rhône-Alpes) m. Marie-Louise Charland (Jacques and Marie Deniau) in Laprairie, QC in 1755.*

Traversy, apparently from *Traversy,* a placename in Haute-Savoie (Rhône-Alpes). — Amer. **Traversie.**

— *Noël Langlois dit **Traversy**, son of Noël from Saint-Léonard-des-Parcs in Orne (Basse-Normandie), m. Geneviève Parent (Pierre and Jeanne Badeau) in Beauport, QC in 1686.*

Trayah, see **Trahan.**

Treado, Tredo, see **Trudeau.**

Tremblay, from *(Le) Tremblay,* a placename in France. — Amer. **Tremble, Trembler, Trembly, Trimble, Tromblay, Tromblee, Trombley, Trombly, Tromley, Trumbla, Trumble, Trumbley, Trumbly.**

— *Pierre **Tremblay** (Philibert and Jeanne Coignet) from Randonnai in Orne (Basse-Normandie) m. Anne/Ozanne Achon (Jean and Hélène Regnaud) in Québec, QC in 1657.*

Trépanier, alteration of *Étrépagny* via *(de) Trépagny,* a placename in Eure (Haute-Normandie). — Amer. **Trippany.**

— *Romain **Trépanier**/(de) Trépagny (Charles and Marie Marette) from Muchedent in Seine-Maritime (Haute-Normandie) m. Geneviève Drouin (Robert and Anne Cloutier) in Québec, QC in 1656.*

Trickey, see **Trottier.**

Trimble, see **Tremblay.**

Trinque, from *(La) Trinque,* a placename in France. — Amer. **Trank.**

— *François **Trinque** (Joseph and Thérèse Puneau) from Tarerach in Pyrénées-Orientales (Languedoc-Roussillon) m. Marie-Françoise Garand (Pierre and Marie-Louise Molleur) in Québec, QC in 1748.*

Trippany, see **Trépanier.**

Trokey, see **Trottier.**

Tromblay, Tromblee, Trombley, Trombly, Tromley, see **Tremblay.**

Trottier, from Old French *trotier* 'messenger; stableboy'. — Amer. **Trackey, Trickey, Trokey, Trotchie, Truckey.**

— *Jules **Trottier** from Igé in Orne (Basse-Normandie) m. Catherine Loiseau in Igé c. 1625.*

Troville, see **Tourville.**

Truchon, alteration of *(Le) Trugeon,* same origin as **Turgeon.** — Amer. **Trucheon, Trushaw.**

— *Louis **Truchon** dit Léveillé (Pierre and Perrine Sirouet) from Abbaretz in Loire-Atlantique (Pays de la Loire) m. Marie-Françoise Beauchamp (Jean and Jeanne Loisel) in Pointe-aux-Trembles, QC in 1687.*

Truckey, see **Trottier.**

Trudeau, same origin as **Trudel.** — Amer. **Treado, Tredo, Trudo.**

— *Étienne **Trudeau**/Truteau (François and Catherine Matinier) from La Rochelle in Charente-Maritime (Poitou-Charentes) m. Adrienne Barbier (Gilbert and Catherine Delavaux) in Montréal, QC in 1667.*

Trudel, derived from *Touroude* via *Tr(o)ude,* from the Germanic name *Turold* composed of *tur* 'giant' or *Thor,* the god of thunder, and *wald* 'power, authority'. — Amer. **Trudell.**

— *Jean **Trudel** (Jean and Marguerite Noyer) from Parfondeval in Orne (Basse-Normandie) m. Marguerite Thomas (Jean and Marguerite Fredry) in Québec, QC in 1655.*

Trudo, see **Trudeau.**

Trumbla, Trumble, Trumbley, Trumbly, see **Tremblay.**

Trushaw, see **Truchon.**

Tucker, see **Beauparlant.**

Tugaw, see **Tougas.**

Tulip, see **Latulippe.**

Turcot(te), derived from *Turc* 'Turk', the nickname of an individual with a tanned complexion. — Amer. **Churco, Churcott, Gilcott, Turcott.**

— *Abel **Turcot** from Mouilleron-en-Pareds in Vendée (Pays de la Loire) m. Marie Giraud in Château-Richer, QC in 1662.*

— *Jean **Turcot** (François and Joseph Guinaudeau) from Fontenay-le-Comte in Vendée (Pays de la Loire) m. Françoise Capel (Julien and Laurence Lecomte) in Trois-Rivières, QC in 1651.*

Turgeon, alteration of *esturgeon* 'sturgeon', a nickname related to some characteristic of this fish. — Amer. **Turgen.**

— *Charles **Turgeon** (Jean and Sébastienne Liger) from Mortagne-au-Perche in Orne (Basse-Normandie) m. Pasquière Lefebvre in Mortagne-au-Perche c. 1649.*

Turner, see **Létourneau.**

Turville, see **Tourville**.
Tusa, Tuson, see **Toussaint**.
Twine, see **Thouin**.
Tyo, see **Taillon**.

U

Upell, see **Riopel**.

V

Vachereau, same origin as **Vachon.** — Amer. **Vashro.**
— *Julien* **Vachereau** *dit Versailles (Pierre-Louis and Anne Aufroy) from Versailles in Yvelines (Île-de-France) m. Françoise-Angélique Leber (Gabriel and Marie Vacher) in Montréal, QC in 1749.*

Vachon, derived from *vacher* 'cowherd'. — Amer. **Cowan, Vashaw, Vashon.**
— *Paul* **Vachon** *(Vincent and Sapience Rabeau) from La Copechagnière in Vendée (Pays de la Loire) m. Marguerite Langlois (Noël and Françoise Grenier) in Québec, QC in 1653.*

Vadeboncoeur, from *va de bon coeur* 'goes with a brave heart', a soldier's nickname. — Amer. **Goodheart, Hart, Verboncoeur, Verboncouer, Verbunker.**
— *Jean Chabrier dit* **Vadeboncoeur** *(Jean and Jeanne Dubois) from Maruéjols-lès-Gardon in Gard (Languedoc-Roussillon) m. Marie-Angélique Sicard (Jean and Marie-Angélique Lupien) in Maskinongé, QC in 1760.*

Vadnais, alteration of *Vadenay,* a placename in France. — Amer. **Vadney, Varney, Vedner.**
— *Jean* **Vadnais**/*Vadenay dit d'Argenteuil (Rémi and Louise Morié) from Auguaise in Orne (Basse-Normandie) m. Marie-Anne Mousseau (Jacques and Marie-Anne Daunay) in Saint-Sulpice, QC in 1723.*

Vague, see **Veilleux.**

Vaillancourt, alteration of *Willencourt* via *Villencourt,* a placename in Pas-de-Calais (Nord-Pas-de-Calais). — Amer. **Smart, Valencour, Vancor, Vancore, Vancour, Vianco, Viancour, Viancourt.**
— *Robert* **Vaillancourt**/*Villencourt (Robert and Jacqueline Papin) from Saint-Nicolas-d'Aliermont in Seine-Maritime (Haute-Normandie) m. Marie Gobeil (Jean and Jeanne Guyet) in Château-Richer, QC in 1668.*

Valade, from *(La) Valade,* a placename in France. — Amer. **Vallad, Vallard.**
— *Jean* **Valade** *dit Lajeunesse (Pierre and Marguerite Denis) from La Rochefoucauld in Charente (Poitou-Charentes) m. Marie Godeau (Étienne and Marie-Françoise Simon) in Montréal, QC in 1712.*

Valencour, see **Vaillancourt.**

Valiquet(te), derived from the Germanic name *Walho,* from *walh* 'stranger'. — Amer. **Veliquette, Velliquette.**
— *Jean* **Valiquet** *dit Laverdure (Jean and Nicole Langevin) from Le Lude in Sarthe (Pays de la Loire) m. Renée Loppé (Jean and Marie Desprez) in Montréal, QC in 1658.*

Vallad, Vallard, see **Valade.**

Vallée, from *(La) Vallée,* a placename in France. — Amer. **Valley, Vallie.**
— *Jean* **Vallée** *dit Lavallée (Pierre and Madeleine Dumesnil) from Saint-Saëns in Seine-Maritime (Haute-Normandie) m. Marie Martin (Jacques and Marie Lemaistre/Bonneau) in Château-Richer, QC in 1666.*

— Pierre **Vallée** (*Pierre and Madeleine Dumesnil*) *from Saint-Saëns in Seine-Maritime (Haute-Normandie) m. Thérèse Leblanc (Léonard and Marie Riton) in Québec, QC in 1665.*

Vallière, from *(La) Vallière*, a placename in France. — Amer. **Valyear, Value, Valyou.**

— Pierre **Vallière** (*Louis and Perrine Fournier*) *from Segonzac in Charente (Poitou-Charentes) m. Anne Lagou (Pierre and Marie *Boiscochin) in Québec, QC in 1670.*

Vanasse, alteration of the Flemish name *Van Asse* 'from Asse', a placename in Belgium. — Amer. **Anas, Vanouse.**

— François **Vanasse** (*Paul and Barbe Monsel/Monteil*) *from Rouen in Seine-Maritime (Haute-Normandie) m. Jeanne Fourrier (Pierre and Jeanne Buson) in Québec in 1671.*

Vancelette, see **Vincelette.**

Vancor, Vancore, Vancour, see **Vaillancourt.**

Vandal, probable alteration of *Vandel* or *Vendel*, placenames in France. — Amer. **Vandale, Vandel, Vondell, Vondle.**

— François **Vandal** (*Étienne and Julienne Grole*) *from Vernantes in Maine-et-Loire (Pays de la Loire) m. Marie-Madeleine Pinel (Gilles and Anne Ledet) in Neuville, QC in 1680.*

Vandet(te), probable alteration of *Vendet*, a placename in Vienne (Poitou-Charentes). — Amer. **Vondett, Vondette.**

— René **Vandet** (*René and Andrée *Ligouneresse*) *from Montournais in Vendée (Pays de la Loire) m. Marie Ariot (Bernardin and Marguerite Dely) in Québec, QC in 1671.*

Vanne, see **Venne.**

Vanouse, see **Vanasse.**

Vanslett, see **Vincelette.**

Varney, see **Vadnais.**

Varno, see **Véronneau.**

Vashaw, Vashon, see **Vachon.**

Vashro, see **Vachereau.**

Vasseur, alteration of **Levasseur.**— Amer. **Vassar, Vasser.**

— Laurent **Levasseur** (*Jean and Marguerite Maheu*) *from Bois-Guillaume in Seine-Maritime (Haute-Normandie) m. Marie Marchand (Louis and Françoise Morineau) in Québec, QC in 1670.*

Vassau, Vassaw, see **Vincent.**

Vautrin, derived from *Vautier*, same origin as **Gauthier.** — Amer. **Vautrain, Votra, Votraw.**

— Charles **Vautrin** dit Bienvenu (*Charles and Catherine Richard*) *from Vaudoncourt in Meuse or Vosges (Lorraine) m. Marie-Catherine Boire (Henri and Marie-Louise Thuot) in Saint-Constant, QC in 1760.*

Vayo, see **Veilleux.**

Vedner, see **Vadnais.**

Veilleux, alteration of *Vérieu*, origin undetermined. — Amer. **Vague, Vayo, Vehue, Vigue.**

— Nicolas **Vérieu/Vérieul** (*Nicolas and Perrette/Colette Roussel*) *from Dieppe in Seine-Maritime (Haute-Normandie) m. Marguerite Hiardin (René and Jeanne Serré) in Château-Richer, QC in 1665.*

Veine, see **Venne.**

Veivia, see **Vivier.**

Velandra, see **Vilandré.**

Veliquette, Velliquette, see **Valiquet(te).**

Venia, Venier, see **Vigneux.**

Venne, probable alteration of *Voyne/Voine*, from the Germanic name *Wano*, derived from *wan* 'expectation, hope'. — Amer. **Vanne, Veine.**

— *Jean Venne/Voyne from France m. Françoise Manseau in France c. 1645.*

Veno, see **Vigneau.**

Verboncoeur, Verboncouer, Verbunker, see **Vadeboncoeur.**

Verge, see **Thivierge.**

Vermet(te), probably from Flemish *ver* 'lady' and *Met*, derived from *Mathilde*, from the Germanic name *Mahthild* composed of *maht* 'powerful' and *hild* 'combat'. — Amer. **Vermett.**

— *Antoine Vermet dit Laforme (Fleury Asquet and Marie Leblanc) from Arras in Pas-de-Calais (Nord-Pas-de-Calais) m. Barbe Ménard (René and Judith Veillon) in Sainte-Famille, Île d'Orléans, QC in 1669.*

Véronneau, derived from *Véron*, probably from Old French *ver* 'boar', the nickname of a bawdy, coarse individual. — Amer. **Varno.**

— *Denis Véronneau (Louis and Perrine Bary) from Bournezeau in Vendée (Pays de la Loire) m. Marguerite Bertault (Jacques and Gillette Banne) in Trois-Rivières, QC in 1668.*

Verreau, probably from Old French *verel* 'bolt, padlock', the nickname of a locksmith. — Amer. **Verrow.**

— *Barthélemi Verreau dit Le Bourguignon (Michel and Claudine Rocher) from Dijon in Côte-d'Or (Bourgogne) m. Marthe Quintel (Denis and Louise Bénard) in Château-Richer, QC in 1665.*

Verret(te), probably derived from Old French *ver* 'boar', the nickname of a coarse, debauched individual. — Amer. **Verrett.**

— *Michel Verret dit Laverdure (Jean and Jeanne de la Prés) from Saintes in Charente-Maritime (Poitou-Charentes) m. Marie Galarneau (Jacques and Jacqueline Héron) in Charlesbourg, QC in 1683.*

Verrow, see **Verreau.**

Versailles, from *Versailles*, a placename in Yvelines (Île-de-France). — Amer. **Versaw.**

— *Julien Vachereau dit Versailles (Pierre-Louis and Anne Aufroy) from Versailles in Yvelines (Île-de-France) m. Françoise-Angélique Leber (Gabriel and Marie Vacher) in Montréal, QC in 1749.*

Vertefeuille, from *verte feuille* 'green leaf', a soldier's nickname. — Amer. **Greenleaf.**

— *Nicolas Bachand dit Vertefeuille (Nicolas and Marie Pinson) from Saint-Cloud in Hauts-de-Seine (Île-de-France) m. Anne Lamoureux (Louis and Françoise Boivin) in Boucherville, QC in 1692.*

Vevea, Vevia, see **Vivier.**

Vézina, probable alteration of *Le Vézinat*, a placename in Dordogne (Aquitaine). — Amer. **Bazinaw, Visina, Visnaw, Visneau.**

— *Jacques Vézina/Voisinat from Puyravault in Charente-Maritime (Poitou-Charentes) m. Marie Boisdon (Jean and Marie Bardin) in France c. 1641.*

Vianco, Viancour, Viancourt, see **Vaillancourt.**

Viau, from the Latin name *Vitalis,* from *vitalis* 'vital'. — Amer. **Vieau, Vieaux, Vieu, Vieux.**

— *Jean **Viau** (Michel and Marie *Ulet) from Ozillac in Charente-Maritime (Poitou-Charentes) m. Françoise Prévost (Jean and Françoise Leblanc) in Montréal, QC in 1711.*

Vien(s), derived from *Vivien,* from the Latin name *Vivianus,* from *vivus* 'alive'. — Amer. **Come, Comings, Cumm, Cummings, Vient.**

— *Vivien Jean dit **Vien** (Vivien and Suzanne Hérault) from Écoyeux in Charente-Maritime (Poitou-Charentes) m. Catherine Gateau (Odart and Geneviève Doucet) in Québec, QC in 1671.*

Vieu, Vieux, see **Viau.**

Vigneau, either an alteration of *Le Vignault* or *Le Vigneau,* placenames in France, or from Old French *vignel* 'vine, vineyard', the nickname of a wine grower. — Amer. **Veno, Vigneaux.**

— *Paul Vignault/**Vigneau** dit Laverdure (Jean and Renée ...) from Poitiers in Vienne (Poitou-Charentes) m. Françoise Bourgeois (Antoine and Marie Piedmont) in Sainte-Famille, Île d'Orléans, QC in 1670.*

Vigneux, probable alteration of *Le Vignault,* a placename in France. — Amer. **Venia, Venier.**

— *François Vignault/**Vigneux** dit Tranchemontagne (Gabriel and Françoise Bernard) from Limoges in Haute-Vienne (Limousin) m. Catherine Laurence (Noël and Élisabeth Bertault) in Repentigny, QC in 1705.*

Vigue, see **Veilleux.**

Vilandré, apparently an alteration of *Villandry,* a placename in France. — Amer. **Velandra.**

— *Pierre Duteau dit **Vilandré**/Villandré, son of Charles from La Rochelle in Charente-Maritime (Poitou-Charentes), m. Marie-Françoise Casaubon (Martin and Françoise Le Pellé) in Sorel, QC in 1718.*

Villemaire, alteration of the Flemish name *Wilmer* via *Villemer,* from the Germanic name *Wilmar* composed of *wil* 'will' and *mar* 'famous'. — Amer. **Villemere.**

— *Nicolas Réal dit Villemer/**Villemaire** (Pierre and Marguerite Dupens) from Waremme in Belgium m. Marie-Anne Galarneau (Jacques and Marguerite Panneton) in Sainte-Foy, QC in 1726.*

Villemure, apparently an alteration of *Villemures,* a placename in Indre (Centre). — Amer. **Villmore.**

— *Joseph Lefebvre dit **Villemure,** son of Gabriel from Paris (Île-de-France), m. Marie-Jeanne Lafond (Pierre and Marie-Madeleine Rivard) in Batiscan, QC in 1724.*

Villeneuve, from *(La) Villeneuve,* a placename in France. — Amer. **Newcity, Newton, Newtown, Newvine, Villenave, Villenueve, Villnave, Villneff, Vilneff, Vinlove.**

— *Mathurin **Villeneuve** (Mathieu and Jeanne Chauché) from Sainte-Marie-de-Ré in Charente-Maritime (Poitou-Charentes) m. Marguerite Lemarché (Jean and Catherine Hurault) in Québec, QC in 1669.*

— *André Arnould dit **Villeneuve** (Pierre and Marie-Madeleine Gobin) from Préguillac in Charente-Maritime (Poitou-Charentes), m. Marie-Madeleine Marié (Charles and Marie-Françoise Sédilot) in Québec, QC in 1722.*

Villmore, see **Villemure.**

Villnave, Villneff, Vilneff, see **Villeneuve.**

Vincelette, alteration of *Vincelet,* derived from **Vincent.** — Amer. **Vancelette, Vanslett.**
 — *Geoffroy* **Vincelet** *dit Laboissière (Julien and Françoise Frenel) from Plumelec in Morbihan (Bretagne) m. Catherine Barsa (André and Françoise Pilois) in Montréal, QC in 1698.*

Vincent, from the Latin name *Vincentius,* derived from *vincens* 'victor, conqueror'. — Amer. **Vassau, Vassaw.**
 — *Pierre* **Vincent** *from Martaizé in Vienne (Poitou-Charentes) m. Anne Gaudet (Denis and Martine Gauthier) in Port-Royal, NS c. 1663.*

Vinlove, see **Villeneuve.**

Visina, Visnaw, Visneau, see **Vézina.**

Vivelamour, from *vive l'amour* 'long live love', a soldier's nickname. — Amer. **Vivlamore.**
 — *Jean-Baptiste Ménard dit* **Vive L'Amour** *(Poncet and Jeanne-Marie Dupuis) from Pontarlier in Doubs (Franche-Comté) m. Marie-Josèphe Éthier (Étienne and Marie-Madeleine Roy) in Repentigny, QC in 1758.*

Vivier, from *(Le) Vivier,* a placename in France. — Amer. **Veivia, Vevea, Vevia.**
 — *Pierre* **Vivier** *(Grégoire and Clémence *Adjourné/*Ajounan) from Thiré in Vendée (Pays de la Loire) m. Marguerite Roy (Mathurin and Marguerite Biré) in Québec, QC in 1665.*

Vivlamore, see **Vivelamour.**

Vondell, see **Vandal.**

Vondett, Vondette, see **Vandet(te).**

Vondle, see **Vandal.**

Votra, Votraw, see **Vautrin.**

W

Walker, see **Lamarche** and **Marcheterre**.
Wallett, Wallette, see **Ouellet(te)**.
Ward, see **Benoit** and **Guérin**.
Wedge, see **Aucoin**.
Welcome, see **Bienvenu**.
Wellet, Wellette, see **Ouellet(te)**.
Wells, see **Dupuis**.
Wemett, Wemette, see **Ouimet(te)**.
Wheel, see **Rouet(te)**.
Wheeler, see **Leroux**.
White, see **Leblanc**.
Wideawake, see **Léveillé**.
Wilette, Willet, Willete, Willett, Willette, see **Ouellet(te)**.
Wimett, Wimette, see **Ouimet(te)**.
Wisell, Wissell, see **Loisel(le)**.
Wood, see **Dubois**, **Gadbois** and **Houde**.
Woods, see **Charlebois**, **Dubois** and **Gadbois**.

Y

Yaddow, see **Guindon**.

Yandeau, Yando, see **Riendeau**.

Yandon, Yandow, see **Guindon**.

Yarneau, Yarno, see **Guernon**.

Yarter, Yartin, Yatta, Yattaw, Yatter, see **Guertin**.

Yelle, alteration of *Diel*, derived from the Germanic name *Theodoric* via *Dietel* composed of *theod* 'people' and *ric* 'powerful'. — Amer. **Yell**.

— *Charles **Diel** (Philippe and Marie Hanctin) from Sainte-Colombe in Seine-Maritime (Haute-Normandie) m. Marie-Anne Picard (Hugues and Antoinette de Liercourt) in Montréal, QC in 1676.*

Yennard, Yenor, see **Léonard**.

Yettaw, Yetter, Yetto, see **Guertin**.

Yeupell, see **Riopel**.

Yon, see **Guyon**.

Yondo, see **Riendeau**.

Yott, see **Huot**.

Youmell, see **Duhamel**.

Young, see **Dion**, **Dionne**, **Guyon**, **Lajeunesse** and **Lejeune**.

Youngs, see **Guyon**.

Youtt, see **Huot**.

Yvon, derived from the Germanic name *Ivo*, from *iv* 'yew'. — Amer. **Evon**.

— *Yves Phlem dit **Yvon** (Guillaume and Marguerite Péroine) from Morlaix in Finistère (Bretagne) m. Marie Lereau (Sixte and Reine Deblois) in Sainte-Famille, Île d'Orléans, QC in 1724.*

Z

Zace, alteration of the German name *Sasse*, from Middle Low German *sasse* 'Saxon'. — Amer. **Zastre**.
— *Heinrich **Sasse** (Christian and Catherine Sporleder) from Magdeburg in Germany m. Marie-Reine Contré (François and Marguerite Tessier) in Sainte-Geneviève, QC in 1785.*
Zeno, see **Lusignan**.
Zercie, see **Desorcy**.

CPSIA information can be obtained at www.ICGtesting.com
Printed in the USA
LVOW07s2119250913

353949LV00009B/168/P